T4-ALE-364

Using Experimental Methods in Environmental and Resource Economics

NEW HORIZONS IN ENVIRONMENTAL ECONOMICS

Series Editors: Wallace E. Oates, *Professor of Economics, University of Maryland, USA* and Henk Folmer, *Professor of General Economics, Wageningen University and Professor of Environmental Economics, Tilburg University, The Netherlands*

This important series is designed to make a significant contribution to the development of the principles and practices of environmental economics. It includes both theoretical and empirical work. International in scope, it addresses issues of current and future concern in both East and West and in developed and developing countries.

The main purpose of the series is to create a forum for the publication of high quality work and to show how economic analysis can make a contribution to understanding and resolving the environmental problems confronting the world in the twenty-first century.

Recent titles in the series include:

Managing Wetlands for Private and Social Good
Theory, Policy and Cases from Australia
Stuart M. Whitten and Jeff Bennett

Amenities and Rural Development
Theory, Methods and Public Policy
Edited by Gary Paul Green, Steven C. Deller and David W. Marcouiller

The Evolution of Markets for Water
Theory and Practice in Australia
Edited by Jeff Bennett

Integrated Assessment and Management of Public Resources
Edited by Joseph C. Cooper, Federico Perali and Marcella Veronesi

Climate Change and the Economics of the World's Fisheries
Examples of Small Pelagic Stocks
Edited by Rögnvaldur Hannesson, Manuel Barange and Samuel F. Herrick Jr

The Theory and Practice of Environmental and Resource Economics
Edited by Thomas Aronsson, Roger Axelsson and Runar Brännlund

The International Yearbook of Environmental and Resource Economics 2006/2007
A Survey of Current Issues
Edited by Tom Tietenberg and Henk Folmer

Choice Modelling and the Transfer of Environmental Values
Edited by John Rolfe and Jeff Bennett

The Impact of Climate Change on Regional Systems
A Comprehensive Analysis of California
Edited by Joel Smith and Robert Mendelsohn

Explorations in Environmental and Natural Resource Economics
Essays in Honor of Gardner M. Brown, Jr.
Edited by Robert Halvorsen and David Layton

Using Experimental Methods in Environmental and Resource Economics
Edited by John A. List

Using Experimental Methods in Environmental and Resource Economics

Edited by

John A. List

Professor of Economics, University of Chicago, USA
Research Associate, NBER and University Fellow, RFF, USA

NEW HORIZONS IN ENVIRONMENTAL ECONOMICS

Edward Elgar
Cheltenham, UK • Northampton, MA, USA

HD
75.6
.U85
2006

ML

© John A. List 2006

All rights reserved. No part of this publication may be reproduced, stored in a retrieval system or transmitted in any form or by any means, electronic, mechanical or photocopying, recording, or otherwise without the prior permission of the publisher.

Published by
Edward Elgar Publishing Limited
Glensanda House
Montpellier Parade
Cheltenham
Glos GL50 1UA
UK

Edward Elgar Publishing, Inc.
William Pratt House
9 Dewey Court
Northampton
Massachusetts 01060
USA

A catalogue record for this book
is available from the British Library

Library of Congress Cataloguing-in-Publication Data

Using experimental methods in environmental and resource economics / edited by John A. List.
p. cm. – (New horizons in environmental economics series)
Includes bibliographical references and index.
1. Environmental economics–Methodology. 2. Natural resources–Management–Methodology. I. List, John A., 1968– II. Series.
HD75.6.U85 2006
333.7072′4–dc22

2006005886

ISBN-13: 978 1 84542 855 6
ISBN-10: 1 84542 855 2

Printed and bound in Great Britain by MPG Books Ltd, Bodmin, Cornwall

This book is dedicated to:
Jennifer, Annika, Eli, Noah, Greta and Mason

University Libraries
Carnegie Mellon University
Pittsburgh, PA 15213-3890

Contents

Contributors

Wiktor Adamowicz, Department of Rural Economy, University of Alberta, Edmonton, Canada.

Jonathan E. Alevy, Department of Resource Economics, University of Nevada, Reno, NV, USA.

Ian Bateman, School of Environmental Sciences, University of East Anglia, Norwich, UK.

Ronald G. Cummings, Department of Economics, Andrew Young School of Policy Studies, Georgia State University, Georgia, USA.

Ariel Dinar, Agriculture and Rural Development Department, World Bank, Washington, DC, USA.

Paul J. Ferraro, Department of Economics, Andrew Young School of Policy Studies, Georgia State University, Georgia, USA.

Glenn W. Harrison, Department of Economics, College of Business Administration, University of Central Florida, USA.

John Horowitz, Department of Agricultural and Resource Economics, University of Maryland, USA.

Richard E. Howitt, Department of Agricultural and Resource Economics, University of California, Davis, USA.

John A. List, Department of Economics, University of Chicago, National Bureau of Economic Research, Chicago, USA.

Jayson L. Lusk, Department of Agricultural Economics, Oklahoma State University, Stillwater, USA.

Erin Mastrangelo, Department of Resource Economics, University of Massachusetts, Amherst, USA.

Alistair Munro, Department of Economics, Royal Holloway, University of London, Egham, UK.

James J. Murphy, Department of Resource Economics and Center for Policy and Administration, University of Massachusetts, Amherst, USA.

Stephen J. Rassenti, Interdisciplinary Center for Economic Science, George Mason University, Fairfax, USA.

Bruce Rhodes, Department of Economics, University of KwaZulu-Natal, Durban, South Africa.

Matthew Rousu, Department of Economics, Susquehanna University, Selinsgrove, USA.

Vernon L. Smith, Interdisciplinary Center for Economic Science, George Mason University, Fairfax, USA.

Chris V. Starmer, Department of Economics, University of Nottingham, Nottingham, UK.

Robert Sugden, School of Economics, University of East Anglia, Norwich, UK.

Daan van Soest, Department of Economics and CentER, Tilburg University, Tilburg, the Netherlands.

Jana Vyrastekova, Department of Economics and CentER, University of Tilburg, Tilburg, and Center for Research in Experimental Economics and Political Decision-Making, University of Amsterdam, Amsterdam, the Netherlands.

Introduction

This book includes a collection of research that makes use of the experimental method to explore important issues in environmental and resource economics. My goal in choosing these studies was to attract a group of premier scholars who would provide cutting-edge research in some of the most important areas in environmental and resource economics. I believe this book was able to accomplish this task.

The early chapters in the book, Chapters 1–4, focus on improving benefit–cost analysis, which remains the hallmark of public policy decision-making around the globe. For example, currently contingent valuation (CV) is the only game in town to provide both use and non-use values of non-marketed goods and services. Recognizing this, in the USA, the Office of Management and Budget has recently confirmed the use of CV in their revision of the benefit–cost guidelines, which every federal agency must follow when performing a formal benefit–cost analysis. The research in Chapters 1–4 provides innovative avenues to credibly lead to more efficient policies. These insights should prove to be fundamental components of the valuation process.

In the latter chapters, 5–8, the authors explore, in a myriad of clever ways, important aspects associated with optimal resource use and regulation of resources. Clearly these issues remain of utmost importance, both in a positive and normative sense; and this lot of studies should also aid in the policy-making process. From my discussion with agency officials, it is clear that resource issues will soon represent some of the most important policy issues of the day. In this spirit, Chapters 5–8 provide a good introduction to some of those problems and represent logical solutions. The ultimate chapter is an overview that includes a discussion of behavioural economics and non-market valuation.

In closing, I would like to sincerely thank this fine set of authors for participating in this endeavour. Each chapter in this volume was peer reviewed and the authors in many cases made extensive revisions to improve their work. For this I am most appreciative. I had great pleasure working with each author on this project. I also thank the anonymous reviewers who spent a considerably amount of time and effort to lend insights that significantly improved the work herein. While your work is rarely lauded and you are truly 'behind the scenes', without your contributions this work would not have been able to rise to its current level.

John A. List
University of Chicago
NBER

1. Anchoring and yea-saying with private goods: an experiment

Ian Bateman, Alistair Munro, Bruce Rhodes, Chris V. Starmer and Robert Sugden

INTRODUCTION[1]

Elicitation effects in contingent valuation methodology (CVM) are said to occur when responses gathered from subjects are sensitive to the method of elicitation in a manner inconsistent with standard, Hicksian consumer theory. Two widely reported elicitation effects are starting point effects and yea-saying. Starting point effects (SPE) occur when reported valuations are correlated with some initial valuation cue, such as the bid value in dichotomous choice (DC) questions. Yea-saying describes the phenomenon of a subject agreeing to a proposal in the form of a direct question that she or he would reject under other conditions. For instance, a subject may agree to a bid price in a dichotomous choice format but then provide a lower stated valuation in a subsequent valuation exercise. A key difference between the two elicitation effects is that yea-saying is a unidirectional phenomenon, that is, it raises willingness-to-pay or reduces willingness-to-accept, whereas starting point bias can work in either direction depending on the value of the cue.

This chapter reports on an experiment designed to test for both types of elicitation effect within the context of a real market for two private goods in an incentive-compatible setting. One aim of the experiment is to examine the robustness of such effects; specifically, do they occur when subjects must make real rather than hypothetical choices and when the objects of choice are private rather than public goods? The second aim of the experiment is to distinguish between the two effects.

BACKGROUND

In the context of valuation, anchoring occurs when an individual's reported or revealed valuation is correlated with some prior numerical cue. Since its preliminary identification by Slovic and Lictenstein (1971), manifestations of anchoring have been identified in numerous and diverse settings, including the guessing of answers to multiplication problems and estimating the number of African countries in the United Nations (Kahneman et al., 1982). In these sorts of problems, subjects have the seemingly simple task of saying whether the true answer is above or below some initial suggested answer that has been offered by the organizer. A particularly stark example of anchoring can be found in the recent work of Ariely et al. (2003), who asked subjects for the final two digits of their US social security number and found that it was closely correlated with individuals' subsequent valuations of a variety of unfamiliar goods.

In the popular iterative bidding format of CVM, subjects are offered a controlled sequence of opportunities to give information about their valuation of a good. For instance, the experimenter may ask the subject if they are willing to pay x (the 'starting point') for an improvement in a public good and then, in a follow-up question, ask the subject to state a maximum willingness-to-pay. Intended as an improvement upon the open-ended (OE) format, the iterative bidding CVM revealed that final open-ended valuations were often correlated with the initial value of x – hence the term, starting point effect (Bateman et al., 1995; Boyle and Bishop, 1985; Boyle and Bishop, 1988; Brookshire et al., 1982; Cameron and Quiggin, 1994; Herriges and Shogren, 1996; Kealy et al., 1988; Rowe et al., 1980; Schulze et al., 1981).

Anchoring is one possible reason for SPE, with the anchor provided by the initial value of x offered to subjects. The initial bid value might act as a clue or hint regarding the good's value, especially when respondents are confused or unfamiliar with the good concerned (Bishop et al., 1983; Brookshire et al., 1982; Brown et al., 1996; Kealy and Turner 1993; McFadden, 1994). Since the domain of CVM largely involves the valuation of unfamiliar, non-marketed goods, this starting point problem has become recognized as a potentially serious flaw inherent in iterative bidding techniques (Boyle and Bishop, 1985, p. 193).

The DC protocol offers an alternative to bidding games. It has been suggested that this approach might simulate a more market-like setting, since it involves a simple accept–reject bid decision. The increased simplicity might help subjects to feel more comfortable answering a CVM valuation question (Seller et al., 1985). Furthermore, CVM surveys are typically limited by time, information, interaction, consultation and market experience, all of which may cause subjects to become rather uncertain about their responses. If subjects only have to think whether their true value is above or below some suggested amount, the whole valuation process may be simplified (Bishop et al., 1983). Comparisons between OE and DC formats have shown that OE mean and median estimates of willingness-to-pay (WTP) are consistently lower than the DC estimated means (Bateman et al., 1995; Bishop et al., 1983; Boyle et al., 1996; Brown et al., 1996; Cummings et al., 1995; Ready et al., 1996; Seller et al., 1985). One view is that these results demonstrate that OE questioning is typically subject to strategic behaviour. This serves to confirm strong priors of free-riding incentives in the public good context. A second explanation is that just as in iterative bidding processes, anchoring may occur in the DC format.

An alternative explanation of these results is however offered by yea-saying. This phenomena is documented in the existing psychology literature (Arndt and Crane, 1975; Crouch and Keniston, 1960), and is also becoming an issue of growing concern in the economics CVM literature (Brown et al., 1996; Kanninen, 1995; Kriström, 1993) as a possible influence on DC responses.

Brown et al. (1996) proposed that the simplicity of the take-it-or-leave-it choice might generate a conflicting objective in response. Torn between answering truthfully and showing a positive preference, if a DC bid is above her/his maximum WTP, a subject may still respond positively because she/he would like to demonstrate a positive preference for the good in question. In addition to this we might include the notion of the 'good respondent' (Orne, 1962). Orne described how subjects, when faced with officialdom, might respond positively to questions, only because they wrongly believe that such a response is exactly what the interviewer (in a position of perceived authority) wishes to hear.

Although some results can be interpreted as evidence for yea-saying, some caution is warranted. Point estimates from DC data which are used to compare with moments from open-ended data, have been found to be rather dependent upon the original specification of the bid function, and the Hanemann (1984) specifications have not been wholly supported (Cooper and Loomis, 1992). Given that many of the previous studies cited above compare OE with DC estimates based upon these functional specifications, it would be unwise to place too much emphasis on these studies as evidence of yea-saying.

Another approach, thereby avoiding the functional form problem entirely, is to test using synthetic data-sets or implicit preferences. The synthetic DC responses are constructed by allocating a 'yes' if an OE valuation is greater than or equal to those bids used in the actual DC questioning. Differences between actual and implicit responses can then be tested. Studies which have previously used these 'synthetic' data-sets have revealed evidence to support the yea-saying tendency (Bateman et al., 1995; Boyle et al., 1996; Holmes and Kramer, 1995; Kriström 1993; Ready et al., 1996). The studies cited produce evidence based on stated preference exercises with hypothetical goods. It is not clear whether the results can be replicated with individuals making real choices about real goods, hence the value of a controlled experiment.

Perhaps the closest investigation to ours is that reported in Frykblom and Shogren (2000) who use real choices and a split-sample design to value an environmental economics text using 108 Swedish university students. One group of students faced a Vickrey auction while the rest faced dichotomous choice questions with various bid levels. The authors argue that both yea-saying and anchoring will increase the acceptance of the proposal at high bid levels, while the two effects work in opposite directions for low bid levels. Hence it is possible to test between the impact of these two effects by comparing the distribution of values derived from the Vickrey auction with the upper and lower parts of the distribution derived from the DC exercise. In our experiment we have a larger sample size, two goods of different familiarity rather than one, and we use a Becker-de Groot-Marschak (BDM) mechanism rather than the Vickrey auction. However, the major difference is that for some subjects, after the DC questions we also have follow-up open-ended (OE) valuation questions. If only anchoring occurs, the values derived from open-ended questions should be consistent with the values from the DC questions, but if only yea-saying is present then the distribution of values derived from the OE questions should be independent of the bid level in the DC question and equal to the distribution obtained from subjects who face an open-ended question without a prior DC question. This provides a clear-cut means of distinguishing between anchoring and yea-saying. As we shall see, despite the differences in design between the two experiments, we obtain broadly the same results: there is little evidence of anchoring, but the data shows large-scale yea-saying in the responses of the subjects.

EXPERIMENTAL DESIGN

Consider an agents' valuation of a unit increase in the level of a private good. Let $wtp(v)$ be the maximum willingness-to-pay for the increase when the subject receives a prior exposure to the anchor value v and let wtp be the maximum willingness-to-pay when the subject faces no such anchor. For willingness-to-pay, an anchoring effect occurs if,

$$\begin{aligned} wtp(v) > wtp \quad & v > wtp \\ wtp(v) < wtp \quad & v < wtp. \end{aligned}$$

Let $P(x)$ be the proportion of the population whose wtp exceeds x in the absence of a common anchor and let $P(x/v)$ be the proportion whose wtp

exceeds x when each subject is exposed to the anchor value v. If anchoring occurs then,

$$P(x/v) > P(x) \quad x < v$$
$$P(x/v) < P(x) \quad x > v$$

It follows that,

$$\text{Median } wtp(v) > \text{median } wtp \quad v > \text{median } wtp$$
$$\text{Median } wtp(v) < \text{median } wtp \quad v < \text{median } wtp.$$

Figure 1.1 illustrates these relationships for the case where $v <$ median wtp.

Meanwhile, let $\pi(x)$ be the proportion of the population who agree that they are willing to pay at least x. Yea-saying occurs when,

$$\pi(x) > P(x).$$

For decreases in the level of the good, we can define similar notions. Let $wta(v)$ be the minimum willingness-to-accept compensation for a unit decrease in the private good when the subject receives a prior exposure to

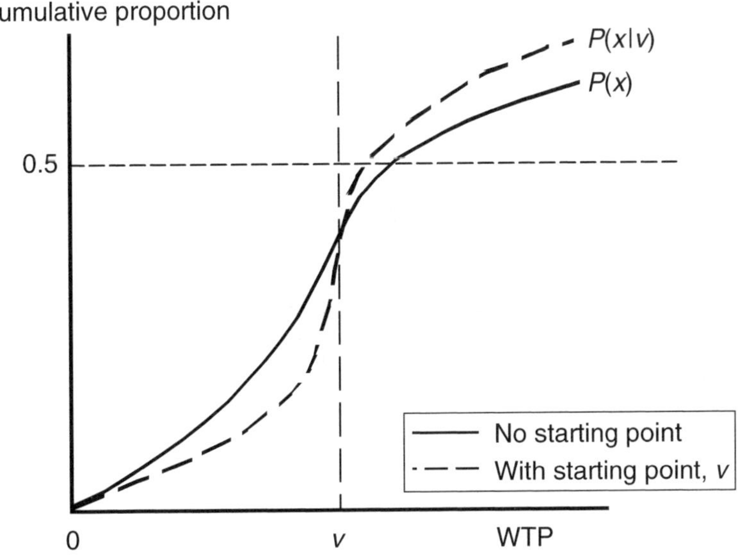

Figure 1.1 The effect of a starting point, with anchoring

the anchor value v and let wta be the minimum willingness-to-accept in the absence of such anchor. An anchoring effect occurs if,

$$\begin{array}{ll} wta(v) > wta & v > wta \\ wta(v) < wta & v < wta \end{array}$$

Let $R(x)$ be the proportion of the population whose wta exceeds x in the absence of a common anchor and let $R(x/v)$ be the proportion whose wta exceeds x when each subject is exposed to the anchor value v. If anchoring occurs then,

$$\begin{array}{ll} R(x/v) > R(x) & x < v \\ R(x/v) < R(x) & x > v \end{array}$$

Meanwhile, let $1-\rho(x)$ be the proportion of the population who agree that they are willing to accept x. Yea-saying occurs when,

$$1-\rho(x) > 1-R(x) \text{ or } R(x) > \rho(x).$$

Table 1.1 summarizes the predictions for anchoring and yea-saying as a whole.

The basic design of the experiment follows from these definitions. In the first treatment, valuations are elicited from subjects who receive no common anchor.[2] In the second treatment, subjects face two related questions, with the second immediately following the first. The first involves a choice where an anchoring value is provided (for example, are you willing to pay v?). In the second, valuations are elicited in a format identical to that used in the first treatment.

Table 1.1 Summary of predictions

	WTP		WTA	
	$x>v$	$v>x$	$x>v$	$v>x$
Hicksian	$P(x\|v)=P(x)$ $P(x)=\pi(x)$	$P(x\|v)=P(x)$ $P(x)=\pi(x)$	$R(x\|v)=R(x)$ $R(x)=\rho(x)$	$R(x\|v)=R(x)$ $R(x)=\rho(x)$
Anchoring and yea-saying	$P(x)>P(x\|v)$ $P(x)<\pi(x)$	$P(x)<P(x\|v)$ $P(x)<\pi(x)$	$R(x)>R(x\|v)$ $R(x)>\rho(x)$	$R(x)<R(x\|v)$ $R(x)>\rho(x)$
Anchoring, no yea-saying	$P(x)>P(x\|v)$ $P(x)=\pi(x)$	$P(x)<P(x\|v)$ $P(x)=\pi(x)$	$R(x)>R(x\|v)$ $R(x)=\rho(x)$	$R(x)<R(x\|v)$ $R(x)=\rho(x)$
Yea-saying, no anchoring	$P(x\|v)=P(x)$ $P(x)<\pi(x)$	$P(x\|v)=P(x)$ $P(x)<\pi(x)$	$R(x)=R(x\|v)$ $R(x)>\rho(x)$	$R(x)=R(x\|v)$ $R(x)>\rho(x)$

Experimental Details[3]

The goods

We used two private goods (a bottle of Cava semi-sparkling wine and a box of 240 tea bags). As noted earlier, the results of previous studies (for example, Kealy et al., 1993) have shown that if a subject has a high degree of familiarity with the good in question, the incidence of biases such as starting point and yea-saying could be significantly reduced. In this case, the intention was to select goods that encouraged some variance in familiarity and characteristics. Tea bags (a staple of British culture) were felt to be the most well-known and the most regularly consumed, relative to the sparkling wine. Thus subjects would be more certain of their preferences and find it easier to formulate an OE value for the more familiar good (teabags as opposed to wine) and hence less vulnerable to the influence of yea-saying and starting point effects when familiarity is high. Subjects are more likely to be influenced by suggested bid levels if they have not previously thought about their preferences for a good (such as the Cava wine) and, being less certain of their preferences, they may be more liable to certain stochastic variation and error.

The questions

By analogy with CVM, in what follows we shall label choice questions as 'DC' and label the questions where subjects had to fill in valuations as 'OE'.

Each task was described by a display on a visual display unit (VDU) screen. At the top of the screen were the words, '*If this question is selected, you will be given . . .*' followed by a specific endowment of money only, for example, '*£6*' or an endowment of a single unit quantity of one of the goods, for example, '*A bottle of wine*'. The next line of text read, '*In addition to this, you will be required to accept either A or B*'.

The letters (the pairs varied) labelled alternative options where the first option described possible transfers of money, or the good, from the subject to the experimenter ('*You give us*') or from the experimenter to the subject ('*We give you*'). The second option was fully described in both elicitation formats but the first option varied according to the format being used. For a DC question, the first option involved a pre-specified amount as one of the high or low bids. The subject was asked to select which option they preferred, for example, for a DC WTP for wine question:

A: *You give us £3 and we give you a bottle of wine.*
B: *No change.*

'No change' here meant that the subject kept their original endowment (£6 here).[4]

Similarly, the open-ended questioning involved two options. In the first option, the quantity of money was unspecified and in its place was an empty box. If the unspecified amount of money was a transfer of cash from subject to experimenter, the subject had to state the most they would be willing to pay such that they would prefer the first option. If the transfer of money was from the experimenter to the subject, the subject had to state the least amount they would receive in order to prefer the first option.

The incentives and the sequence of events

Incentives were provided by a random lottery device. If, at the end of the experiment, one of the choice questions were selected by the lottery device, then the subject received his or her choice. For questions where valuations were required, the widely used Becker de Groot-Marschak (BDM) mechanism was employed. In this incentive-compatible mechanism a random price is generated. If the valuation stated by the subject is less favourable to them than the generated price, then exchange occurs at the random price. If the generated price is less favourable then no trade is made. A computer-generated 'roulette-wheel' was employed to illustrate how the BDM worked.

After a brief introduction, the experimenters described the goods involved in the experiment, using a script, and allowed the subjects to inspect samples of the goods displayed in the laboratory. The random lottery and incentive mechanisms were then explained to the subjects. To ensure they fully understood the incentive compatibility of the BDM device, each subject was required to run through five practice questions before they proceeded to the experiment proper. In each session, half an hour was spent on instructing subjects through these practices using a familiar brand of individually wrapped biscuits as a dummy good. The first practice involved a demonstration of the DC question. For subsequent practices, involving WTP and willingness-to-accept (WTA) in an open-ended format, subjects were shown the BDM 'roulette wheel' after they had completed the statement. This was to clearly demonstrate what would happen if the practice question was in fact the one to be played out 'for real'.

As a check to see if subjects were understanding the design, two multiple-choice questions were asked as part of practices number 2 and 4. These questions were presented on screen after the subject had confirmed their amount in the statement, but before the BDM wheel was displayed. As an example, the two options in the third practice for an equivalent gain type question were '*C: We give you . . . biscuits*' and '*D: We give you £2.00*'. Suppose the subject had written 10 as their answer. The computer would then present the multiple-choice question which might read: *If the computer wrote 11 as the amount for option C, which of these outcomes would you be required to accept? a: We give you 11 biscuits. b: We give you 10 biscuits. c: We give you £2.00.* The other multiple-choice question had the same format. Subjects were not given advice on how to answer the question, but if they got it wrong they were then asked to repeat the question under individual instruction.

Once subjects had completed the fifth practice they were then faced with the 18 decision tasks.

Parameters and subject groups

Table 1.2 summarizes the treatments. Subjects were randomly divided into three groups, I, II and III. For each good (tea bags, wine) and each valuation type (WTA, WTP) we used two bid levels as potential anchors – high and low.[5] So, for instance, Group I faced four questions relevant to our study: one where they were asked their WTP for tea with no anchoring price provided and three where there was an initial DC question followed by an open-ended question on the same valuation. We can see from Table 1.2 that, for each combination of good and valuation type, one group faced a DC question with the high bid level, with a follow-up OE question, a second group faced the same sequence but with a low bid level and the third group faced the OE question only. All subjects faced both valuation types for each of the two goods. So as to reduce any cross-task contamination, no subject faced all the high bids or all the low bids for any single good. Furthermore, the order of related tasks was randomized so that if contamination were to occur it would not have any systematic effects on the final results.[6]

Subjects facing a WTP question were given money endowments of £6 for wine and £3 for tea bags. For a WTA question, subjects were given the good to sell back to the experimenter.

Table 1.2 Parameter values

	Group I	Group II	Group III
WTP tea	—	£1.00	£2.00
WTA tea	£2.50	—	£1.50
WTP wine	£3.00	—	£1.50
WTA wine	£3.00	£5.50	—

RESULTS

Overall we have data from 185 subjects, principally undergraduates from the University of East Anglia, none of whom had experience of a similar experiment. In common with many other experiments (for example, Bateman et al., 1997) we find a significant difference between mean values for WTP and WTA gathered from the no anchor subjects: for tea bags, mean WTP was £0.74 while mean WTA was £1.74; for wine, mean WTP was £1.82 while mean WTA was £3.79.

Table 1.3 summarizes the main evidence from the experiment. In the column headed DC it shows the percentages agreeing with the explicit valuation question. In the subsequent three columns we have the percentages of the subjects whose stated valuations mean that they agree *implicitly* with the valuation question. Recall that there are three such columns because there are three treatments: subjects facing a high anchor, subjects facing a low anchor and subjects facing no common anchor. As can be

Table 1.3 Actual and implicit valuations (percentages accepting offer)

Valuation	DC	OE no anchor	OE low anchor	OE high anchor	Z1	Z2	F
WTP £1.00, tea bags	43.1	39.7	34.5	39.1	0.58	0.95	1.71
WTP £2.00, tea bags	14.5	5.2	5.2	5.8	1.73**	1.69**	0.02
WTA £2.50, tea bags	86.2	74.1	68.1	65.5	1.63*	2.60***	1.56
WTA £1.50, tea bags	68.1	39.7	34.2	20.7	3.21***	3.92***	3.59**
WTP £1.50, wine	85.5	63.7	56.5	60.3	2.84***	3.75***	0.84
WTP £3.00, wine	39.7	17.2	7.2	12.1	2.68***	3.91***	1.05
WTA £5.50, wine	91.4	85.5	89.7	83.9	2.12***	2.22***	0.55
WTA £3.00, wine	60.3	47.8	39.7	37.5	1.409*	2.23***	0.77

Notes:
Z1: Z test of equality of DC and OE no anchor proportions.
Z2: Z test of equality of DC and corresponding anchor proportions.
F: Anova test of equality of all three anchor proportions.
*** 1% level.
** 5% level.
* 10% level.

seen, in all cases the figure for implicit agreement is lower than that for agreement with the explicit question. Broadly speaking, it also appears that the percentages for implicit agreement are the same within each valuation task.

The final three columns of Table 1.3 summarize the results of tests of the main hypotheses. Z1 gives the z value for a test that the proportion of subjects who agree with the explicit question is equal to the proportion of the no-anchor subjects who implicitly agree with the question. In all eight cases the difference between these two proportions is in the direction predicted by both anchoring and yea-saying. In five of the cases, this difference is statistically significant at 5 per cent or lower significance levels (1-tailed test). Z2 then gives the z test values for a test of the hypothesis that the proportion of subjects who agree with the explicit question is equal to the proportion of the same subjects whose answers in the follow-up valuation question implies that they agree with the question. If there is yea-saying, the first of these proportions should be higher, whereas with anchoring or with no anchoring, the proportions should be equal. As can be seen, in all cases the differences are in the direction predicted by yea-saying and in seven out of the eight cases the difference is significant at the 5 per cent level or lower. The final column reports the results of an anova test that the values of the three OE proportions are equal. If there is anchoring then the proportions should differ, whereas with no-anchoring or with yea-saying the proportions should be equal. In only one case is the F value significant at the 5 per cent level. In the other cases the result is not significant and in several instances the differences between the proportions are not in the directions predicted by anchoring.

Summing up, the evidence supports the notion that yea-saying rather than SPE best explains the data. To explore this further, we examine the full distribution of answers to the OE questions (Figures 1.2–1.5). For each valuation type the y axes show the cumulative percentage of values at or below the figure on the x axis, for the three OE treatments (no anchor, low anchor and high anchor). Kolmogorov-Smirnoff tests are not remotely significant for any of the differences between the distributions.

Table 1.4 gives the median values from the experiment, together with tests of their difference. Recall that if anchoring occurs, then the impact of an anchor depends on the sign of the difference between the anchor value and the median in the absence of an anchor. When this median is higher than the anchor, the effect of the anchor should be to lower the median; conversely when the anchor is higher, the effect of the anchor should be to raise the median. Broadly speaking, the differences between medians have the anticipated sign, although in two instances there is no

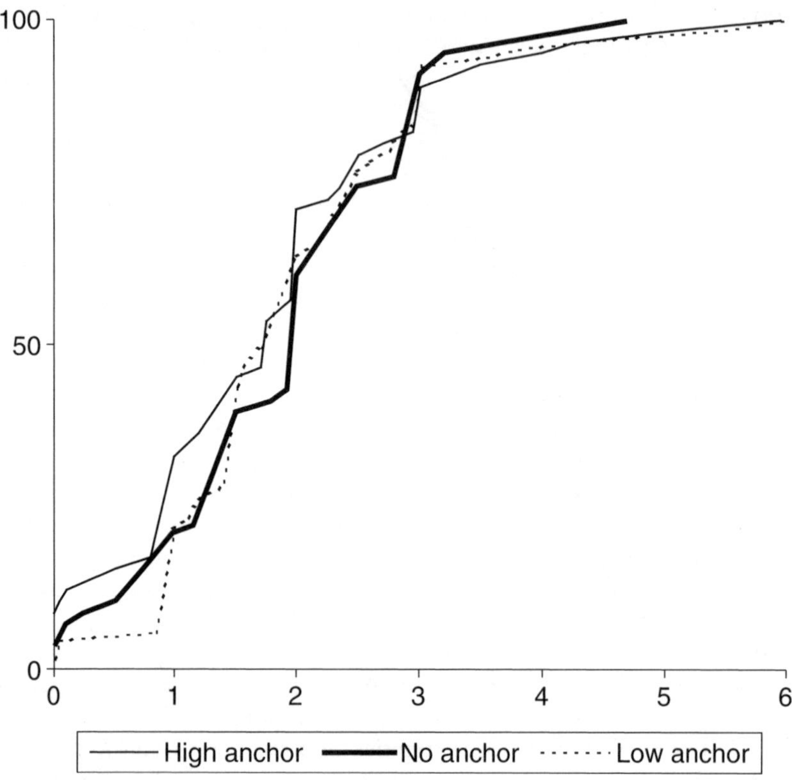

Figure 1.2 Cumulative valuations: WTP for wine

difference in the medians and in one case (WTP for wine) the median with the low anchor is higher than that without an anchor; the anchoring argument would clearly predict otherwise. Moreover, in six comparisons between the no-anchor medians and the medians with an anchor none are significantly different from one another at the 5 per cent level (one-tailed test).[7]

We examine the consistency of responses from individuals who faced both the DC question and the OE follow-up. Let us define a *nay-sayer* as a subject who refuses a WTP (WTA) but then gives an OE value higher (lower) than the DC bid value. If the incidence of yea-saying and nay-saying is equal, then there would be no evidence to say that yea-saying is caused by anything other than random error. The results are shown in Table 1.5, where, for instance it, can be seen that out of 59 individuals who agreed that they were WTP at least £1.50 for the Cava, 12 subsequently gave

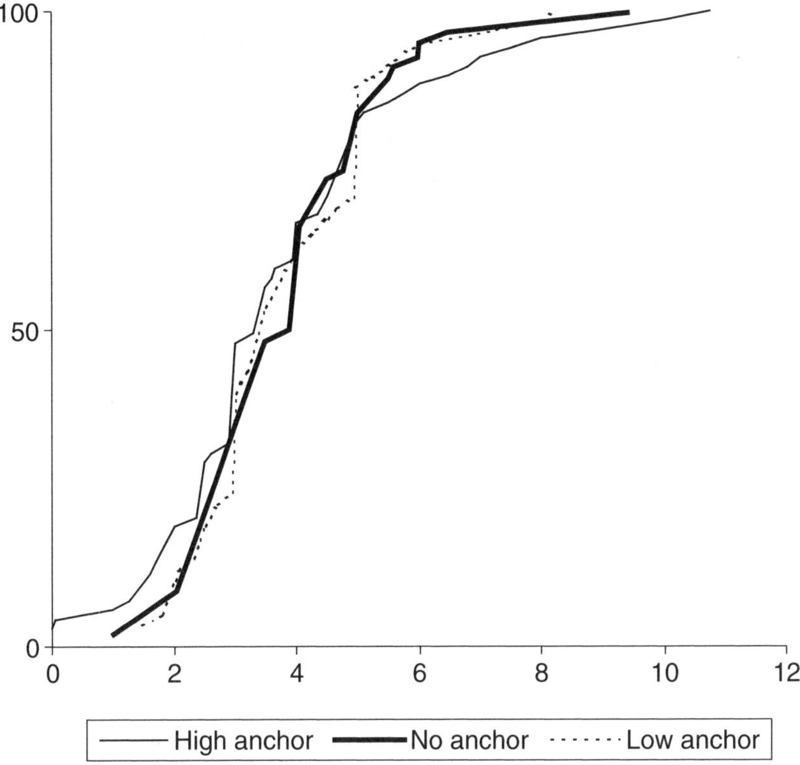

Figure 1.3 Cumulative valuations: WTA for wine

valuations strictly below £1.50. Meanwhile, out of the ten people who would not pay £1.50, only one subsequently gave a WTP value at or above £1.50. We can see that, with the exception of two of the WTA formats, preference reversals were much more likely to be of the yea-saying kind rather than nay-saying.

DISCUSSION

We find that simple models of anchoring do not explain our data well – the distributions of values for subjects who faced different anchoring treatments are remarkably similar. As a result we conclude that anchoring effects are not a significant part of the explanation here. This is in contrast to evidence of strong anchoring effects found widely in other

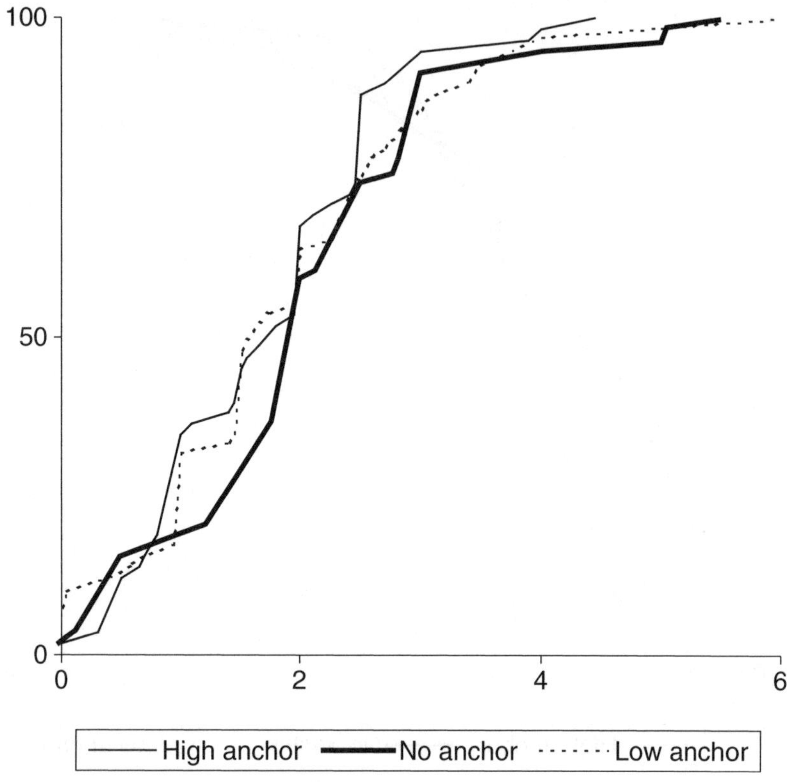

Figure 1.4 Cumulative valuations: WTA for tea bags

studies (for example, Ariely et al., 2003) where unfamiliar goods are involved. On the other hand, it is consistent with Frykblom and Shogren, (2000) and with the evidence on US consumption presented by van Soest and Hurd (2003). Partly the difference may lie in the goods involved. In our experiment and in the last two studies cited, familiar goods were the objects of valuation, whereas anchoring effects seemed to have been found most clearly when subjects were facing new or unfamiliar valuation tasks, which is often the case in environmental valuation.

Nearly all of our evidence is consistent with the yea-saying phenomenon. We obtain significantly higher rates of acceptance of explicit questions posed to subjects, compared with the rates of implicit acceptance computed from the valuation questions. On the other hand, psychological explanations of yea-saying are often grounded in the idea that subjects are conforming with what they perceive as the interviewer's views or seeking to

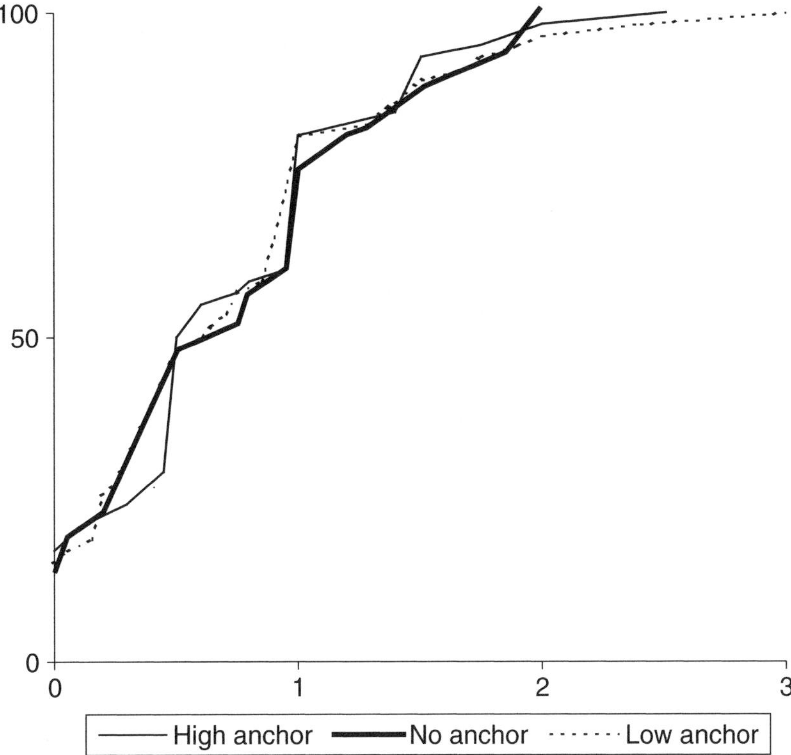

Figure 1.5 Cumulative valuations: WTP for tea bags

please the interviewer in a face-to-face setting (Arndt and Crane, 1975). Our subjects were faced with a computer screen and, although the experimenters were in the room during the experiment, they were not closely monitoring individual responses. It is possible therefore that the results we have obtained do not necessarily reflect yea-saying as it is normally interpreted.[8]

Whatever the source of our results, they do not suggest that the DC format is necessarily superior to open-ended valuation questions when it comes to CVM. Open-ended questions create well-known cues and incentives for strategic bidding. On the other hand, even with familiar goods in a non-hypothetical setting our experiments shows strong evidence of yea-saying in DC questions, which must raise questions about their suitability in the field.

Table 1.4 Medians of WTP and WTA for all groups

Medians	Anchor			Median differences		
	None	Low	High	None v. Low	None v. High	Low v. High
WTP for tea bags	0.550	0.625	0.65	−0.075 (0.686)	−0.100 (0.953)	−0.025 (0.226)
WTA for tea bags	1.800	1.600	2.00	0.200 (1.010)	−0.200 (1.010)	−0.400 (1.880**)
WTP for wine	1.750	2.000	2.00	−0.250 (1.210)	−0.250 (1.190)	0
WTA for wine	3.500	3.500	3.95	0	−0.450 (1.340)	−0.450 (1.620)

Note: Figures in parenthesis denote Mann-Whitney z value (*** 1% ** 5%).

Table 1.5 The extent of yea-saying

	Yea-saying	Nay-saying
Wine		
Are you WTP £1.50?	12/59	1/10
Are you WTP £3.00?	10/23	1/35
Are you WTA £3.00?	14/35	1/23
Are you WTA £5.50?	6/56	2/2
Tea		
Are you WTP £1.00?	6/25	0/33
Are you WTP £2.00?	6/10	0/59
Are you WTA £1.50?	16/47	1/22
Are you WTA £2.50?	8/50	3/8

NOTES

1. This research was supported by the Economic and Social Research Council of Great Britain (award No. W 119 25 1014). We are also grateful to Jan Anderson for help with running the experiment, and to Xiangping Liu for comments on an earlier draft.
2. There may still be individual anchoring effects or self-generated anchors, depending on the history of the individual subject.
3. Other parts of this experiment involved testing for reference point effects in individual valuations of chocolates and cans of coke. This reference-dependent part of the experiment is reported separately in Bateman et al. (1997).
4. So we interpret choosing option A as saying 'yes'.
5. A pilot study was conducted (n = 52) to identify reasonable bid levels using open-ended questioning.
6. But follow-up OE questions always followed on immediately after the relevant DC question.
7. What is not immediately clear from the figures is the significant proportion of subjects who gave 'round number' valuations such as £1.50 or £2.00. In the most extreme example of this, 40 out of 58 subjects gave valuations ending in .50 or .00 when asked their WTA to give up tea bags. Tests based on median differences are likely to be particularly affected by the presence of such effects, but as Figures 1.2–1.5 demonstrate there is very little evidence for the anchors having a major impact on the distribution of reported values.
8. We can discount the possibility that the results are due to the kinds of psychological mechanisms which underpin preference reversals (see Cubitt et al., 2004). To see this note the tasks in our experiment involve trade-offs between goods and money. Valuation questions emphasize the monetary dimension of the subject's dilemma, rather than the goods dimension. If money has a higher weighting or if it is more prominent in valuation, then we would expect WTP to be lower in valuation compared to choice. This is consistent with our evidence, but we would also expect WTA to be lower in valuation, compared to choice and this is not consistent with our evidence. So it appears that are results are not consistent with standard ideas about preference reversal.

REFERENCES

Ariely, D., G. Loewenstein and D. Prelec (2003), 'Coherent arbitrariness: stable demand curves without stable preferences', *Quarterly Journal of Economics*, **118**, 73–105.

Arndt, J. and E. Crane (1975), 'Response bias, yea-saying, and the double negative', *Journal of Marketing Research*, **12**, 218–20.

Bateman, I., I. Langford, K. Turner, K. Willis and G. Garrod (1995), 'Elicitation and truncation effects in contingent valuation', *Ecological Economics*, **12**, 161–79.

Bateman, I., A. Munro, B. Rhodes, C. Starmer and R. Sugden (1997), 'A test of the theory of reference-dependent preferences', *Quarterly Journal of Economics*, **112**, 479–505.

Bishop, R.C., T.A. Heberlein and M. Kealy (1983), 'Contingent valuation of environmental assets: comparisons with a simulated market', *Natural Resources Journal*, **23**, 619–33.

Boyle, K.J., F.R. Johnson, D.W. McCollum, W.H. Desvousges, R.W. Dunford and S.P. Hudson (1996), 'Valuing public goods: discrete versus continuous contingent-valuation responses', *Land Economics*, **72**(3) No. 3, Aug., 381–96.

Boyle, K.J. and R.C. Bishop (1985), 'Welfare measurements using contingent valuation: a comparison of techniques', *American Journal of Agricultural Economics*, **67**, 20–28.

Boyle, K.J. and R.C. Bishop (1988), 'Valuing wildlife in benefit–cost analysis: a case study involving endangered species', *Water Resources Research*, **23**, 943–50.

Brookshire, D., W.D. Schulze, R.C. D'Arge and M.A. Thayer (1982), 'Valuing public goods: a comparison of survey and hedonic approaches', *American Economic Review*, **72**, 165–77.

Brown, T.C., P.A. Champ, R.C. Bishop and D.W. McCollum (1996), 'Which response format reveals the truth about donations to a public goods', *Land Economics*, **72**, 152–66.

Cameron, T.-A. and J. Quiggin (1994), 'Estimation using contingent valuation data from a dichotomous choice with follow-up questionnaire', *Journal of Environmental Economics and Management*, **27**, 218–34.

Cooper, J. and J. Loomis (1992), 'Sensitivity of willingness-to-pay estimates to bid design in dichotomous choice contingent valuation models', *Land Economics*, **68**, 211–24.

Crouch, A. and K. Keniston (1960), 'Yea-sayer and nay-sayers: agreeing response set as a personal variable', *Journal of Abnormal and Social Psychology*, **60**, 151–74.

Cubitt, R.P., A. Munro and C. Starmer (2004), 'Testing explanations of preference reversal', *Economic Journal*, **114**, 709–26.

Cummings, R.G., G.W. Harrison and E.E. Rutström (1995), 'Home-grown values and hypothetical surveys: is the dichotomous choice incentive compatible', *American Economic Review*, **85**, 260–66.

Frykblom, P. and J.F. Shogren (2000), 'An experimental testing of anchoring effects in discrete choice questions', *Environmental and Resources Economics*, **16**(3), 329–41.

Hanemann, M. (1984), 'Welfare evaluations in contingent valuation experiments with discrete responses', *American Journal of Agricultural Economics*, **66**(3), 332–41.

Herriges, J.A. and J.F. Shogren (1996), 'Starting point bias in dichotomous choice valuation with follow-up questioning', *Journal of Environmental Economic Management*, **30**, 112–31.

Holmes, T.P. and R.A. Kramer (1995), 'An independent sample test of yea-saying and starting point bias in dichotomous-choice contingent valuation', *Journal of Environmental Economic Management*, **29**, 121–32.
Kahneman, D., P. Slovic and A. Tversky (1982), *Judgement Under Uncertainty: Heuristics and Biases*, Cambridge: Cambridge University Press.
Kanninen, B.J. (1995), 'Bias in discrete response contingent valuation', *Journal of Environmental Economics and Management*, **28**, 114–25.
Kealy, M.J., J.F. Dovido and M.L. Rockel (1988), 'Accuracy in valuation is a matter of degree', *Land Economics*, **64**, 158–71.
Kealy, M.J. and R.W. Turner (1993), 'A test of the equality of closed-ended and open-ended contingent valuations', *American Journal of Agricultural Economics*, **75**(2), May, 321–31.
Kriström, B. (1993), 'Comparing continuous and discrete contingent valuation', *Environmental and Resource Economics*, **3**(1), 63–71.
McFadden, D. (1994), 'Contingent valuation and social choice', *American Journal of Agricultural Economics*, **76**(4), Nov., 689–708.
Orne, M.T. (1962), 'On the social psychology of the psychological experiment', *American Psychologist*, **17**, pp. 776–89.
Ready, R.C., J.C. Buzby and D. Hu (1996), 'Differences between continuous and discrete contingent value estimates', *Land Economics*, **72**, 397–411.
Rowe, R., R.C. D'Arge and D.S. Brookshire (1980), 'An Experiment on the economic value of visibility', *Journal of Environmental Economics and Management*, **7**, 1–19.
Sellar, C., J.R. Stoll and J.-P. Chavas (1985), 'Validation of empirical measures of welfare change: a comparison of non-market techniques', *Land Economics*, **61**, 156–75.
Schulze, W.D., B.C. d'Arge and D.S. Brookshire (1981), 'Valuing environmental commodities: some recent experiments', *Land Economics*, **57**(2), May, pp. 151–72.
Slovic, P. and S. Lictenstein (1971), 'Comparison of Bayesian and regression approaches to the study of information processing in judgement', *Organizational Behaviour and Human Performance*, **6**, 649–744.
Van Soest, A. and M. Hurd (2003), 'A test for anchoring and yea-saying in experimental consumption data', RAND Corporation, November.

2. Market price endogeneity and accuracy of value elicitation mechanisms

Jayson L. Lusk and Matthew Rousu

Environmental policies are frequently judged on the basis of cost–benefit analysis. One of the most difficult tasks in environmental and natural resource economics relates to determining benefits of environmental policies because of the lack of well-functioning markets that report individuals' values for goods such as parks, forests and endangered species. As a result, practitioners have turned to hypothetical or contingent markets to measure the value of environmental amenities. Since its inception the contingent valuation method has faced criticism, but perhaps the most profound weakness of the method is the finding that individuals behave differently in hypothetical settings as compared to when real money is on the line. A number of studies with public and private goods have found that individuals overstate the amount they are willing to pay in hypothetical valuation questions (Cummings et al., 1995; Fox et al., 1998; List and Shogren, 1998). In a meta analysis on the issue, List and Gallet (2001) reported that on average subjects overstate their willingness-to-pay in hypothetical settings by a factor of three. Efforts to reduce or eliminate this bias have primarily focused on *ex post* calibration methods that compare hypothetical statements to non-hypothetical statements (for example, Fox et al., 1998; Hofler and List, 2004) or *ex ante* methods such as 'cheap talk' that explain the problem of hypothetical bias to individuals prior to a value elicitation question (Cummings and Taylor, 1999; List, 2001; Lusk, 2003). In either case, true values must be elicited. For calibration methods, true values must be elicited as a basis from which to develop a calibration function. In the case of cheap talk, true values must be elicited from a separate group of participants to verify the accuracy of the cheap talk script.

A variety of value elicitation mechanisms have been utilized in the literature that create incentives for truthful value revelation.[1] These value elicitation mechanisms have been used to test economic theory (for example, List, 2002; Shogren et al., 1994), value novel goods and services (for example,

Lusk et al., 2001a), investigate effects of policy alternatives (for example, Hayes et al., 1995), value environmental amenities (for example, Boyce et al., 1992) and elicit risk preferences (for example, Kachelmeier and Shehata, 1992). However, one issue that has received little attention is the effect of market price endogeneity on the accuracy of value elicitation mechanisms. In incentive-compatible auctions, such as the Vickrey second price and random *n*th price auctions, subjects bid against one another in an active market environment, and the market price is determined endogenously. In contrast, other incentive-compatible mechanisms, such as the Becker-de Groot-Marschak (BDM) mechanism (Becker et al., 1964), have an exogenously determined market price. Theoretically, both frameworks (endogenous and exogenous price determination) yield equivalent results.

Despite the theoretical equivalence between elicitation mechanisms that employ exogenous and endogenous clearing prices, empirical evidence suggests the two approaches might generate divergent results. Some have suggested that the existence of an active market environment is necessary to generate economic rationality and that individual decisions made outside a market context are of little relevance to economists (for example, Shogren, forthcoming). This contention is supported by several studies that have found that certain economic anomalies persist in an individual decision-making environment but cease to exist in market-based environments. For example, Shogren et al. (2001a) found that the willingness-to-pay/willingness-to-accept disparity disappeared in active market environments such as the second and random *n*th price auctions but that the anomaly remained when values were elicited with the BDM mechanism. Chu and Chu (1990), Cox and Grether (1996), Cherry et al. (2003) and Cherry and Shogren (2001) have found that the preference reversal anomaly, although persistent on an individual level, can be eradicated in a market setting. Despite these findings, little is known about the effect of market price endogeneity on bidding behaviour in value elicitation mechanisms.

To explore the role of market price endogeneity on subject behaviour, we compare bids across three incentive-compatible value elicitation mechanisms: the second price auction, the random *n*th price auction, and the BDM mechanism.[2] Each of these mechanisms has been shown to be empirically demand revealing in the aggregate (for example, Cox et al., 1982; Irwin et al., 1998; Shogren et al., 2001b),[3] but little is known about the relative predictive ability of mechanisms involving endogenous pricing versus exogenous pricing.

A couple of studies have highlighted how relative accuracy across different incentive-compatible mechanism can diverge. In an induced value study, Shogren et al. (2001b) found that although both the second and random *n*th price auctions were demand revealing in the aggregate, the random *n*th (second) price auction was more accurate for off-margin (on-margin) bidders than the second (random nth) price auction. That is, the random *n*th price auction had the ability to engage bidders with relatively low values that were far away from the market price, whereas the second price auction had the ability to engage bidders with relatively high values that were close to the market price. Intuitively, in a random nth price auction, every individual has a reasonable probability of winning, regardless of their true value; however, in a second price auction only those individuals with a relatively high value have a meaningful chance of winning the auction. In another induced value study, Noussair et al. (2004) found that the second price auction tended to generate bids closer to true values than the BDM mechanism for all high and low induced values. This finding partially contradicts that in Shogren et al. (2001b) because the BDM mechanism and the random *n*th are similar in terms of an individual's probability of winning and, as such, the BDM should better engage individuals with relatively low values. The contention in Shogren et al. (2001b) that the second price auction should be more accurate than the random *n*th for higher-valued individuals is supported by the analytical results in Lusk et al. (2005), which indicate that the expected cost of sub-optimal bidding (for example, not bidding true value) is increasing as an individual's value increases for the second price auction but so for the BDM or random *n*th. In fact, Lusk et at. show that the expected costs of sub-optimal bidding (for example, not bidding true value) are virtually equivalent for the BDM and random *n*th. Their results suggest that any observed differences in bidding behaviour between the BDM and random nth are not likely due to differences in the shape of the pay-off function but perhaps to the psychological effect of an individual bidding against other humans in a competitive market as opposed to bidding against a sterile random price generator as with the BDM.[4]

In this chapter, we first test the demand-revealing properties of the second price, random *n*th price, and BDM mechanisms in an induced value experiment. We then compare the accuracy of the three mechanisms by comparing absolute and squared deviations between bids and induced values across elicitation mechanisms. We find that accuracy differed across mechanisms lending support to the notion that market-price endogeneity influenced bidding behaviour. Although we find evidence that all three mechanisms were demand revealing in the aggregate, the two market-based mechanisms generated bids closer to induced values than the non-market mechanism. Results highlight the importance of an active market environment in generating behaviour consistent with theoretical predictions.

EXPERIMENTAL DESIGN

The BDM mechanism, the random *n*th -price auction, and the second price auction are all theoretically demand revealing (that is, each participant has a dominant strategy to bid his/her true value), yet the three mechanisms are, procedurally, quite different. The BDM works as follows. An individual submits a bid for one unit of a good. The monitor then selects a random number drawn from a uniform distribution over some fixed interval. This randomly drawn number serves as the price, and if the individual's bid price is higher than this price, he/she purchases one unit of the good at the clearing price. In contrast to the BDM, individuals bid against one another in second and random *n*th price auctions and the market clearing price is endogenously determined from individuals' bids. The second price auction, originally introduced by Vickrey (1961), involves each of k bidders submitting bids for one unit of a good. The highest bidder purchases one unit of the good at the second highest bid amount, which is the market price. Shogren et al. (2001b) introduced the random *n*th price auction to incorporate advantages of the BDM (all bidders are engaged because every participant can potentially win the auction) and the second price auction (market price is endogenously determined). The random *n*th price auction is similar to the second price auction except that the market price is randomly determined from the sample of bids rather than being fixed at the second highest bid amount. Specifically, each of k bidders submits a bid for one unit of a good; then each of the bids is rank-ordered from highest to lowest. The auction monitor then selects a random number (n), which is drawn from a uniform distribution between 2 and k, and the monitor sells one unit of the good to each of the $(n - 1)$ highest bidders at the *n*th highest bid amount. For instance, if the monitor randomly selects $n = 5$, the four highest bidders each purchase one unit of the good priced at the fifth highest bid. Again, despite the procedural differences, theoretically, an individual's dominant strategy is to bid his or her true value in all three elicitation mechanisms.

In this study, an induced value experiment was designed to determine the performance of the BDM mechanism relative to two auction mechanisms with endogenous clearing prices: the random *n*th and second price auctions. Thirty-nine students were recruited from undergraduate economics courses to take part in the study, where they had the chance to win a cash prize. Recruited subjects were assigned to one of four experimental treatments. Each experimental treatment consisted of three sessions. In the first session, subjects either participated in a second, random *n*th, or BDM exercise. Within the first session, subjects participated in four bidding rounds. Then subjects moved to the second session, which involved a change in elicitation

Table 2.1 Elicitation mechanisms used in each of the sessions

Treatment	Auction Elicitation Procedure – Session			
	BDM	Second price	Random *n*th price	BDM
1 (9 participants)			X	X
2 (10 participants)		X		X
3 (10 participants)	X		X	
4 (10 participants)	X	X		

mechanism. Within the second session, subjects again participated in four bidding rounds. The four experimental treatments are summarized in Table 2.1. In the first treatment, nine subjects participated in four rounds of a random *n*th price auction in the first session and then participated in four rounds of the BDM mechanism in the second session. Similarly, in treatment 2, ten subjects participated in four bidding rounds of a second price auction and then participated in four bidding rounds with the BDM mechanism. Treatments 1 and 3 and treatments 2 and 4 are the same except the order of the elicitation mechanisms is reversed. As Table 2.1 shows, all subjects participated in a BDM exercise (in either the first or second session) and in either the second or random *n*th price auction. This design allows for a within-subject comparison of bids in endogenous and exogenous price environments and controls for order effects. The third experimental session, which is part of a separate analysis not discussed in this chapter, involved subjects bidding in an induced value auction with uncertainty regarding assigned induced values. This chapter focuses solely on the results from the first two experimental sessions from each treatment.

The following outlines the steps in the experiment.[5] In Step 1, participants arrived and received a recording sheet that listed their individual and private induced values for each of the rounds of the experiment. We used the same ten induced values for each bidding round. These values were randomly drawn from a uniform distribution with bounds 1 and 40. The selected induced values were 3, 9, 11, 14, 16, 20, 24, 29, 33, and 38. The induced values were assigned to individuals such that each person had a different induced value in each round, although the distribution of induced values across individuals was identical in each round. The induced values were described as tokens. Subjects were informed that at the end of the experiment they would participate in a lottery for $30, where their chances of winning were directly related to the number of earned tokens. At the end of the experiment, all subjects' (individually labelled) tokens were placed in a bin, and one token was drawn to determine the winner of the $30 cash prize.[6]

In Step 2, bidding procedures were explained to participants. Subjects were told that they would earn profits each round equal to

$$iv_i - b^* \quad \text{if } b_i > b^* \tag{2.1}$$

and

$$0 \quad \text{if } b_i \leq b^*, \tag{2.2}$$

where iv_i is participant i's induced value, b_i is participant i's bid, and b^* is the market price. Following the instructions, participants were allowed to ask any clarification questions. In Step 3, each participant wrote his/her bids on the bid sheet. In Step 4, the monitors collected all of the bids and ranked them from highest to lowest. In Step 5, the monitors determined and announced the market price. For the BDM, the market price was drawn from a uniform distribution of 1 through to 40 tokens; for the second price auction, the market price was the second highest bid, and the market price for the random *n*th price auction was determined by randomly drawing one bid from the sample bids. In Step 6, individuals who bid above the market-clearing price purchased one unit of the good at the market price. In Step 7, profits were determined according to Equations (2.1) and (2.2). In Step 8, the round ended, and the process was repeated again starting at Step 3.

RESULTS

Table 2.2 reports the mean and median bid deviation (bid minus induced value) for each elicitation mechanism for the third and fourth bidding rounds for each auction mechanism.[7] On average, subjects overbid in all three mechanisms, although the mean overbid was small, ranging from 0.70 tokens to 0.94 tokens (for example, an expected value of about \$0.15 to \$0.20). As an initial attempt to determine whether the mechanisms were empirically demand revealing, we tested whether the average deviations were significantly different from zero. Parametric t-tests and non-parametric Wilcoxon signed rank tests for each of the three auction mechanisms indicate that we cannot reject the null hypothesis that each mechanism is, on average, demand revealing. Although somewhat informative, the average deviation can be misleading. For example, if one bidder bids 20 tokens less than his/her induced value, while another bidder bids 20 tokens more than his/her induced value, their behaviour would offset and produce an average deviation of zero. As a result, absolute or squared

Table 2.2 Aggregate deviations and tests for incentive compatibility

	Elicitation mechanism		
	BDM	Second price	Random *n*th price
Mean deviation[a]	0.821 (6.028)[b]	0.700 (4.800)	0.974 (3.894)
Median deviation	0.000	0.000	0.000
t-test[c]	1.202 [0.23][d]	0.922 [0.36]	1.541 [0.13]
Wilcoxon signed rank test[e]	14.5 [0.91]	26 [0.49]	70 [0.07]
Number of observations	78	40	38

Notes:
[a] Bid minus induced value. Using the bids from both the third and fourth rounds of bidding.
[b] Numbers in parentheses are standard deviations.
[c] t-statistic associated with the null hypothesis that the mean deviation = 0.
[d] Numbers in brackets are p-values from two-tailed t-test.
[e] Test statistic from non-parametric signed rank tests of the null hypothesis that the mean deviation = 0.

deviations provide more information about the demand-revealing nature of each of the auction mechanisms. Perhaps more importantly, from an applied viewpoint, absolute and squared deviations indicate the accuracy of the elicitation mechanism.

Table 2.3 reports mean squared and absolute deviations of each of the three elicitation mechanisms. The second and random *n*th price auctions yielded similar mean squared and absolute deviations. The BDM mechanism had larger mean squared and absolute deviations than both the second and random *n*th price auctions. However, the differences are only marginally statistically significant. The hypothesis that the mean squared deviation is equivalent across the BDM and second (random *n*th) price auction can only be rejected at the $p=0.20$ ($p=0.31$) level according to a two-sided non-parametric Mann–Whitney test. We also calculated the percentage of bids that were equal to induced values (the weakly dominant strategy) and the percentage of bids within two tokens of induced values. The percentage of bids within two units of induced values is similar across the three mechanisms, with the BDM having the lowest percentage at 64.10 per cent and the random *n*th price having the largest percentage at 67.50 per cent.[8] In contrast, the percentage of bids exactly equal to induced values varied widely across the auction mechanisms. The BDM mechanism performed the worst, with only 20.51 per cent of bids exactly demand revealing. In contrast, over 31 per cent and 37 per cent of random *n*th and second price bids, respectively, were exactly demand revealing. Both parametric t-tests ($p=0.04$) and non-parametric Mann–Whitney U tests ($p=0.04$) indicate that the percentage of perfectly demand-revealing bids

Table 2.3 Squared and absolute deviations of the elicitation mechanisms

	Elicitation mechanism		
	BDM	Second price	Random *n*th price
Mean absolute deviation	3.44 (5.01)[a]	2.70 (4.01)	2.45 (3.16)
Mean squared deviation	36.54 (120.47)	22.95 (65.77)	15.71 (35.06)
Bid = induced value	20.51%	37.50%	31.58%
Bid within 2 tokens of induced value	64.10%	67.50%	65.79%
Number of observations	78	40	38

Note: [a] Numbers in parentheses are standard deviations.

is significantly different across the BDM mechanism and the second price auction.

Results reported in Tables 2.2 and 2.3 only provide weak evidence of differences across mechanisms because each subject submitted multiple bids and the statistical tests assume that observations are independent. Following Shogren et al. (2001b), we use the following equation to address this issue:

$$BID_{it} = \beta(IV_{it}) + \alpha_i + \gamma_t + \varepsilon_{it} \tag{2.3}$$

where BID_{it} is subject *i*'s bid in trial *t*, (IV_{it}) is subject *i*'s induced value in trial *t*, α_i represents subject-specific effects, γ_t represents trial-specific effects, and ε_{it} is the overall bidding error. If bids from a particular mechanism are perfectly demand revealing, then $\beta = 1$, $\alpha_i = 0 \ \forall \ i$ and $\gamma_t = 0 \ \forall \ t$. For each elicitation mechanism, we estimated equation (2.3) and carried out a variety of specification tests to determine whether subject-specific and trial-specific effects should be incorporated and whether random or fixed effects was the appropriate specification. First, equation (2.3) was estimated imposing the assumption that $\alpha_i = \alpha \ \forall \ i$ and $\gamma_t = \gamma \ \forall \ t$; this is the OLS specification. Then, random and fixed effects models were estimated. An LM test was used to determine whether the random effects specification was preferred to the ordinary least squares (OLS) and a Hausman test was used to determine whether the random effects specification was preferred over a fixed effects specification. For the random *n*th price auction, test results indicated that a random effects model incorporating trial-specific effects only was the appropriate specification. For the BDM and the second price auction, test results indicated that ordinary least squares with one overall constant was appropriate.

Table 2.4 Regression results: test for behaviour consistent with dominant strategy[a]

Variable	Elicitation mechanism		
	BDM[b]	Second price[c]	Random nth price[d]
Intercept	2.758*[e] (1.414)[f]	1.185 (1.615)	2.184 (1.723)
Induced value	0.902* (0.069)	0.975* (0.072)	0.937* (0.052)
Wald test[g]	3.901 [0.14][h]	0.948 [0.62]	1.947 [0.38]
R^2	0.73	0.83	0.88

Notes:
[a] Dependent variable is bid.
[b] Results from ordinary least squares.
[c] Results from ordinary least squares.
[d] Results from random effects model incorporating trial-specific effects.
[e] One asterisk (*) represents 0.05 level of statistical significance.
[f] Numbers in parentheses are standard errors.
[g] Test of joint hypothesis that intercept = 0 and induced value = 1; distributed chi-square with 2 d.f.
[h] Numbers in brackets are p-values from Wald test.

Regression results are reported in Table 2.4. For all three elicitation mechanisms, the intercepts are greater than zero and slopes are less than unity. However, the null hypotheses that the intercepts equal zero and the slope terms equal one cannot be rejected by Wald tests for any of the three auction mechanisms. These results provide evidence that all three auction mechanisms are demand revealing on average.

On- and Off-Margin Bids

Shogren et al. (2001b) found that the random *n*th price auction worked better for off-margin subjects (those with bids far away from the market price in the previous round), but the second price auction worked better for on-margin subjects (those with bids close to the market price in the previous round). Although our experiment was structured differently, we were interested in investigating whether a similar effect exists here. Similar to Shogren et al. (2001b), we analyse, separately, deviations at the upper and lower portions of the demand curve (referred to as on-margin and off-margin by Shogren et al.). In Shogren et al. (2001b), individuals were assigned the same induced values across several bidding rounds and an individual was defined as on- or off-margin in the current round based on their bid in the previous round relative to the price in the previous round. In this study, individuals were assigned different values each round, so we

Table 2.5 Deviations for low and high induced values

Variable	BDM	Second price	Random *n*th price
On-margin bidders (> 29 tokens)			
Mean squared deviation	13.38 (26.67)[a]	9.33 (16.36)	33.18 (57.29)
Mean absolute deviation	2.38 (2.84)	2.00 (2.41)	3.91 (4.44)
Bid = induced value	25.00%	33.33%	27.27%
Bid within 2 tokens of induced value	70.83%	75.00%	45.45%
Number of observations	24	12	11
Off-margin bidders (< 29 tokens)			
Mean squared deviation	46.83 (142.92)	28.79 (77.60)	8.59 (17.46)
Mean absolute deviation	3.91 (5.67)	3.00 (3.67)	1.85 (2.32)
Bid = induced value	18.52%	39.29%	33.33%
Bid within 2 tokens of induced value	61.11%	64.29%	74.07%
Number of observations	54	28	27

Note: [a]Numbers in parentheses are standard deviations.

could not utilize the same definitions of on- and off-margin as in Shogren et al. (2001b). However, the general concept still applies: individuals with relatively low values are likely to perceive a very low chance of winning in a second price auction, but not so in the BDM and random *n*th. Because we are investigating behaviour after two initial bidding rounds, all of which used the same distribution of values, individuals are likely to get a feel for whether their assigned induced value in a particular round was relatively high or low. If a subject received one of the three highest induced values in a particular round (29, 33 and 38), we classified them as on-margin. If the subject received one of the seven lowest induced values in a particular round (3, 9, 11, 14, 16, 20, 24), we classified them as off-margin. Admittedly, this definition is somewhat ad hoc, but it provides a useful preliminary means of investigating bidding behaviour. In subsequent regression analysis, we investigate the effect of an individual's value on mean and absolute deviation such that we avoid the ad hoc nature of defining a cut-off between on- and off-margin individuals.

Summary statistics for deviations of on-margin and off-margin bidders are reported in Table 2.5. Our results confirm the findings of Shogren et al. (2001b): the second price auction does a better job of estimating the top of the demand curve, while the random *n*th price auction does a better job of estimating the rest of the demand curve. The random *n*th price auction had a lower mean absolute deviation (and a higher percentage of bids within two tokens of the induced value) for off-margin bids than the second price auction; whereas the second price auction had a lower mean absolute deviation (and a higher percentage of bids within two tokens of the induced value) at high induced values than the random *n*th price auction. These differences are only marginally significant (two-tailed, t-test p-value = 0.20), likely because of the low number of observations in the high categories, but they are consistent with the results of Shogren et al. (2001b).

Results in Table 2.5 also illustrate that the mean absolute and squared deviations for the BDM mechanism are greater than that for the second price auction. This result holds for both the on- and off-margin values. Also, the second price auction had a higher percentage of bids exactly equal to and within two tokens of the induced value than the BDM. Again, this result is true for both on- and off-margin values, a result consistent with that presented in Noussair et al. (2004). Thus, the second price auction appears to be more accurate than the BDM mechanism at all points of the demand curve. These results suggest that the random *n*th price auction is more accurate than the BDM at the lower end of the demand curve, but the opposite is the case at the upper end of the demand curve.

Accuracy of Elicitation Mechanisms

To investigate whether the differences in the absolute and squared deviation are statistically different across elicitation mechanisms, we estimated tobit models to account for the significant frequency of zero deviations.[9] The estimated model is given by:

$$D_{it}^{*} = \alpha + \beta(second\ price) + \lambda(nth\ price) + \delta(second\ price)(iv_{it}) + \theta(nth\ price)(iv_{it}) + \mu(BDM)(iv_{it}) + v_{it},\ D_{it} = \max[0, D_{it}^{*}] \quad (2.4)$$

where D_{it} is the deviation (either squared or absolute) for the *i*th subject in the *t*th trial, which is observed only at positive levels; $(second\ price)$, $(nth\ price)$ and (BDM) are dummy variables identifying deviations for the second price auction, random *n*th price auction and BDM, respectively; $(iv)_{it}$ is subject *i*'s induced value in trial *t*; α, β, λ, δ, θ and μ are coefficients to be estimated; and v_{it} is the overall error term. This specification allows for differences in mean squared and absolute deviations by elicitation mechanism and by magnitude of induced value, which, as shown in Table 2.5, has the potential to affect bidding behaviour.

Tobit estimates are reported in Table 2.6. For the squared deviation model, the negative coefficients on the dummy variables for the second price and random *n*th price auctions are statistically significant, indicating

Table 2.6 Tobit estimates: accuracy of elicitation procedures

Variable	Squared deviation[a]	Absolute deviation[b]
Intercept	61.771**[d] (27.140)[c]	4.374** (1.316)
Second price	−85.395* (49.029)	−3.659 (2.356)
Random nth price	−91.558* (47.589)	−4.565** (2.302)
Induced value * BDM	−2.151* (1.222)	−0.084 (0.059)
Induced value * second price	0.579 (1.791)	0.026 (0.086)
Induced value * nth price	0.821 (1.761)	0.072 (0.085)
Log-likelihood	−722.0	−386.5

Notes:
[a] Dependent variable is squared deviation of bid from induced value.
[b] Dependent variable is absolute value of deviation of bid from induced value.
[c] Numbers in parentheses are standard errors.
[d] One (*) and two (**) asterisks represents 0.05 and 0.10 levels of statistical significance, respectively.

that these endogenous price mechanisms generated significantly lower squared deviations from true values compared to the BDM. Similar results are obtained from the absolute deviation model, with the second price auction dummy variable only marginally significant (p = 0.12) in this specification. The results in Table 2.6 also indicate that the BDM became more accurate as subjects received higher induced values: the induced value * BDM effect was negative and statistically significant at the 0.07 and 0.15 levels for the squared and absolute deviation models, respectively. The results in Table 2.6 indicate that the magnitude of the induced value did not have a statistically significant effect on the second price or random *n*th price auctions. In summary, results in Table 2.6 indicate that, even after controlling for the magnitude of the induced value, the BDM was less accurate than either of the two mechanisms using endogenous prices.

IMPLICATIONS AND CONCLUSION

Accurate elicitation of individuals' values is essential for credible cost–benefit analysis. In this study, we explore whether value elicitation mechanisms that rely on endogenous market-clearing prices are more accurate at truthfully revealing values than mechanisms that rely on exogenous market-clearing prices. Our results indicate that an active market environment generates bids more consistent with true values than bids elicited outside a market context. We found that the BDM mechanism was less accurate at generating bids consistent with induced values than the second and random *n*th price auctions that used endogenously determined market-clearing prices. These results suggest that more precise estimates of demand for non-market goods might be obtained using mechanisms with endogenous market-clearing prices.

In some cases, it might be infeasible to conduct valuation exercises with an endogenous price mechanism. For example, in some field experiments (for example, Lusk et al., 2001a) it is often difficult or impossible to use an active market-based elicitation mechanism, and the BDM is a natural alternative.[10] In such applications, practitioners might take some comfort in our finding that the BDM mechanism was demand revealing on average and that the BDM performed relatively well for high values on the demand curve. Nevertheless, if it is possible to employ the second or random *n*th price auctions, our results suggest that these mechanisms are preferable to the BDM in terms of accuracy.

Although we find evidence that the BDM is demand revealing in aggregate, it is less accurate than endogenous price auctions. One interpretation of our results might be that subjects are more familiar with auction-based mechanisms such as the second and random *n*th price auction, perhaps due to online auctions like e-Bay, than with the BDM mechanism and that this familiarity is the cause of more accurate bidding. More research will have to be conducted to further isolate the effect of a competitive market on bidding behaviour. Such work is important as some have criticized the BDM mechanism and other individual-based decision-making experiments because of the lack of market feedback and lack of an endogenous clearing price (for example, Shogren and Hayes, 1997; Shogren et al., 2001a). Our findings are partially supportive of these views. Our results lend credence to the idea that violations of economic theory are most likely to be found in contexts where individuals are not subjected to the scrutiny of competition provided via markets. Unfortunately, markets for environmental amenities rarely exist. In some cases it might be possible to create markets by trading permits for pollution or trading ideas/knowledge in prediction or events markets. In other cases, the experimental laboratory might be a valuable resource for environmental economists to create real and simulated markets.

NOTES

1. These mechanisms, and the ones investigated in this chapter, provide incentives for truthful value revelation under the assumption of expected utility preferences; the mechanisms are not incentive compatible for some non-expected utility preferences.
2. We examine these three mechanisms because they are commonly used in the literature. For examples of the second price auction see Fox et al. (2002), Hayes et al. (1995) or

Lusk et al. (2001b); for examples of the BDM see Lusk et al. (2001a) or Boyce et al. (1992); and for examples of the random *n*th price auction see Huffman et al. (2003).
3. Evidence on whether the second price auction is demand revealing is mixed. Kagel et al. (1987) and Kagel and Levin (1993) found a tendency for subjects to overbid in second price auctions.
4. Differences in bidding behaviour between the two mechanisms could also result from differences in subject understanding or familiarity with the mechanisms.
5. Complete instructions are in the appendix to this chapter.
6. Assuming that each subject earned an equal amount any individual had a 1 out of 10 chance of winning the lottery. Under the assumption of equal earnings of 65 tokens per individual, the expected value of an additional token to any particular individual would be about $0.22. That is, with the addition of the extra token, the total number of tokens in the lottery would be 651 (rather than 650), and the individual with the extra token would increase his/her odds of winning from 10 per cent to 10.7 per cent, which results in the expected value of the lottery for that individual increasing by $0.22. Using this line of reasoning, the expected value of our induced values ranged from about $0.66 to $8.40.
7. In the analysis, we focus only on the third and fourth bidding rounds because the extant literature suggests that it takes individuals time for the market to converge to equilibrium (for example, Smith, 1962). By focusing our analysis only on the last two rounds, we only investigate behaviour after a brief period of learning (note, all bidding rounds were binding). We tested whether first participating in an endogenous-price mechanism affected bidding behaviour in the BDM. Both parametric t-tests and non-parametric Mann–Whitney U tests cannot reject the null hypothesis that deviations were equivalent regardless of whether the BDM was performed before or after the second or random *n*th price auction. Similarly, we find that order of elicitation procedure had no significant effect on second or random *n*th price deviations. As a result, we pooled observations across sessions for the discussion that follows.
8. These percentages compare favourably with previous induced value studies. Shogren et al. (2001b) found that 65 per cent and 63 per cent of bids were within 10 cents of induced values in second and random *n*th price auctions, respectively. Similarly, Irwin et al. (1998) found that 62 per cent of BDM bids were within 25 cents of induced values.
9. We also estimated tobit models incorporating subject and trial-specific effects in a random effects framework. For the squared deviation model, the standard deviation for the individual or trial-specific error was not significantly different from zero. For the absolute deviation model, a random effects model would not converge. As a result, traditional tobit models are reported. Although this approach might yield inefficient estimates, it is consistent with our statistical tests that indicated ordinary least squares was the appropriate specification for equation (2.3) for two out of three auctions.
10. On some occasions it is possible to use endogenous price mechanisms in field experiments (for example, List, 2002).

REFERENCES

Becker, G., M. DeGroot and J. Marschak (1964), 'Measuring utility by a single-response sequential method', *Behavioral Science*, **23**, 226–32.

Boyce, R.R., T.C. Brown, G.H. McClelland, G.L. Peterson and W.D. Schulze (1992), 'An experimental examination of intrinsic values as a source of the WTA-WTP disparity', *American Economic Review*, **82**, 1366–73.

Cherry, T.L. and J.F. Shogren (2001), 'Rationality crossovers', working paper, Department of Economics, Appalachian State University.

Cherry, T., T. Crocker and J.F. Shogren (2003), 'Rationality spillovers', *Journal of Environmental Economics and Management*, **45**, 63–84.

Chu, Y.P. and R.L. Chu (1990), 'The subsidence of preference reversals in simplified and marketlike experimental settings: a note', *American Economic Review*, **80**, 902–11.

Cox, J.C. and D.M. Grether (1996), 'The preference reversal phenomenon: response mode, markets and incentive', *Economic Theory*, **7**, 381–405.

Cox, R.C., B. Roberson and V.L. Smith (1982), 'Theory and behavior of single object auctions', in V.L. Smith (ed.), *Research in Experimental Economics*, vol. 2. Greenwich, CT: JAI Press.

Cummings, R.G. and L.O. Taylor (1999), 'Unbiased value estimates for environmental goods: a cheap talk design for the contingent valuation method', *American Economic Review*, **89**, 649–65.

Cummings, R.G., G.W. Harrison and E.E. Rutström (1995), 'Homegrown values and hypothetical surveys: is the dichotomous choice approach incentive-compatible?', *American Economic Review*, **85**, 260–66.

Fox, J.A., D.J. Hayes and J.F. Shogren (2002), 'Consumer preferences for food irradiation: how favorable and unfavorable descriptions affect preferences for irradiated pork in experimental auctions', *Journal of Risk and Uncertainty*, **24**, 75–95.

Fox, J.A., J.F. Shogren, D.J. Hayes and J.B. Kliebenstein (1998), 'CVM-X: calibrating contingent values with experimental auction markets', *American Journal of Agricultural Economics*, **80**, 455–65.

Hayes, D.J., J.F. Shogren, S.U. Shin and J.B. Kliebenstein (1995), 'Valuing food safety in experimental auction markets', *American Journal of Agricultural Economics*, **77**, 40–53.

Hofler, R.A. and J.A. List (2004), 'Valuation on the frontier: calibrating actual and hypothetical statements of value', *American Journal of Agricultural Economics*, **86**, 213–21.

Huffman, W.E., M. Rousu, J.F. Shogren and A. Tegene (2003), 'The public good value of information from agribusinesses on genetically modified food', *American Journal of Agricultural Economics*, **85**, 1309–15.

Irwin, J.R., G.H. McClelland, M. McKee, W.D. Schulze and N.E. Norden (1998), 'Payoff dominance vs. cognitive transparency in decision making', *Economic Inquiry*, **36**, 272–85.

Kachelmeier S.J. and M. Shehata (1992), 'Examining risk preferences under high monetary incentives: experimental evidence for the People's Republic of China', *American Economic Review*, **82**, 1120–40.

Kagel, J.H. and D. Levin (1993), 'Independent private value auctions: bidder behavior in first-, second-, and third price auctions with varying numbers of bidders', *Economic Journal*, **103**, 868–79.

Kagel, J.H., R.M. Harstad and D. Levin (1987), 'Information impact and allocation rules in auctions with affiliated private values: a laboratory study', *Econometrica*, **55**, 1275–1304.

List, J.A. (2001), 'Do explicit warnings eliminate the hypothetical bias in elicitation procedures? Evidence from field auctions for sports cards', *American Economic Review*, **91**, 1498–507.

List, J.A. (2002), 'Preference reversals of a different kind: the "more is less" phenomenon', *American Economic Review*, **92**, 1636–43.

List, J.A. and C. Gallet (2001), 'What experimental protocol influence disparities between actual and hypothetical stated values? Evidence from a meta-analysis', *Environmental and Resource Economics*, **20**, 241–54.

List, J.A. and J.F. Shogren (1998), 'Calibrating the differences between actual and hypothetical valuations in a field experiment', *Journal of Economic Behavior and Organization*, **37**, 193–205.

Lusk, J.L. (2003), 'Effect of cheap talk on consumer willingness-to-pay for golden rice', *American Journal of Agricultural Economics*, **85**, 840–56.

Lusk, J.L., C.E. Alexander and M. Rousu (2005), 'Designing experimental auctions for marketing research: effect of values, distributions, and mechanisms on incentives for truthful bidding', working paper, Department of Agricultural Economics, Oklahoma State University.

Lusk, J.L., M.S. Daniel, D.R. Mark and C.L. Lusk (2001b), 'Alternative calibration and auction institutions for predicting consumer willingness-to-pay for nongenetically modified corn chips', *Journal of Agriculture and Resource Economics*, **26**, 40–57.

Lusk, J.L., J.A. Fox, T.C. Schroeder, J. Mintert and M. Koohmaraie (2001a), 'In-store valuation of steak tenderness', *American Journal of Agricultural Economics*, **83**, 539–50.

Noussair, C., S. Robin and B. Ruffieux (2004), 'Revealing consumers' willingness-to-pay: a comparison of the BDM mechanism and the Vickrey auction', *Journal of Economic Psychology*, **25**, 725–41.

Shogren, J.F. (forthcoming), 'Experimental methods and valuation', in K.G. Mäler and J. Vincent (eds), *Handbook of Environmental Economics*, Amsterdam: Elsevier.

Shogren, J.F. and D. Hayes (1997), 'Resolving differences in willingness to pay and willingness to accept: reply', *American Economic Review*, **87**, 241–4.

Shogren, J.F., S. Cho, C. Koo, J.A. List, C. Park, P. Polo and R. Wilhelmi (2001a), 'Auction mechanisms and the measurement of WTP and WTA', *Resource and Energy Economics*, **23**, 97–109.

Shogren, J.F., M. Margolis, C. Koo and J.A. List (2001b), 'A random *n*th-price auction', *Journal of Economic Behavior and Organization*, **46**, 409–21.

Shogren, J.F., S.Y. Shin, D. Hayes and J.B. Kliebenstein (1994), 'Resolving differences in willingness to pay and willingness to accept', *American Economic Review*, **84**, 255–70.

Smith, V.L. (1962), 'An experimental study of competitive market behavior', *Journal of Political Economy*, **70**, 111–37.

Vickrey, W. (1961), 'Counterspeculation, auctions, and competitive sealed tenders', *Journal of Finance*, **16**, 8–37.

APPENDIX: INSTRUCTION SHEET GIVEN TO PARTICIPANTS

Instructions for the BDM Mechanism (Limit Price Auction)

Today you will be involved in a decision-making exercise where you will have the opportunity to earn money. Each of you should have been assigned a random number, which you will use to identify yourself throughout the exercise. In this exercise, you will participate in an auction in which you will make bids using tokens for an 'item'. We will not specify the name for the good you are attempting to buy; we will simply refer to an 'item'.

What we are playing for in this auction is tokens. Everyone starts with an initial balance of 20 tokens. The auctions will give you the opportunity to try to win more tokens.

At the end of the experiment, each person's tokens will go into a drawing for $30 – which will be paid in cash to someone in this room at the end of this experiment. So, the more tokens you have, the better chance you have of winning.

The auction will proceed as follows. Each of you should have been assigned a bidder 'record sheet' that lists your value from an item in several repeated rounds as shown below:

A Round	B Prize value of item (in tokens)	C Your bid (in tokens)	D Winner? (1 = Yes; 0 = No)	E Limit price (in tokens)	F Token earnings (B – E)*D
Example 1	20	19	0	32	0
Example 2	8	12	1	10	−2
Example 3	33	31	1	20	13

In each round you are assigned a 'prize value' for an item, which represents the amount of tokens the item is worth to you. These prize values are in column B of the record sheet. Note: you will only participate in one round at a time. For example, in example 2, your prize value is 8 tokens. Note: your prize values are private information and should not be shared with anyone around you.

In the auction, all bidders will submit bids to buy an item in a particular round. Suppose you are participating in round 1. You will write your bid on the enclosed 'bid sheet' AND on the 'record sheet' in column C next in the row marked Round 1. The monitor will then go around the room and collect the bid sheets from each individual. Then the limit bid will be randomly chosen randomly, and it can be any amount of tokens from 1–40. Everyone should write the limit price in column D on the record sheet in the row marked Round 1. Everyone who bid (as much or) higher than the limit price wins the auction – and pays the limit price for the item. Those who bid less than the limit price do not purchase the item. If you bid higher than the limit price and your number has been posted on the board, you should place a 1 in column E or the record sheet; otherwise, you should place a 0 in column E.

The winning bidders will earn the difference between their own prize value and the second highest bid. Non-winning bidders will earn no tokens. Earnings are determined by subtracting the amount in column B from the amount in column E and multiplying this value by the number in column D. In general, earnings are as follows:

Earnings = your own prize value – the limit price (if your bid is higher than the limit price)
Earnings = 0 tokens (if your bid is not higher than the limit price)

After completing the auction for round 1, we will proceed to round 2, then to round 3, and so on. At the end of the session, your earnings will be added up for all of the rounds to determine your total earnings.

Example 1
Suppose you are participating in an auction for an item and have been assigned a prize value of 20 tokens as shown in example 1 of the game record sheet. Suppose you bid 19 tokens for the item. Also assume that there were 3 other people participating in the auction and participant #1 bid, 37 tokens, participant #2 bid 17 tokens and participant #3 bid 34 tokens. The limit price that is randomly chosen is 32 tokens. Would you win the auction? No. Participant #1 and participant #3 would win the auction because their bids are higher than the limit price. How much would participants #1 and #3 pay for the item? They would pay the limit price, which was 32 tokens. How many tokens would participants #1 and #3 earn? They would earn the difference between their own prize value and 32 tokens. How much money would you earn in this auction? Because your bid was not higher than the limit price, you would earn 0 tokens for that round.

Example 2
Suppose you are participating in an auction for an item and have been assigned a prize value of 8 tokens as shown in example 2 of the game record sheet. Suppose you bid 12 tokens for the item. Also assume that there were

3 other people participating in the auction and participant #1 bid, 8 tokens, participant #2 bid 7 tokens and participant #3 bid 3 tokens. Suppose the randomly selected limit price was 10 tokens. Would you win the auction? Yes! You would win the auction because your bid was higher than the limit price. How many tokens will you earn? You will earn the difference between your own prize value (8 tokens) and the limit price (10 tokens). Thus, you will earn (8−10) tokens, or −2 tokens. So in this round, you actually lose 2 tokens. *This illustrates that it is important to place your bids in the auction carefully*. The other participants would not win or lose any tokens, since you had the only bid higher than the limit price.

Example 3

Suppose you are participating in an auction for an item and have been assigned a prize value of 33 tokens. You bid 31 tokens for the item. Also assume that there were 3 other people participating in the auction and participant #1 bid 24 tokens, participant #2 bid 16 tokens and participant #3 bid 5 tokens. Suppose the randomly selected limit price is 20 tokens. Would you win the auction? Yes! You (and participant #1) would win the auction because you had the highest bids. How many tokens will you earn? You will earn the difference between your own prize value 33 tokens and the second highest bid amount 20 tokens. Thus, you will earn 33−20 = 13 tokens. How much will participant #1 win? That depends upon their private value for the product. Participants #2 and #3 would earn 0 tokens that round.

Instructions for the Second Price Auction

The next four rounds work similar to the first four, except for how the winners are determined. Once again, for these four rounds you will have private values for an 'item'. This time, however, instead of a random price being drawn between 1–40 tokens, the top bidder wins the auction and pays the second highest bid price (once again in tokens). For this auction, there can only be one winning bidder per round. Now consider a modified version of example 2, to fit the rules of this particular auction.

A Round	B Prize value of item (in tokens)	C Your bid (in tokens)	D Winner? (1 = Yes; 0 = No)	E 2nd Price	F Earnings (B – E)*D
Example 2A	8	12	1	8	0

Example 2A

Suppose you are participating in an auction for an item and have been assigned a prize value of 8 tokens as shown in example 2A of the game record sheet. Suppose you bid 12 tokens for the item. Also assume that there were 3 other people participating in the auction and participant #1 bid 8 tokens, participant #2 bid 7 tokens and participant #3 bid 3 tokens. Would you win this auction? Yes, because you are the top bidder. How many tokens will you earn? You will earn the difference between your own prize value 8 tokens and the second highest price which was also 8 tokens. Thus, you will earn $8-8=0$ tokens. How much money would everyone else earn? Zero, because only the top bidder wins this auction. Although in this case, everybody earned zero tokens.

Instructions for the Random *n*th Price Auction

The next four rounds work similar to the first four, except for how the winners are determined. Once again, for these four rounds you will have private values for an 'item'. This time, however, instead of the limit price being determined by selecting a price at random, a random price is drawn from one of the bids. Each bid from the 2nd highest to the lowest has an equal chance of being the limit price. Everyone who bids higher than the 'limit' price will win the product and pay the 'limit' price. Similar to before, there can be multiple winners in this section of the experiments, depending on the 'limit' price. Now consider a modified version of example 2, to fit the rules of this particular auction.

A Round	B Prize value of item (in tokens)	C Your bid (in tokens)	D Winner? (1 = Yes; 0 = No)	E Limit bid price	F Earnings (B – E)*D
Example 2B	8	12	1	8	0

Example 2B

Suppose you are participating in an auction for an item and have been assigned a prize value of 8 tokens as shown in example 2B of the game record sheet. Suppose you bid 12 tokens for the item. Also assume that there were 3 other people participating in the auction and participant #1 bid, 8 tokens, participant #2 bid 7 tokens and participant #3 bid 3 tokens. Suppose the randomly selected limit bid was the 2nd highest bid. Would you win this auction? Yes, because you bid higher than the randomly selected limit price. How many tokens will you earn? You will earn the difference between your own prize value 8 tokens and the limit price which was also 8 tokens. Thus, you will earn $8-8=0$ tokens. How much money would everyone else earn? Zero, because only the top bidder wins this auction. Although in this case, everybody earned zero tokens.

3. Hypothetical bias over uncertain outcomes

Glenn W. Harrison*

One of the major contributions of experimental methods to environmental economics has been the characterization of hypothetical bias. A long series of experiments has established evidence of differences in responses to tasks that involve real economic commitments when compared to comparable tasks involving hypothetical economic commitments. In addition, there have been constructive attempts to use the laboratory environment to design instruments to mitigate the extent of the bias or to correct for it.[1] One gap in the previous literature has been the examination of hypothetical bias for outcomes that are uncertain. Although some of the commodities used in previous studies may have had some subjectively uncertain characteristics, those were not controlled for or explicit. This study fills that gap, by reviewing evidence for differences in responses to outcomes that are explicitly uncertain, focusing specifically on exogenous lotteries where the uncertainty is controlled and known a priori. In effect, we ask if estimates of risk attitudes defined over monetary outcomes suffer from hypothetical bias.

The relevance of characterizing hypothetical bias over uncertain outcomes should be apparent in the context of environmental valuation. Virtually every important environmental project includes some scientific or perceptual uncertainty. Many of the scenarios that are presented to subjects try to remove artificially any uncertainty, but often this entails less control than one might hope for, since subjects are then likely to doubt the credibility of the artificially certain scenario. The danger is that they might then employ subjective assumptions that cannot be controlled for in the experiment. The implication is that one might elicit very different valuations if the scenario was presented openly as a policy lottery.

Sections 3.1 and 3.2 consider two series of experiments that considered the issue of hypothetical bias over uncertain outcomes: Battalio et al. (1990) and Holt and Laury (2002; 2005). Other experiments provide indirect opportunities for checking for hypothetical biases, but these studies had this as one of their primary treatments.[2] Section 3.3 presents the results of a new experiment considering the effects of hypothetical bias, using subjects and procedures that match the salient experiments of Harrison, Johnson, McInnes and Rutström (2005). Section 4 considers the sensitivity of inferences about hypothetical bias to alternative specifications of the underlying decision process, by allowing for probability weighting of choices. Section 3.5 draws implications from the results for the design and interpretation of contingent valuation surveys, and section 3.6 discusses implications for related debates in 'behavioural economics'.

3.1 BATTALIO, KAGEL AND JIRANYAKUL

3.1.1 Overall Design

Battalio et al. (1990) and Kagel et al. (1990), hereafter BKJ and KMB, use a similar experimental design to collect information on human lottery choices. The subject is given a number of choice tasks, and told that one will be selected at random for payment at the end. Each subject received a $30 endowment, and since only one choice will be paid out and the losses never exceed $20, the subject knows that they will always leave the experiment with a gain of at least $10. Some of the lotteries involve gains, and some involve losses, all relative to the initial stake: we refer to these as a gain frame or a loss frame. The experiments of BKJ and KMB span prizes of $10, $16, $18, $30, $44 and $50, roughly equally.

In some cases expected utility theory (EUT) makes predictions over triples of choice pairs, and in some cases it makes predictions of doubles of choice pairs. Those predictions are of no immediate import for our use of these data to characterize risk attitudes of the sample, other than for the fact that the data is reported in terms of frequencies of choice patterns over these triples or doubles, and not over the constituent choice pairs.

3.1.2 Hypothetical Bias Treatments

BKJ included a controlled test of hypothetical bias in their design. Their 'Series 1 design' in fact consisted of *in-sample* comparisons of hypothetical and real responses to the same lotteries: there were 41 hypothetical choices in the loss (gain) frame, matched with 15 real choices in the loss (gain) frame. The only substantive difference, apart from the salience of the consequences of the choices, was that the subjects in the hypothetical experiments did not receive any endowment.[3] Since there were some 'prizes' in the hypothetical loss *and gain* frame experiments that entailed significant losses, we could proceed by assuming that the subjects behaved as if those losses would be covered by the experimenter out of an initial endowment.[4] Doing so, and pooling responses across individuals, we confirm the conclusion of BKJ that there is no qualitative effect of using hypothetical responses instead of real responses.[5] Since their conclusion has been widely cited, it is worth stating explicitly: 'despite these systematic and at times significant quantitative differences between responses to real versus hypothetical pay-offs, qualitative conclusions regarding differences in risk attitudes over gains and losses were quite similar across both real and hypothetical choices' (p. 28). Their support for this conclusion consists of examination of hypothetical and real responses on a *between-sample* basis.

However, the *in-sample* comparisons allowed by their design reveal that there is indeed a significant difference between risk attitudes in hypothetical and real settings. Figure 3.1 reports these comparisons. The left panels refer to choices in the loss frame, and the right panels to choices in the gain frame.[6] The top panels show the fraction of choices that were different when the same subject was asked in hypothetical or real mode.[7] These are all well above zero, and a t-test on each question confirms this conclusion. The direction of the change in risk preferences is also quite clear. In the loss frame more than 50 per cent of the changes were in the direction of the subject expressing a reduction in risk aversion (or increase in risk loving), with one solitary exception. In the gain frame the reverse pattern obtains, with hypothetical responses being more risk averse (or less risk loving). Both sets of differences are again statistically significant from 0.5 using t-tests for each paired comparison.

How can one reconcile this conclusion with the one stated by BKJ (p. 28)? The answer is that their conclusion was based on between-sample responses,[8] and referred to their conclusions about specific violations of EUT. Just because there is a change in the degree of risk aversion, there may not be a change in the extent to which the aggregate sample exhibits EUT violations. Unfortunately, the carefully worded conclusion of BKJ, which is correct as far as it goes, has been mis-characterized in some widely cited surveys of the effects of hypothetical response on lottery choices. For example, Camerer (1995: 634) notes that several 'studies have compared hypothetical choices with real choices (in which one choice was played). They found either no effect or a slight tendency for playing gambles to yield more risk aversion'. Although this conclusion admittedly refers to several studies all at once, it overstates the inferences appropriate from the BKJ data. There is an effect on risk attitudes, and it differs in sign as one changes from a loss frame to a gain frame.[9]

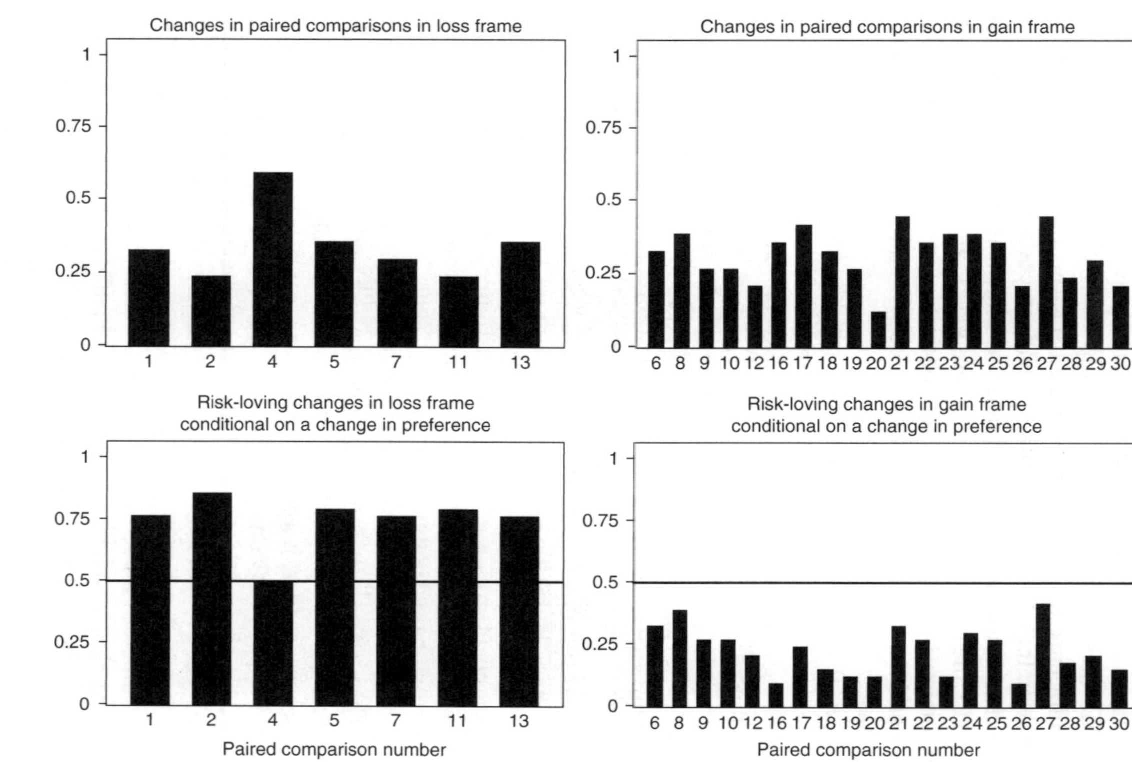

Figure 3.1 Hypothetical bias in BKJ experiments: fraction of within-sample responses (N = 33)

3.2 HOLT AND LAURY

3.2.1 Overall Design

Holt and Laury (2002) (HL) provide a relatively transparent task for eliciting risk attitudes using a Multiple Price List (MPL).[10]

Each subject is presented with a choice between two lotteries, which we can call A or B. Table 3.1 illustrates the basic pay-off matrix presented to subjects. The first row shows that lottery A offers a 10 per cent chance of receiving $2 and a 90 per cent chance of receiving $1.60. The expected value of this lottery, EV^A, is shown in the third-last column as $1.64, although the EV columns were not presented to subjects.[11] Similarly, lottery B in the

Table 3.1 Design of the Holt and Laury (2002) experiments

A. Lottery pay-off alternatives at pay-off scale 1 level

Lottery A				Lottery B				EV^A	EV^B	Difference
p($2)		p($1.60)		p($3.85)		p($0.10)				
0.1	$2	0.9	$1.60	0.1	$3.85	0.9	$0.10	$1.64	$0.48	$1.17
0.2	$2	0.8	$1.60	0.2	$3.85	0.8	$0.10	$1.68	$0.85	$0.83
0.3	$2	0.7	$1.60	0.3	$3.85	0.7	$0.10	$1.72	$1.23	$0.49
0.4	$2	0.6	$1.60	0.4	$3.85	0.6	$0.10	$1.76	$1.60	$0.16
0.5	$2	0.5	$1.60	0.5	$3.85	0.5	$0.10	$1.80	$1.98	−$0.17
0.6	$2	0.4	$1.60	0.6	$3.85	0.4	$0.10	$1.84	$2.35	−$0.51
0.7	$2	0.3	$1.60	0.7	$3.85	0.3	$0.10	$1.88	$2.73	−$0.84
0.8	$2	0.2	$1.60	0.8	$3.85	0.2	$0.10	$1.92	$3.10	−$1.18
0.9	$2	0.1	$1.60	0.9	$3.85	0.1	$0.10	$1.96	$3.48	−$1.52
1.0	$2	0.0	$1.60	1.0	$3.85	0.0	$0.10	$2.00	$3.85	−$1.85

B. Sample sizes and design

Scale of pay-offs	Task				Total
	1	2	3	4	
1	212			212	424
20		118	150		268
50		19	19		38
90		18	18		36
All	212	155	187	212	766
Hypothetical?	No	Yes	No	No	

first row has chances of pay-offs of \$3.85 and \$0.10, for an expected value of \$0.48. Thus the two lotteries have a relatively large difference in expected values, in this case \$1.17. As one proceeds down the matrix, the expected value of both lotteries increases but the expected value of lottery B becomes greater than the expected value of lottery A.

The subject chooses A or B in each row, and one row is later selected at random for pay-out for that subject. The logic behind this test for risk aversion is that only risk-loving subjects would take lottery B in the first row, and only risk-averse subjects would take lottery A in the second last row.[12] Arguably, the last row is simply a test that the subject understood the instructions, and has no relevance for risk aversion at all. A risk-neutral subject should switch from choosing A to B when the EV of each is about the same, so a risk-neutral subject would choose A for the first four rows and B thereafter.

3.2.2 Experimental Design

HL examine two main treatments with 212 subjects. The first is the effect of incentives. They vary the scale of the pay-offs in the matrix shown in panel A of Table 3.1, which we take to be the scale of 1. Every subject was presented with the first matrix of choices shown in Table 3.1, and with the exact same matrix at the end of the experiment. These two choices were always given to all subjects, and we refer to them as task 1 and task 4. All subjects additionally had one *or* two intermediate choices, referred to here as task 2 and task 3. The question in task 2, if asked, was a *higher-scale, hypothetical* version of the initial matrix of pay-offs. The question in task 3, if asked, was the *same* higher-scale version of pay-offs but with *real* pay-offs. Some subjects were asked one of these intermediate task questions; most subjects were asked both of them.[13] Thus we obtain the tabulation of individual responses shown in panel B of Table 3.1.

We see from panel B of Table 3.1 how each subject experienced different scales of pay-offs in task 2 and/or task 3. This provides in-sample tests of the hypothesis that risk aversion does not vary with wealth, an important issue for those that assume specific functional forms such as Constant Relative Risk Aversion (CRRA) or Constant Absolute Risk Aversion (CARA), where the ‘constant’ part in CRRA or CARA refers to the scale of the choices. A rejection of the ‘constancy’ assumption is not a rejection of expected utility theory in general, of course, but just these particular (popular) parameterizations.

The second treatment in the HL design is the effect of hypothetical pay-offs, which is why the questions in task 2 are included. We focus on these treatments below in more detail.

Although having in-sample responses is valuable, it comes at a price in terms of control since there may be wealth effects from the subjects having earned some profit in the previous choice. To handle this potential problem HL use a nice trick: when the subjects proceed from task 1 to task 3, they are first asked if they are willing to give up their earnings in task 1 in order to play task 3. Since the stakes are so much higher in task 3, all subjects chose to do so. This means that the subjects face tasks 1 and 3 with no prior earnings from these experiments, although they do have experience with the type of task when facing task 3. No such trick can be applied for task 4, since the subjects would be unlikely to give up their earnings in task 3 in this instance. Thus the responses to task 4 have no controls for wealth built in to the design. However, we do know the actual earnings of the subjects from the experimental data.[14]

HL also ask each subject to fill out a detailed question of individual demographic information, so their data include a rich set of controls for differences in risk preferences due to these characteristics.

Figure 3.2 shows the main responses in the HL experiments with real responses. Consider the top-left panel, which shows the average number of choices of the 'safe' option A in each problem. Thus in problem 1, which is row 1 in Table 3.1, virtually everyone chooses option A (the safe choice). By the time the subjects get to problem 10, which is the last row in Table 3.1, virtually everyone has switched over to problem B, the 'risky' option. The dashed line shows the prediction if each and every subject were risk neutral: in this case everyone would choose option A up to problem 4, then everyone would choose option B thereafter. The solid line marked 1x shows the observed behaviour in task 1, the low pay-off case. The solid line marked 20x shows the observed behaviour in task 3, the high pay-off case that scales up the values in Table 3.1 by 20. The top-right panel in Figure 3.2 shows comparable data for the 50x problems, and the bottom-left panel shows comparable data for the 90x problems.[15]

We examine the bottom-right panel later.

HL proceed with their analysis by looking at the first three pictures and drawing two conclusions. First, that one has to introduce some 'noise' into any model of the data-generation process, since the observed choices are 'smoother' than the risk-neutral prediction. A more general way of saying this is to allow subjects to have a specific degree of risk aversion, but to assume that they all have exactly the same degree of risk aversion. Thus, if subjects were a little risk averse the line marked 'Risk neutral' (RN) would shift to the right and drop down a bit to the right, perhaps at problem 6 or 7 instead of problem 5.[16] Of course, it would no longer represent risk-neutral responses, but it would still drop sharply, and that is the point being made by HL when arguing for a noise parameter. Second, and related to the previous explanation, the best-fitting line that assumes homogenous risk preferences

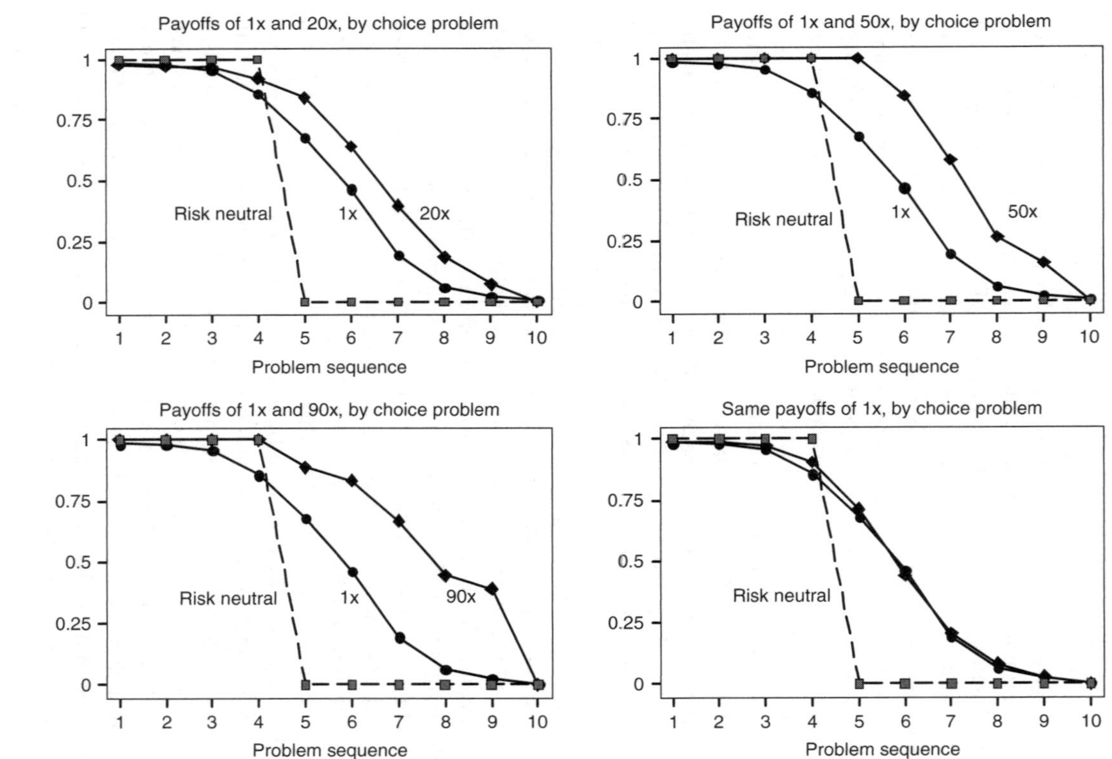

Figure 3.2 Real responses in HL (2002) experiments

would have to be a bit to the right of the risk-neutral line marked 'Risk neutral'. So some degree of risk aversion, they argue, is needed to account for the *location* of the observed averages, quite apart from the need for a noise parameter to account for the *smoothness* of the observed averages.

Both conclusions depend on the assumption that every subject in the experiment has the same preferences over risk. The smoothness of the observed averages is easily explained if one allows heterogenous risk attitudes and no noise at all at the individual level: some people drop down at problem 4, some more at problem 5, some more at problem 6, and so on. The smoothness that the eye sees is in Figure 3.1 is then just a counterpart of averaging over this heterogeneous process. The fact that *some* degree of risk aversion is needed for *some* subjects is undeniable, from the positive area above the RN line and below the other lines from problems 5 through to 10. But it simply does not follow without further statistical analysis that all subjects, or even the typical subject, exhibit significant amounts of risk aversion.

These conclusions follow from inspection of each of the first three panels, and just the RN and 1x lines in each for that matter. Now turn to the comparison of the lines of observed choices *within* each of the first three panels. The eyeball suggests that the 20x, 50x and 90x lines are to the right of the 1x lines, which implies that risk aversion increases as the scale of pay-offs increases. But this conclusion requires some measures of the uncertainty of these averages. Not surprisingly, the standard deviation in responses is the largest around problems 5 through to 7, suggesting that the confidence intervals around these lines of observed choices could easily overlap. Again, this is a matter for an appropriate statistical analysis, not eyeball inspection of the averages.

Finally, compare the differences between the lines of observed choices as one scans across the first three panels in Figure 3.2. As the pay-off scale gets larger, from 20x to 50x and then to 90x, it appears that the gap widens. That is, if one ignores the issue of standard errors around these averages, it appears that the degree of risk aversion increases. This leads HL to reject CRRA and CARA, and to consider generalized functional forms for utility functions that admit of increasing risk aversion. However, as panel B of Table 3.1 shows, the sample sizes for the 50x and 90x treatments were significantly smaller than those for the 20x treatment: 38 and 36 subjects, respectively, compared with 268 subjects for the 20x treatments. So one would expect that the standard errors around the 50x and 90x high pay-off lines would be much larger than those around the 20x high pay-off lines. This could make it difficult to statistically draw the eyeball conclusion that scale increases risk aversion.

Finally, one needs to account for the fact that all of the high pay-off data in the HL experiments were obtained in a task that followed the low pay-off task. Income effects were controlled for, in an elegant manner described above. But there could still be *simple order effects* owing to experience with the qualitative task. HL recognize the possibility of order effects when discussing why they had the high hypothetical task before the high real task: 'Doing the high hypothetical choice task before high real allows us to hold wealth constant and to evaluate the effect of using real incentives. For our purposes, it would not have made sense to do the high real treatment first, since the careful thinking would bias the high hypothetical decisions.' The same (correct) logic applies to comparisons of the second real task with the first real task.

The bottom-right panel of Figure 3.2 examines the data collected by HL in task 1 and task 4, which have the same scale but differ only in terms of the order effect and the accumulated wealth from task 3. These lines appear to be identical, suggesting no order effect, but a closer statistical analysis that conditions on the two differences shows that there is in fact an order effect at work.

Figures 3.3, 3.4 and 3.5 show in detail the paired real and hypothetical responses for each of the scales used by HL. The same general conclusion emerges from each comparison: the real responses exhibit greater risk aversion than the hypothetical responses.

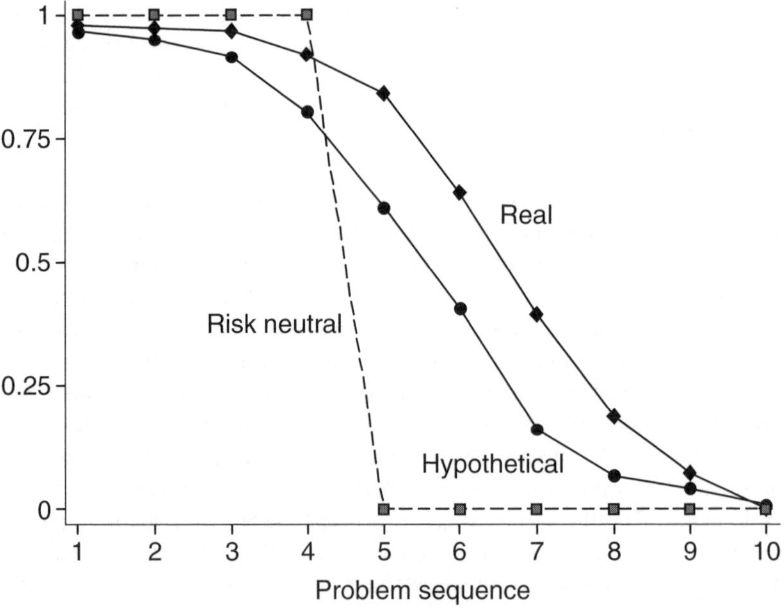

Figure 3.3 Hypothetical bias in HL (2002) experiments with 20x pay-offs: fraction choosing safe option A in each choice problem

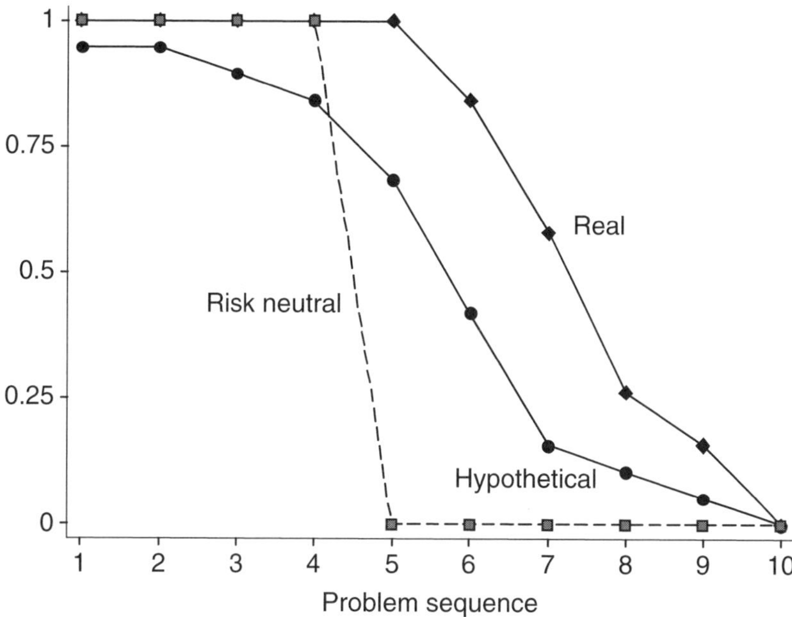

Figure 3.4 *Hypothetical bias in HL (2002) experiments with 50x pay-offs: fraction choosing safe option A in each choice problem*

3.2.3 Design Issues

An obvious design issue with the HL experiments is that inferences about scale and hypothetical bias are confounded by order. This effect is quite distinct from the effect of order on 'income effects', although that is also an issue for some of the responses. Harrison et al. (2005) demonstrated that the order effects in the real responses of HL were in fact statistically significant, and reduced by about one-half the effects of scale on risk aversion.

Holt and Laury (2005) agreed with the potential and estimated effects of order, and extended their earlier experiments to consider the effects of hypothetical bias without any potential confounds from order. Specifically, they conducted four sessions. One session had 1x pay-offs with real rewards, and one session had 1x pay-offs with hypothetical rewards. The other two sessions were the same but with 20x pay-offs. Each session used different subjects, so the comparisons are all between-subjects. Each of the sessions with real rewards used 48 subjects, and each of the sessions with hypothetical rewards used 36 subjects.[17] We therefore use these new data to consider the effect of hypothetical bias in their design, since they do not suffer from order effects.

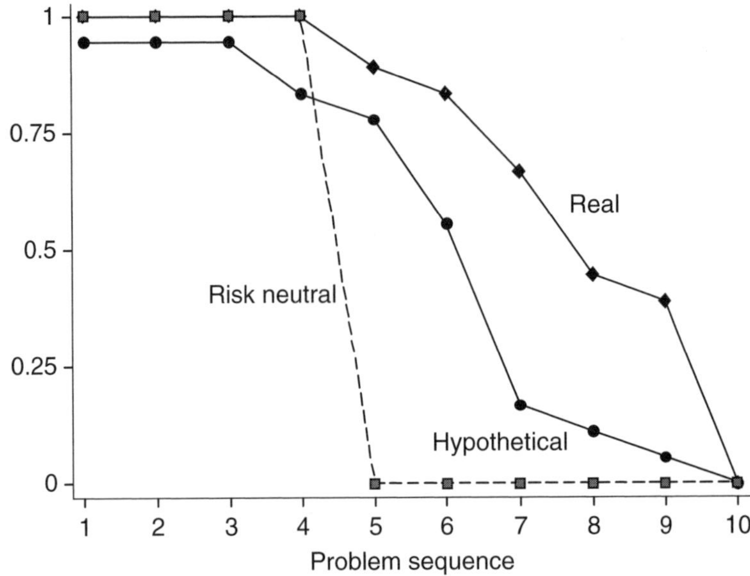

Figure 3.5 *Hypothetical bias in HL (2002) experiments with 90x pay-offs: fraction choosing safe option A in each choice problem*

3.2.4 Hypothetical Bias Treatments

HL were concerned with two issues at once: the constancy of risk aversion over the income domain that they scaled pay-offs over, and the effect of hypothetical responses compared to real responses. To allow for the possibility that relative risk aversion is not constant we follow HL and estimate a flexible functional form, such as the Expo-Power (EP) function proposed by Saha (1993). The EP function can be defined as $u(y) = [1 - \exp(-\alpha y^{1-r})]/\alpha$, where y is income and α and r are parameters to be estimated using maximum likelihood methods. Relative risk aversion (RRA) is then $r + \alpha(1 - r)y^{1-r}$. So RRA varies with income if $\alpha \neq 0$. This function nests CARA (as r tends to 0), but is not defined for α equal to 0.

Maximum likelihood estimates of the EP model can be used to calculate the RRA for different income levels. The likelihood function we use here employs the same function used by Holt and Laury (2002) to evaluate their laboratory data, and indeed we replicate their estimates exactly.[18] Their likelihood function takes the ratio of the expected utility of the safe option to the sum of the expected utility of both options, where each expected utility is evaluated conditional on candidate values of α and r. Their likelihood specification also allow for a 'noise parameter', μ, to capture stochastic errors associated with the choices of subjects.

One important econometric extension of their approach is to allow each parameter, r and α, to be a separate linear function of the task controls and individual characteristics, where we can estimate the coefficients on each of these linear functions. We also allow for the responses of the same subject to be correlated, due to unobserved individual effects. The data from Holt and Laury (2005) do not include information on individual characteristics, which is unfortunate since the treatments involve between-subject comparisons for which it is particularly important to control for observable differences in samples.

Table 3.2 displays the results from maximum likelihood estimation of the EP model. Treatment dummies are included for the tasks in which the order of presentation of the lotteries was reversed (variable 'reverse'). This model allows for the possibility of correlation between responses by the same subject, since each subject provides 10 binary choices.[19] Panel A includes the data pooled from the hypothetical and real samples, and panels B and C estimate the model on each sample.

In general the treatment of 'reversing' the order of presentation has no statistically significant effect on any parameter.

Panel A of Table 3.2 indicates that the real responses differ from the hypothetical responses solely in terms of the α parameter, which controls the non-constancy of RRA in this EP specification. Since CRRA emerges in the limit as α tends to 0, the hypothetical responses are consistent with CRRA roughly equal to 0.38 (the constant term on the r parameter). That is also the value for RRA with real responses when income levels are sufficiently low, since RRA is equal to r at zero income levels. These inferences are confirmed in Figure 3.6, which displays the predicted RRA in each treatment, along with a 95 per cent confidence interval. *At low levels of income there is virtually no discernible difference between RRA for the hypothetical and real responses, but at higher income levels the real responses exhibit much higher RRA*. Thus hypothetical rewards provide reliable results precisely when they save the least money in terms of subject payments.

3.3 HARRISON, JOHNSON, McINNES AND RUTSTRÖM

Harrison, Johnson, McInnes and Rutström (2005) (HJMR) replicated the basic experimental procedures developed by Holt and Laury (2002) to elicit risk attitudes, but avoided the order effects in their original design. The

Table 3.2 Estimates of expo-power model

Maximum likelihood estimates of expo-power utility function $u(y) = [1 - \exp(-\alpha y^{1-r})]/\alpha$, using data from the HL (2005) experiments

Utility function parameter	Parameter covariate	Point estimate	Standard error	t	p-value	Lower 95% confidence interval	Upper 95% confidence interval
A. Pooled data (N = 1680 choices by 168 subjects)							
r	Real responses	−0.018	0.117	−0.155	0.877	−0.250	0.213
	Reverse column order	0.068	0.094	0.726	0.469	−0.117	0.253
	Constant	0.386	0.101	3.808	0.000	0.186	0.586
α	Real responses	0.072	0.034	2.097	0.038	0.004	0.140
	Reverse column order	−0.004	0.028	−0.142	0.888	−0.058	0.051
	Constant	0.005	0.026	0.187	0.852	−0.047	0.057
μ	Real responses	0.014	0.026	0.549	0.584	−0.037	0.066
	Reverse column order	−0.011	0.026	−0.439	0.661	−0.062	0.039
	Constant	0.108	0.015	7.043	0.000	0.078	0.138
B. Real responses only (N = 960 choices by 96 subjects)							
r	Reverse column order	−0.027	0.148	−0.179	0.858	−0.321	0.268
	Constant	0.412	0.099	4.179	0.000	0.216	0.608
α	Reverse column order	−0.015	0.037	−0.390	0.697	−0.089	0.060
	Constant	0.084	0.030	2.794	0.006	0.024	0.144
μ	Reverse column order	−0.008	0.047	−0.180	0.857	−0.101	0.084
	Constant	0.121	0.033	3.661	0.000	0.055	0.187

C. Hypothetical responses only (N = 720 choices by 72 subjects)							
r	Reverse column order	0.197	0.268	0.734	0.465	−0.337	0.730
	Constant	0.347	0.106	3.279	0.002	0.136	0.557
α	Reverse column order	−0.056	0.200	−0.279	0.781	−0.455	0.344
	Constant	0.012	0.019	0.607	0.546	−0.027	0.050
μ	Reverse column order	−0.014	0.027	−0.537	0.593	−0.068	0.039
	Constant	0.108	0.015	7.395	0.000	0.079	0.137

Note: Each utility function parameter is estimated as a linear function of the covariates indicated. For example, in Panel A the utility function parameter r is estimated as $0.386 - 0.018 \times \text{REAL} + 0.068 \times \text{REVERSE}$, where REAL and REVERSE are binary dummy variables reflecting the use of real responses and the reverse column order, respectively.

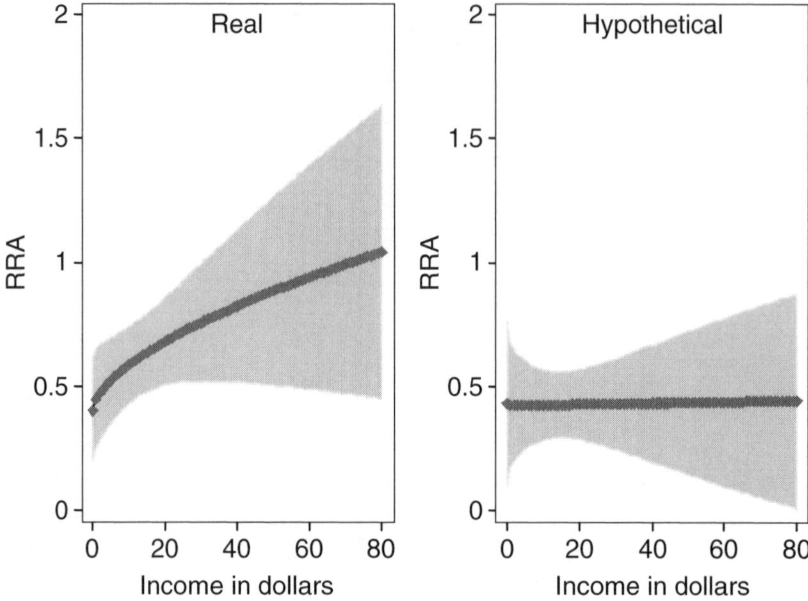

Figure 3.6 Hypothetical bias in HL (2005) experiments: predicated RRA from maximum-likelihood expo-power model

experimental results they reported all used salient incentives, but they also conducted some hypothetical experiments using subjects drawn from the same population and the same instruments. The effect of hypothetical bias can therefore be evaluated using those published and unpublished experiments. The hypothetical experiments only used the 10x design, which is to say that they were not preceded by a 1x treatment. Thus there are no order effects, and the responses should be compared to the real 10x responses reported in HJMR. The results is a sample of 46 hypothetical responses and 55 real responses. One feature of these data is that a rich array of individual characteristics was collected, and can be used to condition responses in the two samples.

Table 3.3 presents estimates from an interval regression model of the elicited CRRA interval. Since there is evidence that hypothetical responses may have different variances from real responses, as well as different means, these estimates also allow for multiplicative heteroskedasticity associated with the response being hypothetical or real.

The results provide further evidence that hypothetical responses are systematically different from real responses. The mean effect is significantly different, as is the variance. Relative risk aversion in the hypothetical setting

Table 3.3 Estimates of CRRA interval regression model

Maximum likelihood estimates of CRRA utility function $u(y) = y^{1-r}/(1-r)$, using published and unpublished data from the HJMR (2005) experiments

Parameter	Parameter covariate	Point estimate	Standard error	p-value	Lower 95% confidence interval	Upper 95% confidence interval
r	Hypothetical responses	−0.208	0.092	0.024	−0.389	−0.027
	Female	0.102	0.078	0.188	−0.050	0.255
	Black	0.052	0.144	0.719	−0.230	0.334
	Age	0.009	0.012	0.434	−0.014	0.032
	Major is in business	−0.089	0.077	0.244	−0.240	0.061
	Sophomore in college	0.211	0.144	0.143	−0.072	0.494
	Junior in college	−0.035	0.133	0.795	−0.296	0.227
	Senior in college	−0.044	0.137	0.747	−0.313	0.225
	High GPA (greater than 3.75)	0.043	0.090	0.632	−0.134	0.221
	Low GPA (below 3.24)	−0.159	0.104	0.126	−0.363	0.045
	Graduate student	−0.100	0.171	0.561	−0.435	0.236
	Expect to complete a higher degree	−0.117	0.091	0.195	−0.295	0.060
	Father completed college	0.171	0.105	0.105	−0.036	0.377
	Mother completed college	−0.139	0.095	0.142	−0.325	0.046
	U.S. citizen	−0.212	0.119	0.074	−0.445	0.020
	Constant	0.568	0.313	0.069	−0.045	1.181
r	Hypothetical responses	0.110	0.064	0.086	−0.016	0.236
	Constant	0.286	0.033	0.000	0.221	0.351

is 0.21 lower than the real setting, and has a standard error that is 0.11 higher. Both effects are statistically significant, with *p*-values of 0.024 and 0.086 respectively.

3.4 SENSITIVITY TO ALTERNATIVE FORMULATIONS

Behaviour under uncertainty is an area in which there have been many alternative theories to standard EUT, starting with prospect theory and rank-dependent utility theory, and encompassing many other subsequent specifications. Starmer (2000) provides an excellent overview of the evolution of this literature, and its relation to experimental evidence.

To illustrate the sensitivity of inferences about hypothetical bias over risk attitudes to alternative specifications, consider the effect of allowing for 'probability weighting' of outcomes. The idea of probability weighting was originally proposed by Edwards (1962), and was extended by other decision theorists in the 1960s and 1970s, and had a longer implicit tradition in psychometrics. Kahneman and Tversky (1979: 280ff.) brought it to the attention of mainstream economists as one component of their prospect theory of choice under uncertainty.

To be specific, consider two functional forms that have been popular. Let $w(p)$ denote the weighting function of probability p. The identity weighting function, $w(p)=p$, is employed by EUT and emerges as a special case of virtually all of the weighting functions employed. One functional form we use is the S-shaped function $w(p)=p^\gamma / \{[p^\gamma+(1-p)^\gamma]^{1/\gamma}\}$ introduced by Tversky and Kahneman (1992), and widely used in other applied work using prospect theory. The other functional form is a generalization due to Prelec (1998), in which $w(p)=\exp[-\delta(-\ln p)]^\gamma$. Previous statistical applications of these weighting functions have typically used restrictive functional forms for the utility (or value) function, such as assuming CRRA or even risk neutrality. We allow the utility function to be flexible, in the sense of using the same EP function employed in Section 3.2, along with these flexible[20] probability weighting functions.

Table 3.4 reports the results of maximum likelihood estimation using these probability weighting functions applied to the experimental data from Holt and Laury (2005). Panel A uses the S-shaped function, and panel B uses the Prelec function.[21] Each lead to dramatically different inferences about the extent of hypothetical bias. Using the S-shaped function one would be led to infer that there is no hypothetical bias in the value function (originally, utility function), but that there is hypothetical bias in the probability weighting function. Using real rewards significantly shifts the

Table 3.4 Effects on hypothetical bias of probability weighting

Maximum likelihood estimates of expo-power utility function $u(y) = [1 - \exp(-\alpha y^{1-r})]/\alpha$, and specified probability weighting function, using pooled data from the HL (2005) experiments

Utility function parameter	Parameter covariate	Point estimate	Standard error	t	p-value	Lower 95% confidence interval	Upper 95% confidence interval
A. S-shaped function $w(p) = p^\gamma / \{[p^\gamma + (1-p)^\gamma]^{1/\gamma}\}$ (N = 1680 choices by 168 subjects)							
r	Real responses	−0.128	0.127	−1.004	0.317	−0.378	0.123
	Reverse column order	0.014	0.079	0.170	0.865	−0.143	0.170
	Constant	0.374	0.119	3.136	0.002	0.139	0.609
α	Real responses	0.014	0.026	0.532	0.595	−0.037	0.065
	Reverse column order	−0.002	0.015	−0.167	0.868	−0.032	0.027
	Constant	0.004	0.021	0.215	0.830	−0.036	0.045
μ	Real responses	−0.032	0.029	−1.124	0.263	−0.089	0.025
	Reverse column order	−0.009	0.022	−0.429	0.669	−0.053	0.034
	Constant	0.100	0.019	5.354	0.000	0.063	0.137
γ	Real responses	−0.483	0.258	−1.873	0.063	−0.993	0.026
	Reverse column order	−0.020	0.184	−0.107	0.915	−0.383	0.344
	Constant	0.855	0.208	4.103	0.000	0.444	1.267
B. Prelec function $w(p) = \exp - \delta(-\ln p)^\gamma$ (N = 1512 choices by 168 subjects)							
r	Real responses	−0.456	0.251	−1.815	0.071	−0.952	0.040
	Reverse column order	0.074	0.176	0.421	0.674	−0.273	0.421
	Constant	0.195	0.110	1.770	0.079	−0.023	0.413

Table 3.4 (continued)

Utility function parameter	Parameter covariate	Point estimate	Standard error	t	p-value	Lower 95% confidence interval	Upper 95% confidence interval
α	Real responses	−0.004	0.005	−0.879	0.381	−0.013	0.005
	Reverse column order	−0.002	0.003	−0.651	0.516	−0.008	0.004
	Constant	0.002	0.004	0.435	0.664	−0.006	0.009
μ	Real responses	−0.218	0.115	−1.884	0.061	−0.445	0.010
	Reverse column order	0.014	0.065	0.221	0.826	−0.114	0.142
	Constant	0.028	0.057	0.493	0.623	−0.084	0.140
γ	Real responses	−0.041	0.175	−0.235	0.814	−0.386	0.304
	Reverse column order	0.047	0.112	0.417	0.677	−0.174	0.268
	Constant	0.460	0.149	3.092	0.002	0.166	0.754
δ	Real responses	−2.016	1.003	−2.010	0.046	−3.995	−0.036
	Reverse column order	0.161	0.786	0.205	0.838	−1.390	1.713
	Constant	0.367	0.771	0.475	0.635	−1.156	1.890

Note: Each utility function parameter and probability weighting function parameter is estimated as a linear function of the covariates indicated. For example, in Panel A the probability weighting function parameter γ is estimated as $0.855 - 0.483 \times$ REAL $- 0.020 \times$ REVERSE, where REAL and REVERSE are binary dummy variables reflecting the use of real responses and the reverse column order, respectively.

estimates of γ down by 0.48 from the default value of 0.85. The effect on the parameter r of the EP value function remains negative, but it is smaller in size at only −0.13 and has a p-value of 0.32. On the other hand, using the Prelec function one would be led to infer that there is a significant effect of hypothetical bias on both the value function *and* the probability weighting function. In this case the r parameter of the EP value function is 0.46 lower with real rewards, and the estimates of the δ parameter of the probability weighting function are much lower with real rewards. Since the Prelec functional form generalizes the S-shaped functional form in terms of the probability weighting behaviour it admits, one might argue a priori that it is to be preferred.

These results are intended to be illustrative of the sensitivity of inferences about hypothetical bias to the precise specifications used. In maximum likelihood, estimation of this kind one must expect some numerical instability, as three sets of parameters are 'competing' to account for observed behaviour: the parameters characterizing the value function, the noise parameter that can explain anything if it is large enough, and the parameters characterizing the probability weighting function. More precise characterizations of hypothetical bias that allow all three to play a role will require larger sample sizes and controls for observable sample differences (for example, sex, race, and so on). It would be invalid to infer from the fragility of the inferences in Table 3.4 that there is no evidence that hypothetical bias matters in a systematic or robust manner. Instead, the correct conclusion is that the inferences one makes about hypothetical bias depend critically on what specifications of the underlying decision-making process one assumes.[22]

3.5 IMPLICATIONS FOR CONTINGENT VALUATION SURVEYS

In contingent valuation surveys a key issue is the credibility of the scenario. One factor encouraging incredibility and scenario rejection must be the need to make the scenario sound overly precise and known. Subjects are likely to respond naturally to scenarios presented with some uncertainty surrounding them. For this reason it becomes important to know that hypothetical bias does exist for uncertain outcomes, and to design scenarios that include explicit statements about uncertainty.

For example, consider the scenario used in the contingent valuation survey undertaken for the state of Alaska after the *Exxon Valdez* oil spill (Carson et al., 1992). The scenario asked subjects to consider willingness-to-pay for an escort ship and an emergency Norwegian sea net programme. The subjects were told that until double-hulling laws take effect in 10 years' time they were to expect another large oil spill in Prince William Sound of the same size and potential scope as the *Exxon Valdez* oil spill. The escort ship and sea net scenario was presented as a way of reducing the chance of such an oil spill effectively to zero during the next 10 years, upon which time the double-hulling laws would presumably reduce the probability to zero. Many features of this scenario defy credibility. Anyone with a passing knowledge of the problems encountered after the actual oil spill would know that plans and implementation were two very different things, so a rational respondent that knew this or intuited it from common sense would correctly be asking what probabilities to attach to the claims of the scenario. Similarly, what probability is there that another large oil spill would occur within precisely 10 years, and how can one hope to state such a thing with any certainty? The subject is presumably filling in some probabilities to these outcomes, and the surveyor has no control over these subjective assessments.

In some settings there have been several scenarios presented to subjects that differ in terms of the 'scope' of the environmental injury. The most notable contingent valuation study to do this was one undertaken for preservation of the Kakadu Conservation Zone in Australia (Imber et al., 1991). In this case a between-subjects design was employed to reflect intrinsic scientific uncertainty about the likely ecological impacts of the proposed mining activity at the time that the survey needed to go out into the field. But each scenario was presented to subjects as if it were 'the truth', when in fact there was scientific uncertainty about which one would obtain. Of course, one could use those responses as the basis for an expected utility calculation of willingness-to-pay, imposing some probabilities on each conditional outcome. But it would be better to build such inferences about uncertain outcomes into the design from the outset, rather than correcting for them by heroic assumption after the fact.

An ideal design would elicit valuations of final outcomes, subjective beliefs that each outcome would occur, and the risk attitudes of the respondent. These would preferably be elicited on a within-subjects basis, but one could use between-subjects designs with sufficient sample size and controls for observable sample characteristics. It would then be possible for the analyst to identify valuations that reflect the subjective uncertainty of outcomes, as well as to infer 'corrected' probabilities of outcomes if the respondents made systematic errors in that area. It would, of course, be appropriate to report the original valuations as well as any that were corrected for errors in probability perception, to avoid concerns that voter sovereignty was being implicitly rejected.[23]

One might object that it is often hard to reduce 'intrinsic uncertainty' about the credibility of features of a contingent valuation survey, just as it is almost always hard to make the good or policy 'deliverable'. This is true, but does not mean that methods for identifying the effects of uncertainty and hypothetical bias cannot be developed, as reviewed in Harrison (2005). It is an open question for future research if those methods will prove reliable in the case of hypothetical bias over uncertain outcomes.

In the case of uncertainty, one might also profit from using ideas from the statistical literature on 'errors in variables' to identify the extent of hypothetical bias due to the uncertainty. For example, consider the simulation-extrapolation approach developed by Cook and Stefanski (1994) and Stefanski and Cook (1995). Their idea is that one can always *add noise* to a variable, using a known random process, and that one can then use information on the relationship between the addition of noise and the coefficient of interest to extrapolate what the coefficient would be if the uncertainty were removed. To be concrete, they suggest generating additional noise with a Gaussian process with zero mean and known variance, where the variance is the estimated sample variance of the variable suspected to have some errors of measurement. Add some noise to the suspect variable with variance scaled by a fixed parameter $\lambda>0$, re-estimate the model, go back and change λ in a known way, add more noise to the original values of the variable, and repeat liberally as the computer runs over a long weekend. Then collect the estimates of the coefficients of interest in the model, and estimate a relationship between those estimates and the values of λ that were tried. Then solve this estimated relationship for $\lambda = -1$ and one has an estimate of the effect of removing the measurement error. This idea is closely related to the notion of a 'reduced-bias jacknife estimator', introduced by Quenouille (1956), and can be readily applied in an experimental setting where one has control over the instruments. It is always easy to add noise to an instrument, and only slightly harder to add controlled and measurable noise.

3.6 IMPLICATIONS FOR BEHAVIOURAL ECONOMICS

There has been a parallel debate in behavioural economics over the validity of hypothetical bias in the context of lottery choices. For some reason, many proponents of behavioural economics insist on using task responses that involve hypothetical choices. One simple explanation is that many of the earliest examples in behavioural economics came from psychologists, who did not use salient rewards to motivate subjects, and this tradition just persisted. Another explanation is that an influential survey by Camerer and Hogarth (1999) is widely misquoted as concluding that there is no evidence of hypothetical bias in such lottery choices. Although one can dismiss this issue as a red herring in the context of debates over the validity of the empirical premises of behavioural economics, such claims are important to evaluate in the context of environmental economics where there is a substantive issue at stake: the validity of choices elicited by hypothetical surveys, such as those employing the contingent valuation method.

What Camerer and Hogarth (1999) conclude, quite clearly, is that the use of hypothetical rewards makes a difference to the choices observed, but that it does not generally change the inference that they draw about the validity of EUT.[24] Since the latter typically involve paired comparisons of response rates in *two lottery pairs* (for example, in common ratio tests), it is logically possible for there to be (1) differences in choice probabilities in *a given lottery* depending on whether one use hypothetical or real responses, and (2) no difference between the effect of the EUT treatment on lottery *pair* responses rates depending on whether one uses hypothetical or real responses.

Furthermore, Camerer and Hogarth (1999) explicitly exclude from their analysis the mountain of data from experiments on valuation[25] that show hypothetical bias. Their rationale for this exclusion was that economic theory did not provide any guidance as to which set of responses was valid. This is an odd rationale, since there is a well-articulated methodology in experimental economics that is quite precise about the motivational role of salient financial incentives (Smith, 1982). Also, the experimental literature has generally been careful to consider elicitation mechanisms that provide dominant strategy incentives for honest revelation of valuations, and indeed in most instances explain this to subjects since it is not being tested. Thus economic theory clearly points to the real responses as having a stronger claim to represent true valuations. In any event, the mere fact that hypothetical and real valuations differ so much tells us that at least one of them is wrong! Thus one does not actually need to identify one as reflecting true preferences, even if that is an easy task a priori, in order to recognize that there are differences in behaviour between hypothetical and real responses.

NOTES

* I am grateful to John Kagel and Susan Laury for making detailed experimental results available, to the Danish Social Science Research Council for research support under project 24-02-0124, and to Steffen Andersen, Morten Lau and Elisabet Rutström for discussions, and an anonymous referee for helpful suggestions. All data and statistical code are stored in the ExLab Digital Library at http://exlab.bus.ucf.edu.

1. See Cummings and Harrison (1994), Shogren (2004). The methods for correcting for hypothetical bias include *ex ante* approaches and *ex post* approaches, and are discussed extensively in Harrison (2005). The former refer to efforts to design hypothetical

instruments that better approximate the responses of instruments with salient incentives, perhaps by the use of 'cheap talk' that brings the problem of hypothetical bias to the respondent's attention. The latter refer to statistical methods for adjusting hypothetical responses to reflect systematic biases identified in comparable settings.

2. For example, Camerer (1989) included tests of hypothetical bias in his design. One of his payment treatments was to have subjects receive $2 for completing the task, but no payments. Another treatment was to let subjects play out one of the small gain gambles, chosen at random. Finally, subjects in the small loss treatment were given $10 and required to play out one of their choices, again chosen at random. Each subject made 12 choices, but only four of these were marked as eligible for selection to be played out. (Subjects were also asked to pick again for one of the 12, so there were actually 13 choices. In addition, half of the subjects that faced salient choices were given the option to change their choice before the final determination of their pay-offs.) Furthermore, four of the choices involved large hypothetical gains, and the subjects were told explicitly that they were not to be played out. So there were, in fact, only eight choices eligible for real pay-offs. Thus the subjects knew in advance which four of this eight were salient in the last two pay-off treatments. There are three ways to check for hypothetical bias in this design. One is to compare the results from the responses to the large gains task, which were explicitly declared to be hypothetical (and the stakes would have implied that as well). Another is to compare the results from the responses to the small gains or small loss task that was implicitly not salient, assuming the subjects figured this out. The third is to compare the results from the subjects in the first payment treatment with those in the second. Each of these three has some advantages and disadvantages, but none provides a clean comparison without additional assumptions.
3. The instructions were also different in many other ways. In tests of hypothetical bias in valuation settings the experimental instructions have been generally designed to be virtually identical apart from the use of subjunctive language to describe the hypothetical task.
4. Apart from ensuring comparability with the actual design of the real experiments, this avoids the problem of zero 'contingent liability' in experiments. This refers to the problem of getting subjects to pay net losses in experiments, and the probability that subjects would then rationally behave as if risk-loving since they are not liable for the losses. This issue was raised by Hansen and Lott (1991) in the context of bidding behaviour in experiments with common values.
5. This conclusion derives from examination of the statistical significance of a dummy variable for hypothetical choices in a maximum-likelihood estimation of the coefficient in a constant relative risk aversion specification for all subjects in their Series 1. The same conclusion is drawn if estimation is solely over choices in the loss frame and choices in the gain frame.
6. In the experimental *session* labelled 'loss frame' subjects were also asked some *questions* in a gain frame, hence there are more paired comparisons in the latter than in the former. These are paired comparisons 6, 8, 9, 10 and 12 in Figure 3.1.
7. To be conservative, and literal, any choice that a subject expressed indifference over is viewed as consistent with any other choice in the other mode. Thus, if a subject expressed indifference over a hypothetical pair and then expressed a strict preference in the paired real pair, we count that as consistent (since it is).
8. Between-sample estimates do not allow one to control for unobserved individual effects with the statistical power that within-sample estimates do.
9. Our focus is solely on risk attitudes. It would be interesting to tabulate the in-sample choices of the BKJ subjects and re do their tests of the effect of real rewards on the extent of their violations of EUT, rather than doing that on a pooled basis.
10. The earliest use of the MPL design in the context of elicitation of risk attitudes is, we believe, Miller et al. (1969). Their design confronted each subject with five alternatives that constitute an MPL, although the alternatives were presented individually over 100 trials. It was subsequently used by Murnighan et al. (1988), although they only used the results to sort subjects into one group that was less risk averse than the other. Beck (1994)

utilized it to identify risk aversion in subjects, prior to them making group decisions about the dispersion of everyone else's potential income. This allowed an assessment of the extent to which subjects in the second stage chose more egalitarian outcomes because they were individually averse to risk or because they cared about the distribution of income. The use of the MPL also has a longer history in the elicitation of hypothetical valuation responses in contingent valuation survey settings, as discussed by Mitchell and Carson (1989: 100, fn. 14).

11. There is an interesting question as to whether they should be provided. Arguably the subjects are trying to calculate them anyway, so providing them avoids a test of the joint hypothesis that 'the subjects can calculate EV in their heads and will not accept a fair actuarial bet'. On the other hand, providing them may cue the subjects to adopt risk-neutral choices. The effect of providing EV information deserves empirical study.
12. Friedman (1981) argues that subjects should never exhibit risk-loving behaviour in the laboratory even if they are risk lovers, since they have cheaper ways to purchase uncertainty in the field (for example, purchase of lottery tickets, or trips to a casino). This amounts to 'field censoring' of lab response by field substitutes.
13. Hence for *some* subjects task 4 was actually their third and last task.
14. All of the risk aversion experiments in Holt and Laury (2002; 2005) appear to have been preceded by other experiments that generated income for the subjects. This could have added some noise to responses, although in principle one could condition on previous earnings.
15. The control data in these three panels, for the 1x problem, are pooled across all task 1 responses. That is, the task 1 responses in the bottom left panel of Figure 3.2 are not just the task 1 responses of the individuals facing the 90x problem. Nothing essential hinges on this at this stage of exposition.
16. One concern with the use of MPL procedures is that subjects might gravitate to the middle of the table, and hence appear to be more risk-neutral than they really are. One can test these 'framing' effects easily by experimental variations. Andersen et al. (2004) reports such experiments, and note that there are some small framing effects with the MPL procedures employed by HL.
17. An additional treatment was to control for the order of presentation of the task within each MPL table.
18. Alternative statistical specifications might be expected to lead to different estimates of risk attitudes, although one would not expect radically different estimates. On the other hand, alternative specifications that deviate from traditional EUT, such as allowance for probability weighting, might lead to very different inferences about hypothetical bias.
19. The use of clustering to allow for panel effects from unobserved individual effects is common in the statistical survey literature. Clustering commonly arises in national field surveys from the fact that physically proximate households are often sampled to save time and money, but it can also arise from more homely sampling procedures. For example, Williams (2000: 645) notes that it could arise from dental studies that 'collect data on each tooth surface for each of several teeth from a set of patients' or 'repeated measurements or recurrent events observed on the same person'. The procedures for allowing for clustering allow heteroskedasticity between and within clusters, as well as autocorrelation within clusters. They are closely related to the 'generalized estimating equations' approach to panel estimation in epidemiology (see Liang and Zeger, 1986), and generalize the 'robust standard errors' approach popular in econometrics (see Rogers, 1993). Wooldridge (2003) reviews some issues in the use of clustering for panel effects, in particular noting that significant inferential problems may arise with small numbers of panels.
20. Flexible relative to the EUT specification of the identity function.
21. The Prelec function is not defined for choices in which there is a probability of 0 or 1, so row 10 of the choices in Panel A of Table 3.1 is dropped when estimating it.
22. It is difficult to come up with *a priori* arguments for the validity of probability weighting, or one or other functional form, being appropriate in specific settings. This may be possible as laboratory experiments provide a better sense of the performance of different

assumptions in different settings, but that evidence is not yet available. In a related area, the choice of which 'stochastic error story' to use when evaluating experimental data testing expected utility theory, Loomes et al. (2002) make the important point that there are likely to be significant interactions between model selection and stochastic specifications.

23. One might also undertake corrections for the use of individual risk attitudes instead of social risk attitudes. Ongoing experimental work is examining the possible differences between these.
24. With one exception, I do not believe that this inference is supported by the existing data and experimental designs, but that is an issue well beyond the scope of the present study. That exception is Beattie and Loomes (1997), an excellent example of the type of controlled study of incentives that is needed to address these issues.
25. The term 'valuation' subsumes open-ended elicitation procedures as well as dichotomous choice, binary referenda and stated choice tasks.

REFERENCES

Andersen, S., G.W. Harrison, M.I. Lau and E.E. Rutström (2004), 'Elicitation using multiple price lists', *Working Paper 04–08*, Department of Economics, College of Business Administration, University of Central Florida, forthcoming, *Experimental Economics*.

Battalio, R.C., J.C. Kagel and K. Jiranyakul (1990),'Testing between alternative models of choice under uncertainty: some initial results', *Journal of Risk and Uncertainty*, **3**, 25–50.

Beattie, J. and G. Loomes (1997),'The impact of incentives upon risky choice experiments', *Journal of Risk and Uncertainty*, **14**, 155–68.

Beck, J.H. (1994), 'An experimental test of preferences for the distribution of income and individual risk aversion', *Eastern Economic Journal*, **20**(2), 131–45.

Camerer, C.F. (1989), 'An experimental test of several generalized utility theories', *Journal of Risk and Uncertainty*, **2**, 61–104.

Camerer, C.F. (1995), 'Individual decision making', in J.H. Kagel and A.E. Roth (eds), *The Handbook of Experimental Economics*, Princeton, NJ: Princeton University Press.

Camerer, C. and R. Hogarth (1999), 'The effects of financial incentives in experiments: a review and capital-labor framework', *Journal of Risk and Uncertainty*, **19**, 7–42.

Carson, R.T., R.C. Mitchell, W.M. Hanemann, R.J. Kopp, S. Presser and P.A. Ruud (1992), *A Contingent Valuation Study of Lost Passive Use Values Resulting From the Exxon Valdez Oil Spill*, November, Anchorage, AK: Attorney General of the State of Alaska.

Cook, J.R. and L.A. Stefanski (1994), 'Simulation-extrapolation estimation in parametric-measurement error models', *Journal of the American Statistical Association*, **89**, December, 1314–28.

Cummings, R.G. and G.W. Harrison (1994), 'Was the *Ohio* court well informed in their assessment of the accuracy of the contingent valuation method?', *Natural Resources Journal*, **34**(1), 1–36.

Edwards, W. (1962), 'Subjective probabilities inferred from decisions', *Psychological Review*, **69**, 109–35.

Friedman, D. (1981), 'Why there are no risk preferrers', *Journal of Political Economy*, **89**(3), 600.

Hansen, R.G. and J.R. Lott Jr (1991), 'The winner's curse and public information in common value auctions: comment', *American Economic Review*, **81**, March, 347–61.

Harrison, G.W. (2005), 'Experimental evidence on alternative environmental valuation methods', *Environmental & Resource Economics*, **31.**

Harrison, G.W. and E.E. Rutström (2005),'Experimental evidence on the existence of hypothetical bias in value elicitation methods', in C.R. Plott and V.L. Smith (eds), *Handbook of Experimental Economics Results*, Amsterdam: North-Holland.

Harrison, G.W., E. Johnson, M.M. McInnes and E.E. Rutström (2005), 'Risk aversion and incentive effects: comment', *American Economic Review*, **95**(3), 897–901.

Holt, C.A. and S.K. Laury (2002), 'Risk aversion and incentive effects', *American Economic Review*, **92**(5), 1644–55.

Holt, C.A. and S.K. Laury (2005), 'Risk aversion and incentive effects: new data without order effects', *American Economic Review*, **95**(3), 902–12.

Imber, D., G. Stevenson and L. Wilks (1991), *A Contingent Valuation Survey of the Kakadu Conservation Zone*, February, Canberra: Australian Government Publishing Service for the Resource Assessment Commission.

Kagel, J.H., D.N. MacDonald and R.C. Battalio (1990),'Tests of "fanning out" of indifference curves: results from animal and human experiments', *American Economic Review*, **80**(4), 912–21.

Kahneman, D. and A. Tversky (1979), 'Prospect theory: an analysis of decision under risk', *Econometrica*, **47**(2), 263–91.

Liang, K.-Y. and S.L. Zeger (1986), 'Longitudinal data analysis using generalized linear models', *Biometrika*, **73**, 13–22.

Loomes, G., P.G. Moffatt and R. Sugden (2002), 'A microeconometric test of alternative stochastic theories of risky choice', *Journal of Risk and Uncertainty*, **24**(2), 103–30.

Miller, L., D.E. Meyer and J.T. Lanzetta (1969), 'Choice among equal expected value alternatives: sequential effects of winning probability level on risk preferences', *Journal of Experimental Psychology*, **79**(3), 419–23.

Mitchell, R.C. and R.T. Carson (1989), *Using Surveys to Value Public Goods: The Contingent Valuation Method*, Baltimore, MD: Johns Hopkins Press.

Murnighan, J.K., A.E. Roth and F. Shoumaker (1988), 'Risk aversion in bargaining: an experimental study', *Journal of Risk and Uncertainty*, **1**(1), 101–24.

Prelec, D. (1998), 'The probability weighting function', *Econometrica*, **66**(3), 497–527.

Quenouille, M.H. (1956), 'Notes on bias in estimation', *Biometrika*, **43**, 353–60.

Rogers, W.H. (1993), 'Regression standard errors in clustered samples', *Stata Technical Bulletin*, **13**, 19–23.

Saha, A. (1993), 'Expo-power utility: a flexible form for absolute and relative risk aversion', *American Journal of Agricultural Economics*, **75**(4), 905–13.

Shogren, J.F. (2004), 'Experimental methods and valuation', in K.-G. Mäler and J. Vincent (eds), *Handbook of Environmental Economics. Volume 2: Valuing Environmental Changes*, Amsterdam: North-Holland.

Smith, V.L. (1982), 'Microeconomic systems as an experimental science', *American Economic Review*, **72**(5), 923–55.

Starmer, C. (2000), 'Developments in non-expected utility theory developments in non-expected utility theory: the hunt for a descriptive theory of choice under risk', *Journal of Economic Literature*, **38**, June, 332–82.

Stefanski, L.A. and J.R. Cook (1995), 'Simulation-extrapolation: the measurement error jackknife', *Journal of the American Statistical Association*, **90**, December, 1247–56.

Tversky, A. and D. Kahneman (1992), 'Advances in prospect theory: cumulative representation of uncertainty', *Journal of Risk and Uncertainty*, **5**, 297–323.

Williams, R.L. (2000), 'A note on robust variance estimation for cluster-correlated data', *Biometrics*, **56**, June, 645–6.

Wooldridge, J. (1993), 'Cluster-sample methods in applied econometrics', *American Economic Review (Papers and Proceedings)*, **93**, May, 133–8.

4. The use of a real-money experiment in a stated-preference survey

John Horowitz[1]

4.1 INTRODUCTION

Environmental economics divides into two sub-disciplines: valuation and regulation. Regulation is the analysis of how regulations work, how much they cost, and how they can be improved. Valuation is the analysis and measurement of the benefits of environmental quality. It primarily means assigning a dollar value to environmental quality. Valuation refers to both revealed and stated preference techniques. Because there are many environmental scenarios for which revealed preference data are difficult or impossible to obtain, a large portion of environmental valuation relies on stated-preference techniques. Stated preference, a general category of which contingent valuation is a part, means the use of surveys and similar instruments to elicit a value for environmental quality.

Environmental valuation is an essential component of economics but its results have been greeted with indifference, scepticism, suspicion, or even hostility.[2] This scepticism extends to both revealed and stated preference findings, although different concerns underlie each of these techniques. This chapter examines stated preference techniques, which I sometimes refer to simply as 'valuation surveys'.

I focus on one of the key reasons for scepticism about stated preference techniques, namely, their hypothetical nature. Because stated preference is hypothetical by definition, its findings will always be open to question. This chapter discusses the nature of this hypothetical-ness and reviews remedies to minimize its effects.[3]

In Section 4.4, I present a new method for overcoming problems of hypothetical-ness. This section reports the results of a real-money experiment used as part of a hypothetical valuation survey.

The survey used a willingness-to-accept (WTA) framework, which is the correct measure for many environmental problems but is often not undertaken because of poor results. In contrast, the WTA results reported here demonstrate 'typical' valuation behaviour. I argue that the real-money experiment helped the survey participants see valuation as a concrete exercise in which money and goods change hands. This experience in turn helped them understand what they were being asked to envisage in the more unfamiliar environmental valuation question.

Before tackling these issues, I first discuss *valuation experiments* in general. I describe how lessons from experimental economics have been used in environmental valuation. Although environmental valuation borrows freely from experimental economics, the exact connection between environmental valuation and valuation experiments has not been much explored. This connection is laid out in section 4.2.

4.2 VALUATION EXPERIMENTS: DEFINITION AND A SHORT HISTORY[4]

Experimental economics and environmental valuation have grown up together, but their exact relationship has not been laid out. This section presents a short discussion of the use of experiments to value things.[5]

4.2.1 Valuation Experiments

Valuation experiments are a relatively new category of economic experiments, albeit with a long pedigree. A valuation experiment is one that elicits values as a tool for studying economic behaviour. An example is the use of a Becker-DeGroot-Marshack mechanism (BDM) to elicit an individual's willingness-to-pay for a lottery (Becker et al., 1964). Another example is the use of an auction to elicit individuals' compensation-demanded to taste the bitter substance SOA (Sucrose octa-acetate) (Coursey et al., 1987).

What makes these two examples 'valuation experiments' rather than some other kind of experiment is that the specific activity subjects engage in is the expression of a dollar value. What makes them 'experiments' rather than simply 'valuation exercises' is that their design allows researchers to study economic behaviour, not simply record the value of the item being investigated. In a sense, valuation experiments attempt to understand behaviour and values jointly, rather than separately.

Further examples of valuation experiments include the difference between willingness-to-pay and willingness-to-accept (Horowitz and McConnell, 2002; Knetsch and Sinden, 1984), the value of risk (Harless and Camerer, 1994; Hey and Orme, 1994), value of timing (Harrison et al., 2002b; Horowitz, 1991; Thaler, 1981), endowment or reference point effects (Horowitz et al., 2005; Kahneman et al., 1990; Samuelson and Zeckhauser, 1988), concavity of values (Horowitz et al., 1999) and some public-goods provision experiments (Bohm, 1972).[6] Hypothetical-versus-real experiments play a special role in the intersection of valuation experiments and environmental valuation (Cummings et al., 1995; 1997). Note that in all of these examples, the actual value of the item being studied is rarely the primary object of interest. On the other hand, the basic format of these experiments is the elicitation of a value.

Valuation experiments are a branch of what Davis and Holt (1993) identify as *individual-choice experiments*, which they define to include experiments on optimality, rationality, choice and related topics. Among this group, the line between valuation experiments and non-valuation 'choice experiments' will always be a shaky one because value and choice are so closely intertwined in economics.

I define valuation experiments as experiments that either (1) explicitly elicit a subject's willingness-to-pay or compensation-demanded for some well-defined item, or (2) entail a choice that bounds the subject's value for some item. Thus, dichotomous choice, iterated dichotomous choice, polychotomous choice (choosing the best from a group of options) and ranking exercises constitute forms of valuation experiment. Although the subjects' values are mostly denominated in money terms, there are some cases in which values may be defined in non-money terms.

Early economic experiments were conducted using what are now known as 'induced values'. Subjects either received money or a token for their actions in the experiment; those actions had no value in and of themselves. As Harrison et al. (2002a) note, early experiments were conducted almost entirely with induced values, although there are some important exceptions involving indifference curves, public goods, and choice under uncertainty (see Roth, 1995).

The alternative to induced values are 'homegrown values'. *Homegrown* means the subject comes to the experiment with the values rather than being assigned them as part of the experiment; in other words, the values come from outside the experiment. The first application we can find of this term is Rutström (1998). Homegrown values are essentially identical to what environmental economists are interested in eliciting.

It should be obvious that most valuation experiments elicit home-grown values. It would be a mistake, however, to think that homegrown values are the only focus on valuation experiments, since several important valuation results have been derived from induced-value experiments. Irwin et al. (1998), for example, studied the BDM using induced values in order to test whether the BDM is truly incentive compatible. Other relevant induced-value experiments include Kagel et al. (1987), Kagel and Levin (1993) and Noussair et al. (2002).

4.2.2 History of Valuation Experiments

Valuation experiments are not a new enterprise. The famous Bernoulli paradox of 1738 is an early example of this kind of experiment: David Bernoulli asked his brother Nicholas his willingness-to-pay for a lottery that paid \$n (in contemporaneous currency, of course) with probability $1/2^n$, where n ranged from 1 to infinity. The expected value of this lottery is infinity, but Nicholas was willing to pay only a finite amount, thus providing early evidence of risk aversion.[7]

This experiment already shows the amorphous mixture of valuation and behaviour. Nicholas Bernoulli is being asked the value he places on the lottery; at the same time, he is demonstrating a behaviour towards risk, by which I mean his predicted pattern of choices in other situations involving uncertainty. But it is clear that this exercise represents a valuation experiment rather than valuation itself. The experimenter is not truly interested in the value of the lottery but in what that value reveals about attitudes towards risk. At the same time, the essence of the experiment is clearly the question about value, in this case, willingness-to-pay.

Other early examples came roughly 250 years later. In the early 1960s, Vickrey (1961) and then Becker et al. (1964) examined methods to induce subjects to reveal their values. These were first applied to valuing lotteries rather than goods. It was several years later that experimental techniques were used for commodities or amenities. The earliest example I can find of a valuation experiment for an environmental commodity is the goose-hunting experiment in Bishop and Heberlein (1979).

4.2.3 History of Stated Preference Surveys

The previous section looked at how experimental methods came to be applied to environmental valuation. One might also ask how environmental valuation came to see the usefulness of the experimental literature. Stated preference surveys first developed independently of the experimental literature. Early stated preference surveys such as Hammack and Brown (1974) were conducted without any recourse to, or acknowledgement of, the experimental literature. Because valuation started out clearly as hypothetical, at about the time when real money became a crucial ingredient of experimental economics, the connection between experiments and environmental valuation was not immediately made. See Hanemann (1992) for discussion of the development of the stated preference approach to environmental valuation.

4.3 THE ROLE OF HYPOTHETICAL BIAS

Hypothetical bias is one of the most important contributions of valuation experiments to environmental valuation. Hypothetical bias means the difference between responses to hypothetical valuation experiments and real choices. Environmental valuation questions are typically considered hypothetical because the choice situations they pose are fabricated and because subjects' responses are not directly tied to the environmental decision ultimately made. The ultimate purpose of environmental valuation, however, is to recover true values. Thus, understanding potential discrepancies between hypothetical and real responses is at the very centre of research for valuation experiments.[8]

Before tackling this issue, however, it is worth asking to what degree stated preference surveys are indeed hypothetical. This is the goal of section 4.3.1.

4.3.1 Are Stated Preference Surveys Hypothetical?

Most analysts discuss contingent valuation surveys as if they were hypothetical. Surveys are hypothetical presumably because the vast majority of environmental decisions are not made on the basis of a benefit–cost analysis (see, for example, Morgenstern, 1997). A large proportion of benefit–cost analyses are conducted for regulations that specifically disallow cost considerations or, more generally, that dictate specific non-benefit–cost decision criteria; many benefit–cost analyses are conducted for regulations that have already been issued. In such situations, the contingent valuation survey *must* be considered hypothetical because the specified environmental decision is unconnected to subjects' responses.

In most cases, hypothetical-ness is obvious from the wording and the situation described, as in this question from Jones-Lee et al. (1985):[9]

> Imagine that you have to make a long coach trip in a foreign country. You have been given £200 for your traveling expenses, and given the name of a coach service which will take you for exactly £200. The risk of being killed on the journey with this coach firm is 8 in 100,000.
>
> You can choose to travel with a safer coach service if you want to, but the fare will be higher, and you will have to pay the extra cost yourself.
>
> (a) How much extra, if anything, would you be prepared to pay to use a coach service with a risk of being killed of 4 in 100,000 – that is half the risk of the one at £200?

Furthermore, even in cases that are much more realistic, this hypothetical-ness remains an obvious feature of the valuation scenario:

> Because everyone would bear part of the cost, we are using this survey to ask people how they would vote if they had the chance to vote on the program . . .
>
> At present, government officials estimate the program will cost your household a total of $50. You would pay this in a special one time charge in addition to your regular federal taxes. This money would only be used for the program to prevent damage from another large oil spill in Prince William Sound.
>
> If the program cost your household a total of $50 would you vote for the program or against it?
>
> (Main interview questionnaire, Alaska Exxon Valdez Study Westat, Inc., undated)

Carson et al. (2002, hereafter CGM) argue that many of these situations should be considered non-hypothetical despite the wording and despite the absence of a concrete connection to environmental policy-making. Their argument runs as follows. Suppose a subject is asked whether her household would be willing to pay $50 for a conservation policy that would preserve spotted owl habitat. Suppose there were no concrete connection between the subject's response and the US government's spotted owl policies. CGM argue that despite the vagueness of the link between subjects' responses and the policy decision, it is reasonable to assume that there is at least some probability that the subject's response will tilt the policy in the direction described. That is, if the subject says yes, then it is more likely that a policy costing $50 and improving spotted owl habitat will be enacted. If she says no, then the policy is less likely to be enacted. Thus, the subject has the incentive to answer truthfully. See also Cummings et al. (1997).

There are two important caveats. First, the subject must believe that the survey accurately describes the costs and environmental quality choices, as CGM note. This condition is almost surely violated by even the best contingent valuation survey. For example, suppose the policy turns out to cost $100 (and this is known before the final regulatory decision is made.) If this subject's response (to the cost of $50) is used to make a decision about the $100 policy, then the 'true cost' incentive compatibility condition is violated. Likewise, if the subject's $50 response will be used to make decisions about policies other than the one being described, then the 'true environmental quality' incentive compatibility condition is violated.

All the common estimation techniques for closed-ended questions introduce the first kind of violation. The reason is that they estimate a distribution of responses rather than using the sample responses at each cost level when predicting population responses at that cost level. That is, a subject's response at a cost of $50 is, through the estimation procedure, part of the econometrician's inference about her responses at all other cost levels. This violates the condition that the reported cost is the true cost, because a subject's discrete-choice response (under a true cost scenario) would provide information only about her willingness-to-pay that cost. Open-ended responses incur similar objections; see section 4.4.2.

Benefits-transfer introduces the second kind of violation. Under benefits-transfer, a subject's response about the spotted owl conservation policy might be used to infer her willingness-to-pay for other endangered species protection policies or even her willingness-to-pay for environmental actions in general. Any respondent who believes that her response may be used for these kinds of inferences will adjust her response accordingly. Note that respondents would be perfectly justified in such a belief.[10]

The second caveat is that even when the scenario is accurate and therefore incentive-compatible, it surely matters, from a practical standpoint, *how much more likely* it is that the policy will be enacted, or not, based on the subject's response.

If the actual policy choice will be determined by subjects' responses, as in a binding referendum, then a respondent has a very strong incentive to answer truthfully. If the actual decision rests on many pieces of information (as is generally the case), and the subject's response makes it 'just a little more likely' that the policy will be enacted or not, then she has a much weaker incentive to answer truthfully. While both of these cases will lead individuals to reveal their true willingness-to-pay according to the theoretical model of CGM, these cases may not lead to the same responses in practice.

Whether these are big violations remains an empirical matter. Valuation experiments would seem to be particularly useful in this regard. (For some evidence, see Taylor et al., 2001.)

4.3.2 Experimental Approaches to Hypothetical Bias

Murphy and Stevens (2004) identify three approaches to hypothetical bias in the literature:

1. *Calibration*. Researchers can measure the ratio of hypothetical to real values in experiments that meet the test of revealing true willingness-to-pay. Calibration means dividing values from stated preference surveys by some number – 2, for example – in order to arrive at the true value. Calibration can attempt to correct for: (a) respondent demographic characteristics, such as income or whether the respondent is a student; (b) respondent certainty about his or her stated value; (c) survey features; or (d) valuation question. For recent studies of calibration, see Hofler and List (2004) and List and Shogren (2002).

   Murphy and Stevens (2004) note that some studies have implied that calibration could be tailored to payment amounts. For example, consider a closed-ended survey. The proportion of subjects who say yes to a real and hypothetical question at the $5 level may be roughly the same (calibration = 1); but, the proportion who say yes at the $50 level may be higher for hypothetical than for real questions (calibration > 1). Thus, with sufficient experimental information, calibration could be tied to the payment amount.

This experimental finding is unusable for calibration, however, since it is impossible to know *ex ante* whether a given payment level is low or high. Put another way, the decision to label a payment amount low or high, and therefore subject to a specific calibration factor, is necessarily based on other information or assumptions such as the income effect or the 'reasonableness' of the payment amount. This information should either be used explicitly, in the case of the income effect, or not at all.

By extension, calibration also cannot be conditioned on a subject's reported value in an open-ended survey. For example, it may be tempting to assume that subjects who say they are willing to pay $5 in a stated-preference survey are probably telling the truth, whereas those who say they are willing to pay $500 are probably not. Indeed, this assumption will often be correct. But no calibration can be formulated from this relationship. Calibration on the payment amount would be due either to the respondent's income, in which case calibration should be treated as a demographic calibration, as in approach (a) above. Or, calibration would be due to the researcher's *ex ante* belief about the ballpark value of the item being assessed. This belief cannot legitimately be used when doing valuation.

2. *Survey design features*. Researchers can use specific survey design features to minimize hypothetical bias.

   When analysis identifies survey features that have calibration levels close to one, an alternative to calibration is to directly incorporate those features in a stated-preference survey. In this case, the two approaches to hypothetical bias, calibration and survey design, are essentially identical. In general, a good survey design feature is one with a calibration ratio close to one.

   Survey design has a broader agenda, however. It refers more broadly to the use of design features that are intellectually appealing but that cannot be reliably calibrated; in other words, constructive validity. Experimental evidence may be either impossible to provide, or currently incomplete or qualitative rather than quantitative. I follow this topic further in section 4.3.3.
3. *Valuation questions*. Researchers can reframe the 'valuation exercise' itself. An example is the use of closed-ended rather than open-ended

questions. This is fundamentally different from survey design, which refers to how a specific valuation exercise, such as an open-ended survey, is presented. In the case of open- vs closed-ended questions, the former elicits an individual value; the latter only bounds that value and provides, with additional assumptions, a population average value.

4.3.3 Control of an Experiment's 'Real-ness'

The benefit of experiments is the control that they afford. Their particular benefit for illuminating hypothetical bias is that they allow the researcher to control the nature and degree of hypothetical-ness in a valuation question. In a non-experimental setting, it is difficult to know how real a valuation question is perceived to be. But in the experimental context it is possible to construct the valuation exercises explicitly as hypothetical or real. This is a necessary step because a quantitative understanding of the effects of survey design features requires a clear measure of the degree to which a valuation task is perceived to be 'real'.

Unfortunately, there are serious limitations on the ability of experiments to provide relevant controls on the real-ness or hypothetical-ness of a valuation experiment.

Harrison et al. (2002a) point out that hypothetical bias is almost always studied for private goods. They note that even in a laboratory experiment the outside market for these goods (that is, the ability to purchase or sell an item outside the experiment) will likely play an important role but beliefs about this outside market are unobservable. Note that because these are private goods, those outside markets necessarily exist. Several experimental papers have attempted to control outside market beliefs, with varying success (for example, Shogren et al., 1994). Horowitz and McConnell (2000) measured the effect of dropping experimental willingness-to-accept observations that deviate too greatly from resale values of items. They cannot, however, determine what the 'right' role for resale is.

The problems for environmental goods are even greater. First, very few research projects have successfully created a real valuation experiment on the scale that is needed for reliable inference. A 'real' experiment involving environmental policy is impossible almost by definition, since those policies must be chosen based on legal procedures that preclude binding valuation exercises. The outstanding exception to this claim is the California referendum study of Carson et al. (1986).

Experiments in which subjects provide funds for a public good that will actually be purchased (Brookshire and Coursey, 1987; Cummings et al., 1997; Landry et al., forthcoming) overcome some of these objections, but other problems remain. The unobservable-outside-options problem remains, since in most cases subjects could donate outside the experiment to the public good. The number of participants is considerably smaller than would be affected by most environmental policies. Many experiments (although not Landry et al., forthcoming) provide subjects with a participation payment, which likely contaminates the experiment. Perhaps most importantly, fund-raising for public goods is a very different kind of public choice from that posed by most environmental policies.

Many dimensions that are important for real-ness have not yet been the focus of survey design, and it will be difficult to make them so. As section 4.3.1 makes clear, it is important that both the cost and environmental quality change being described be concrete and immutable. Yet very few valuation studies focus on these dimensions.

In summary, one of the strongest potential contributions of valuation experiments is to elucidate hypothetical bias and thus improve the reliability of hypothetical environmental valuation questions. However, this task requires that experimenters control the 'real-ness' of their treatments. This is intrinsically difficult for environmental valuation because (1) realistic real environmental valuation situations are extremely difficult to construct, and (2) the nature of environmental regulation often precludes a clear and decisive role for valuation, which is essential for real valuation. Environmental valuation surveys are 'not real' in ways that are difficult for experiments to treat or overcome.

4.3.4 The 'Budget Constraint' Problem

The previous sections have argued that experiments are integral to improving valuation surveys. However, experimental methods to reduce hypothetical bias in environmental surveys are more difficult to devise than has generally been recognized.

The most promising alternative approach is based on construct validity. By construct validity, I mean the adoption of techniques that are intellectually and intuitively valid. Direct empirical evidence is impossible, but indirect empirical is valuable and essential.

Construct validity is most useful for the problem of designing surveys to encourage subjects to take their budget constraints seriously. The goal is to have survey respondents use the same mindset that they use in making familiar spending and savings decisions involving their own money. This mindset is unobservable, of course, and therefore it is difficult, if not impossible, to test whether subjects are 'taking their budget constraints seriously'.

Obvious departures from budget-mindfulness can sometimes be spotted; for example, Horowitz and McConnell (2000) observed some $1 million valuations of binoculars that cost $25. Such a response is clearly wrong.

But there is no obvious line to draw between reasonable answers and unreasonable ones, and any attempt to impose a standard of reasonableness should be resisted.

On the other hand, sharp researchers can recognize whether the survey design (as opposed to its results) adequately encourages participants to take their task seriously. This is the role for construct validity. Survey design is as much art as science; this is the art part.

From the inception of contingent valuation, economists have used a wide range of reminders to help put subjects in the appropriate frame of mind. Tolley and Babcock (1986) used the following approach when valuing the benefits of clean air:

> Before we start, please look at this card showing how a typical family spends its take-home income.
>
> When you pay to avoid symptoms, the money will have to come out of one of the categories shown. We'll leave the card here so that you can think about where the money comes from that you would spend to avoid the symptoms.

The experiment shown in section 4.4 is proposed with this approach in mind. Subjects who make a real-money decision that takes the same form as the valuation decision are more likely to adopt the approach that economists hope they would.

4.4 THE USE OF A REAL-MONEY EXPERIMENT IN A STATED-PREFERENCE SURVEY

This section proposes a technique for improving valuation surveys. A real-money experiment is conducted as part of the survey, before the key valuation question. Its purpose is to use the real-money, real-goods experience to help put survey subjects in the right 'frame of mind' for the environmental valuation question.

This procedure requires that the valuation survey take place in person. Neither mail nor telephone surveys are suitable for this procedure. The procedure works best when the valuation survey is administered to a group of subjects simultaneously. The group format approach is discussed in section 4.4.2.

4.4.1 Procedure

The valuation experiment takes the form of a willingness-to-accept public-choice experiment. The experiment uses an open-ended format and a median-value rule.

Each of the subjects, seated in a room together, is given a small item such as a mug, flashlight, or pair of binoculars. Subjects are asked, individually, the minimum payment they would require to return this item to the experimenter. A public-choice variant of the Becker-de Groot-Marschak mechanism is used to determine whether subjects will keep their items or return them to the experimenter and, if returned, the amount of the payment.

The experimenter draws a random per-item price, called the offered amount. If more than 50 per cent of the subjects are willing to surrender their item for that amount, then all subjects must return their items to the experimenter and all subjects are paid the offered amount. The payment is made on the spot, in real money.[11] If less than 50 per cent of the subjects are willing to surrender their item for that price, then all subjects keep their items and no payment is made. A sample sheet is shown in Figure 4.1.

This is essentially a standard willingness-to-accept experiment, but here used for a collective choice. The experiment highlights for participants both (1) the valuation exercise (each participant must ask himself or herself, 'What is this item really worth to me?') and (2) the public choice decision, namely, how individuals' values are used to make a collective choice. The purpose of these components is to help participants get in the mindset of making value-based decisions about public goods.

4.4.2 Discussion

4.4.2.1 Group presentation format

The group presentation format is useful for making clear the public-choice dimension of environmental valuation. In the absence of a group format, experiments could use a standard BDM.

The group format has long been the norm in behavioural experiments. But its use specifically for valuation (that is, for experiments that might otherwise be conducted one on one) is still not established. The group format was first suggested for contingent valuation (to my knowledge) by Richard Carson. Following Carson's recommendation, Horowitz et al. (1999) used this format to conduct private goods valuation at lower cost to the experimenter than one-on-one valuation. John List has conducted many field experiments using the group format to study both private goods and public goods. Another example is Cummings et al. (1997). Schelling has long advocated using group discussion as part of the (individual) valuation exercise. His reasoning is that most real-world opinions are formed and expressed in open discussion.

4.4.2.2 Willingness-to-accept

This experiment requires a willingness-to-accept format, which is much less common than willingness-to-pay. The alternative willingness-to-pay format

Flashlight Values

Each person in the room has been given a flashlight. You will either get to keep your flashlights or return them to the administrator, in which case everyone will receive some payment. The amount of the possible payment will be determined at the end of the exercise.

What is the smallest payment that would make you on-the-fence between keeping your flashlight and returning it to the administrator?

Amount: ____________________

This is like a vote to keep or return your flashlight. Suppose I offered you 10 cents more than the amount you write down. Would you definitely vote ***for*** accepting the offer, if you knew that was the amount I was offering?

Suppose I offered 10 cents less than the amount you write down. Would definitely vote ***against*** accepting the offer?

At the amount you write down, you should be ***on-the-fence*** about voting for or against accepting the offer.

There is no right or wrong answer; it just depends on how much you like the flashlight.

How the Outcome will be Determined:

1. After everyone has turned in his sheet, I will put all the sheets in order, with the amounts going from lowest to highest.
2. I will draw the payment amount randomly, using the device at the front of the room.
3. Once we know the amount, I will determine whether at least half of the people would have voted for or against accepting that amount.
4. If the amount I am offering is high enough (more than half the people would have voted *for* it), then everyone will return his or her flashlight and receive the offered amount.
5. If the amount I am offering is too low (more than half the people would have voted *against* it), then everyone will keep his or her flashlight and receive no money.

Figure 4.1 Real-money public-choice valuation experiment

is essentially impossible because experimenters cannot compel subjects to pay for a public good. One remedy, an up front payment to subjects (for example, $10, with the specified payments being less than $10), is highly problematic. If the experimenter can compel all subjects to pay for a public good, then that money cannot also be considered the subjects' to spend as they please, which is the key feature of a real-money valuation experiment!

The willingness-to-accept format is not a problem for the experiment but for the subsequent environmental valuation survey. If the valuation survey is framed in terms of willingness-to-pay, some of the lessons of the real-money experiment will be lost, or willingness-to-accept. If the valuation survey is framed in terms of willingness-to-accept, then the experiment's lessons are not lost. However, environmental valuation using willingness-to-accept will almost surely lead to non-credible value estimates.

4.4.2.3 Mean vs median willingness-to-pay

This experiment also requires a median-value approach. Note that many of the real-money public goods experiments such as Cummings et al. (1997) or Horowitz et al. (2005) also adopt a median-value or median-voter approach. For an exception, see Brookshire and Coursey (1987). The median value approach is incentive compatible under a broad range of conditions. In contrast, mechanisms using total or average willingness-to-pay are not incentive compatible even if they are derived from closed-ended surveys. See CGM for a review this literature as it applies to valuation.

Many economists might hope that the total-value approach could be used despite its not being truly incentive compatible. There is a lesson, however, in this body of experimental work using the median value. In a real-world experiment (such as Cummings et al., 1997) it is necessary to explain to subjects how their responses will be used to make the public goods decision. For a closed-ended survey in which subjects are assigned different cost amounts, the required explanation is complicated and, therefore, probably not feasible. Such a mechanism would be difficult to administer even if subjects did not take into account its non-incentive-compatible opportunities.

On the other hand, for an open-ended survey the required explanation would be simple. But subjects could easily understand how to exploit the non-incentive-compatible loopholes, therefore making the open-ended total-value approach also unworkable.

This chapter's proposed experiment, because it is open-ended and incentive compatible, allows economists to observe individual values. This is advantageous for experimental purposes. But this information cannot be used for actual valuation decisions unless the experimenter is willing to be untruthful to the subjects.

H. Wetlands Acreage

One environmental issue that society faces is the preservation of *wetlands*. Wetlands are marshes, forested swamps, and other areas that are under water part of the year. Wetlands vary from less than an acre in size to thousands of acres. Wetlands provide many services to the natural environment such as maintaining water quality and providing habitat for fish, birds, frogs, raccoons and other animals.

Unfortunately, there is competition for the use of wetlands. Wetlands can be drained and used for farms, for houses, or for industries that create jobs and raise incomes.

To preserve wetlands and protect the environment, the state of Maryland purchases wetlands and places them in parks and preserves. There are approximately 300,000 preserved wetlands acres on the eastern shore.

State budget analysts have made a suggestion about some of these wetlands. They have suggested selling 36,000 acres to the highest bidder. If this land is sold, whoever buys it will be free to do with it as he wishes, subject to other state laws. The area will probably be developed.

If these wetlands acres are not sold, there will be 300,000 preserved wetlands acres on the eastern shore. If the 36,000 acres are sold, there will be 264,000 preserved wetlands acres, but there will also be more money available to the state government. This money can be used for schools or police or used to cut state income taxes.

The 36,000 acres are the same kind of wetland as the other 264,000 acres. They do not have any distinguishing environmental characteristics. The acres were chosen to be considered for would be a one-time payment that every household in the state would receive if the wetlands were sold.

Figure 4.2 Environmental valuation survey

It is possible to conduct this experiment with a closed-ended (yes–no) survey. The question format would be the standard dichotomous choice format. The decision rule would be that after the offered amount is drawn, the experiment looks to see whether 50 per cent of the responses at that amount would vote in favour of accepting the offer.

The open-ended survey shown in Figure 4.2 is highly desirable from an experimental point of view. A closed-ended survey might be valuable, however, if the subsequent valuation survey was closed-ended.

H. Wetlands Acreage, cont.

Name: ______________________________

The purpose of this survey is to determine which outcome you prefer.

Suppose that we that we were offering to write you a cheque for $150. This represents how much money the state would receive, per household, by not keeping these acres. We would like to know whether you prefer: (i) a cheque for $150, and keeping 264,000 acres; or (ii) no cheque, and keeping 300,000 acres.

The decision for you is similar to the flashlight survey. The main difference is that now we can tell you ahead of time the dollar amount that is being offered. This would be a one-time payment that every household in the state would receive if the wetlands were sold.

The outcome will depend on whichever option receives the most votes.

QUESTION H:

Please indicate which outcome you would prefer:

__________ A cheque for $150, and keeping 264,000 wetland acres; or

__________ No cheque, and keeping 300,000 wetland acres.

The details and the situation in this question are hypothetical. Our purpose is to explore a 'what if' scenario.

Figure 4.2 Continued

4.4.2.4 Experiments used in valuation surveys

The literature on stated preference surveys that used real experiments on unrelated items as part of the survey is relatively slim.

4.4.3 Results

I conducted, with K.E. McConnell, a real-money individual-choice experiment followed by a hypothetical valuation survey. The real-money experiment is described in Horowitz et al. (1999). It is similar to the

Table 4.1 Wetlands values – raw data

	Payment offer			
	\$48	\$100	\$150	\$300
Yes	2	2	1	6
No	12	12	8	7
(Total subjects)	14	14	9	13
Percentage Yes	14	14	11	46

public-choice experiment shown in Figure 4.1, but the rule about whether the individual kept his item or returned it for money was made at the individual level, not the group level. We did not, however, conduct a public-choice experiment, nor did we conduct a separate treatment that included a valuation survey without the preceding real-money experiment. Thus, the results described here do not fully conform to the research design described in section 4.4.1.

The hypothetical valuation survey examined values for wetlands preservation using a willingness-to-accept framework. The survey instrument is shown in Figure 4.2. It used a one-shot closed-ended format with four possible values for the payment amount: \$48, \$100, \$150 and \$300.

Results are shown in Table 4.1. The subjects were members of a local Parent–Teacher Association. Fifty subjects took part.

4.4.3.1 Discussion

I used the data in Table 4.1 to estimate a mean willingness-to-accept of \$88. There were roughly 1.9 million Maryland households in 1996, which yields a total WTA of \$167.2 million. This works out to \$4644 per acre.

Note that willingness-to-accept experiments are often poorly behaved, so this pattern of responses represents a small victory of experimental technique.

Based on results in Horowitz and McConnell (2002) for public goods, the predicted mean willingness-to-pay would be \$8.45 (= \$88/10.4).

There is one word of caution, however. These results came after several valuation exercises to assess willingness-to-accept reduced protection of sea turtles (using a different subject pool). Protection of sea turtles turned out to be such a high-value issue that the great majority of respondents reported that there was no compensation that they would accept for a diminution of sea turtle populations (even though the survey stated that turtles would not become endangered as a result of the action). Analysis was essentially impossible because there were so few 'yes' responses.

There are two interpretations of the turtle results in comparison with the 'well-behaved' wetlands results. First, it is possible that turtle values are indeed extremely high, in which case the valuation survey should be considered a success. But it is also possible that turtle results are not stratospherically high and that the accompanying real-money experiment was not sufficient to overcome the problem of unfamiliarity that often makes environmental valuation unworkable.

4.5 CONCLUDING REMARKS

This chapter has two themes. First, valuation experiments are a separate category of experiment, to be distinguished from other experiments. Valuation experiments elicit preferences, and from these experiments we learn both about preferences and how individuals express those preferences. This is the very essence of economics.

This joint inquiry into preferences and the expression of those preferences is one of the paramount contributions that environmental economics, together with experimental economics, has made to the economics profession. Environmental economists were among the first economists to recognize the importance of the question, 'What do people really care about and how do we uncover this?' and to take it seriously as an empirical matter.

Second, this chapter has shown how a real-money experiment can be used as part of a stated-preference survey. The real-money experiment provides a useful 'decision context' for subjects without polluting the stated-preference survey. This chapter did not attempt to test hypotheses about this combination of experiments. I leave this for future research.

NOTES

1. I thank John List and Ted McConnell for helpful comments.
2. This chapter does not address the issue of why environmental valuation should be considered 'essential'; for this, see Hanemann (1994) or Epstein (2003), for example. I also leave out the valuation of ecological services, which is better thought of as a form of market, rather than non-market, valuation.
3. The literature on hypothetical bias is vast; see List and Gallet (2001) or Murphy et al. (2005) for reviews.
4. In writing this chapter I benefited greatly from the well-written and amazingly comprehensive *Handbook of Experimental Economics*, especially chapter 1 by Al Roth (1995) and chapter 7 by Kagel (1995).
5. Harrison and List (2004) discuss the definition of an experiment.
6. A full list of valuation experiments is beyond the scope of this chapter. In each case, I have tried to give a seminal article and/or review.

7. One of the curious things about this famous experiment is that the actual value response is not typically reported. Whether the respondent gave an actual money value or merely a qualitative response is not typically reported.
8. The term hypothetical bias is a bit misleading, but like 'contingent valuation', it has stuck. If analysts are able to calibrate actual willingness-to-pay based on hypothetical survey responses, then the goal of survey design should be precision, not accuracy. Of course, accurate calibration is difficult, so survey design must focus on both precision and accuracy.
9. An amusing feature of this question is its framing of the safety decision as taking place 'in a foreign country'.
10. There is a useful opinion-poll analogy: suppose a law is up for consideration and a member of the public is polled about whether he supports the law. The respondent has an incentive to respond truthfully even though he has no say in whether the law is passed because no matter how small his voice, his opinion must sway the vote in the right direction. On the other hand, suppose that a general issue is being debated and there are many potential remedies being considered, and that an opinion poll is conducted about a single concrete proposal to address the issue. Then the respondent will answer the question based on how he thinks his response will shape the general debate or on what he thinks the 'real' issue is, not simply the specific proposal being asked about.
11. In past experiments, I have simply written cheques to all subjects in the event that their responses led them to be paid the offered amount. At the end of the experiment, all subjects will have either a flashlight (or similar item) or a cheque for a small amount of money. Harrison (1992) argues that the BDM is a weak instrument for eliciting values.

REFERENCES

Becker, G., M. DeGroot and J. Marschak (1964), 'Measuring utility by a single-response sequential method', *Behavioral Science*, **9**, 226–36.

Bishop, R.C. and T. Heberlein (1979), 'Measuring values of extramarket goods: are indirect measures biased?', *American Journal of Agricultural Economics*, **61**, 926–30.

Bohm, P. (1972), 'Estimating demand for public goods: an experiment', *European Economic Review*, **3**, 111–30.

Brookshire, D.S. and D.L. Coursey (1987), 'Measuring the value of a public good: an empirical comparison of elicitation procedures', *American Economic Review*, **77**, 554–66.

Carson, R., T. Groves and M. Machina (2002), 'Incentive and informational properties of preference questions', unpublished manuscript.

Carson, R., W.M. Hanemann and R.C. Mitchell (1986), 'Determining the demand for public goods by simulating referendums at different tax prices', unpublished manuscript.

Coursey, D.L., J.L. Hovis and W.D. Schulze (1987), 'The disparity between willingness to accept and willingness to pay measures of value', *Quarterly Journal of Economics*, **102**, 679–90.

Cummings, R., S. Elliott, G.W. Harrison and J. Murphy (1997), 'Are hypothetical referenda incentive compatible?', *Journal of Political Economy*, **105**, 609–21.

Cummings, R., G.W. Harrison and E. Rutström (1995), 'Homegrown values and hypothetical surveys: is the dichotomous choice approach incentive-compatible', *American Economic Review*, **85**, 260–66.

Davis, D.D. and C.A. Holt (1993), *Experimental Economics*, Princeton, NJ: Princeton University Press.

Epstein, R.A. (2003), 'The regrettable necessity of contingent valuation', *Journal of Cultural Values*, **27**, 259–74.
Hammack, J. and G.M. Brown (1974), *Waterfowl and Wetlands: Toward Bioeconomic Analysis*, Baltimore, MD: Johns Hopkins University Press for Resources for the Future.
Hanemann, W.M. (1992), 'Preface', in S. Navrud (ed.), *Pricing the European Environment*, Oslo: Scandinavian University Press.
Hanemann, W.M. (1994), 'Valuing the environment through contingent valuation', *Journal of Economic Perspectives*, **8**, 19–43.
Harless, D. and C. Camerer (1994), 'The predictive utility of generalized expected utility theories', *Econometrica*, **62**, 1251–89.
Harrison, G.W. (1992), 'Theory and misbehavior of first-price auctions: reply', *American Economic Review*, **82**, 426–43.
Harrison, G.W. and J.A. List (2004), 'Field experiments', *Journal of Economic Literature*, **42**, 1009–55.
Harrison, G.W., R. Harstad and E.E. Rutström (2002a), 'Experimental methods and elicitation of values', unpublished manuscript.
Harrison, G.W., M. Lau and M. Williams (2002b), 'Estimating individual discount rates for Denmark: a field experiment', *American Economic Review*, **92**, 1606–17.
Hey, J.D. and C. Orme (1994), 'Investigating generalizations of expected utility theory using experimental data', *Econometrica*, **62**, 1291–326.
Hofler, R. and J.A. List (2004), 'Valuation on the frontier: calibrating actual and hypothetical statements of value', *American Journal of Agricultural Economics*, **86**, 213–21.
Horowitz, J. (1991), 'Discounting money payoffs: an experimental analysis', in S. Kaish and B. Gilad (eds), *Handbook of Behavioral Economics*, vol. 2B, Oxford: JAI Press.
Horowitz, J. and K.E. McConnell (2000), 'Values elicited from open-ended real experiments', *Journal of Economic Behavior and Organization*, **41**, 221–37.
Horowitz, J. and K.E. McConnell (2002), 'A Review of WTA/WTP studies', *Journal of Environmental Economics and Management*, **44**, 426–47.
Horowitz, J., J.A. List and K.E. McConnell (2005), 'Diminishing marginal value', unpublished manuscript.
Horowitz, J., K.E. McConnell and J. Quiggin (1999), 'A test of competing explanations of compensation demanded', *Economic Inquiry*, **37**, 637–46.
Irwin, J., G. McClelland, M. McKee, W. Schulze and N. Norden (1998), 'Payoff dominance vs. cognitive transparency in decision making', *Economic Inquiry*, **36**, 272–85.
Jones-Lee, M.W., M. Hammerton and P. Philips (1985), 'The value of safety: results of a national sample survey', *Economic Journal*, **95**, 49–72.
Kagel, J. (1995), 'Auctions: a survey of experimental research', in J. Kagel and A. Roth (eds), *Handbook of Experimental Economics*, Princeton, NJ: Princeton University Press.
Kagel, J. and D. Levin (1993), 'Independent private value auctions: bidder behaviour in first-, second-, and third-price auctions with varying numbers of bidders', *Economic Journal*, **103**, 868–79.
Kagel, J., R. Harstad and D. Levin (1987), 'Information impact and allocation rules in auctions with affiliated private values: a laboratory study', *Econometrica*, **55**, 1275–304.

Kahneman, D., J. Knetsch and R. Thaler (1990), 'Experimental tests of the endowment effect and the Coase theorem', *Journal of Political Economy*, **98**, 1325–48.

Knetsch, J. and J. Sinden (1984), 'Willingness to pay and compensation demanded: experimental evidence of an unexpected disparity in measures of value', *Quarterly Journal of Economics*, **99**, 507–21.

Landry, C., A. Lange, J.A. List, M.K. Price and N. Rupp (forthcoming), 'Toward an understanding of the economics of charity: evidence from a field experiment', *Quarterly Journal of Economics*.

List, J.A. and C. Gallet (2001), 'What experimental protocol influence disparities between actual and hypothetical stated values?', *Environmental and Resource Economics*, **20**, 241–54.

List, J.A. and J. Shogren (2002), 'Calibration of willingness-to-accept', *Journal of Environmental Economics and Management*, **43**, 219–33.

Morgenstern, R. (1997), *Economic Analyses at EPA*, Washington, DC: Resources for the Future.

Murphy, J.J. and T.H. Stevens (2004), 'Contingent valuation, hypothetical bias, and experimental economics', *Agricultural and Resource Economics Review*, **33**(2), 182–92.

Murphy, J.J., P. Allen, T.H. Stevens and D. Weatherhead (2005), 'A meta-analysis of hypothetical bias in stated preference valuation', *Environmental and Resource Economics*, **30**, 313–25.

Noussair, C., S. Robin and B. Ruffieux (2002), 'Revealing consumers' willingness-to-pay: a comparison of the BDM mechanism and the Vickrey auction', unpublished manuscript.

Roth, A. (1995), 'Introduction to experimental economics', in J. Kagel and A. Roth (eds), *Handbook of Experimental Economics*, Princeton, NJ: Princeton University Press.

Rutström, E.E. (1998), 'Home-grown values and incentive compatible auction design', *International Journal of Game Theory*, **27**, 427–41.

Samuleson, W. and R. Zeckhauser (1988), 'Status quo bias in decision making', *Journal of Risk and Uncertainty*, **1**, 7–59.

Shogren, J., S. Shin, D. Hayes and J. Kliebenstein (1994), 'Resolving differences in willingness to pay and willingness to accept', *American Economic Review*, **84**, 255–70.

Taylor, L.O., M. McKee, S. Laury and R. Cummings (2001), 'Induced-value tests of the referendum voting mechanism', *Economics Letters*, **71**, 61–65.

Thaler, R. (1981), 'Some empirical evidence on dynamic inconsistency', *Economics Letters*, **8**, 201–207.

Tolley, G.S. and L. Babcock (1986), 'Valuation of reductions in human health symptoms and risks', US Environmental Protection Agency, Office of Policy Analysis.

Vickrey, W. (1961), 'Counterspeculation, auctions, and competitive sealed tenders', *Journal of Finance*, **16**, 8–37.

Westat, Inc. (undated), 'National Opinion Survey (Alaska Exxon Valdez Study)', http://econ.ucsd.edu/%7Ercarson/AKsurvey.pdf.

5. Mechanisms for addressing third-party impacts resulting from voluntary water transfers

James J. Murphy, Ariel Dinar, Richard E. Howitt, Erin Mastrangelo, Stephen J. Rassenti and Vernon L. Smith

INTRODUCTION

Voluntary transfers have emerged as a central instrument in balancing and reallocating the changing demand and supply for water in the western United States. These transfers can have significant impacts beyond the benefits realized by the parties engaged in the voluntary transfer, such as environmental degradation due to reduced streamflows or regional economic impacts in the source areas. A viable water transfer mechanism must incorporate not only the direct benefits and costs associated with the transfer, but also the external costs imposed on the environment and local communities. Until it can be demonstrated that a water market institution is capable of adequately accounting for environmental and regional economic impacts, voluntary water transfers will not realize their full potential as an integral part of a comprehensive water management strategy.

We use laboratory experiments to test alternative water market institutions designed to incorporate the value of non-consumptive water uses into the allocation process. A non-consumptive water use includes any activity that derives an economic benefit from the water without actually consuming it. For example, water consumed in an agricultural region may stimulate local economic growth and water flowing instream may provide water quality and environmental benefits. This research was initially motivated by California's objective of avoiding unreasonable disruptions to the local economy in the source areas, which we refer to as third-party impacts. Because these impacts are pecuniary externalities and may be the result of a well-functioning market, some economists might find it troubling to impose restrictions on voluntary exchange in order to protect these third parties. Below, we make the case that, although perhaps unorthodox, the protection of rural economies is an unavoidable reality and any exchange mechanism that ignores these consequences is not viable. More importantly, we emphasize that although the focus of this chapter is on third-party impacts, the results and analysis are applicable to any non-consumptive water use. This includes the environmental benefits of instream flows, which most economists would agree are a classic externality problem that ought to be incorporated into water allocation decisions.

Concern about the social and economic impacts from water transfers has a long history in California and exerts a strong influence on policy decisions today. Memories of Owen's Valley still persist and resistance to water exports can be strong, particularly in some rural areas. Section 1745.05 of the state's Water Code restricts exports to 20 per cent of the local water supply, and 22 of the state's 58 counties have imposed restrictions on groundwater exports (Hanak, 2003). Hanak suggests that these local ordinances reflect a broader intent to discourage any type of transfer that might affect the local economy. Moreover, extensive idling of crops that results in unemployment of manual labourers could be considered an unfair treatment under the state's environmental justice policies (California Department of Water Resources, 2004) and some environmental justice representatives have argued that the public trust doctrine includes broader economic and social concerns (Water Transfer Workgroup, 2002). A recent report for the State Water Resources Control Board (SWRCB) asserts that the highly subsidized rates that agriculture pays for water reflects the high value society places on agriculture, and that this objective could be undermined if water does not remain with its intended use. They therefore recommend that water exports must avoid unreasonable impacts on the overall economy from the source area (Water Transfer Workgroup, 2002). Recognizing the need to minimize these impacts, a recent agreement between the Metropolitan Water District of Southern California and the Palo Verde Irrigation District includes a $6 million payment to the community to offset economic harm from land fallowing (Vogel, 2002).

Non-consumptive rights are often protected by constraints on water transfers such as minimum instream flow requirements, taxes on transfers, restrictions on the quantity of water that may be exported from a region, or 'no injury' rules. When constraints on transfers are binding, the resulting allocation will be inefficient (Weber, 2001). Both Huffman (1983) and Griffin and Hsu (1993) suggest that the creation of property rights for non-consumptive use may lead to more efficient allocations. Since the externalities associated with water transfers vary by location, efficiency will usually require location-specific pricing (Griffin and Hsu, 1993; Weber, 2001). However, a water market with spatially discriminative prices is likely to be complex and face high transaction costs associated with finding trading partners. Thus, institutional design plays an important role in the transmission of information and the evolution of prices such that the water market yields efficient allocations (Weber, 2001).

Successful implementation of an institution that can facilitate water transfers requires a substantial amount of coordination to achieve an efficient water allocation, especially in the presence of non-consumptive uses. The SWRCB observed that an efficient water allocation must balance an 'unusually complex mix of price responsive and non-price responsive social values' including complex interrelations between the multitude of consumptive and non-consumptive uses (Water Transfer Workgroup, 2002). They concluded that market forces alone cannot achieve efficient allocations because of the inherent complexities and externalities not considered during private bargaining.

However, advances in computing technology and high-speed communication networks can facilitate exchange systems in complex environments that were previously considered impractical. 'Smart', computer-coordinated markets can provide a decentralized solution to complex resource allocation problems. McCabe et al. (1989; 1991), have demonstrated the ability of these 'smart' markets to achieve efficient allocations in the natural gas and electricity industries. Dinar et al. (1998) and Murphy et al. (2000) report similar success applying the 'smart' market concept to spot water markets with environmental constraints. These 'smart' markets allow participants to submit bids to buy and offers to sell to a centralized computer center. Using the willingness to exchange provided by participants, the 'smart' market can then compute prices and allocations by maximizing the gains from trade subject to physical constraints on the system (for example, streamflow or reservoir capacity). By doing so, these markets can lower transaction costs, facilitate trades that may not have otherwise been effected and increase overall market efficiency. The ability of these electronic markets to address complex allocation problems is a particularly attractive feature for water markets, especially in the presence of environmental and third-party impacts.

Murphy et al. (2004) find that computer-assisted markets can successfully incorporate instream flow values into the water allocation mechanism. Their results indicate that facilitating direct environmental participation in the market can yield highly efficient outcomes, although it may introduce some volatility. Although motivated by the protection of instream flow values, their results are equally applicable to any non-consumptive use including third-party impacts. The research in this chapter extends their analysis by considering a mechanism that decouples the water allocation decision from the compensation of non-consumptive users adversely affected by water transfers. During droughts, rapid approval of short-term transfers is critical and there may be inadequate time for a lengthy review process to quantify third-party or environmental damages. To account for this, the California Model Water Transfer Act (Gray, 1996) proposes a tax-and-compensate scheme to expedite transfers. The basic process is simple: a regulator sets the tax rate at the beginning of the water year and trading occurs with participants paying the tax on all water transfers. Tax revenue goes directly into a fund that is managed by a neutral arbitrator. At the end of the water year, victims of a water transfer may file a claim requesting compensation from the fund and the arbitrator renders a binding final decision to each claimant. Any surplus or deficit in the fund after compensation is carried over to the next water year.

This chapter describes a series of laboratory experiments designed to test this compensation mechanism and compares it with an alternative institution that allows direct third-party market participation. The key results are: (1) although third-party participation in the market has the advantage of allowing those affected by the transfers to express their willingness-to-trade, it is prone to strategic behaviour and free-riding that may introduce market volatility and could erode the efficiency gains; and (2) taxing transfers to compensate victims as described above may not be able to maximize total social welfare, but the market still yields highly efficient and stable outcomes, and is more flexible than fixed limits on water transfers. Although further research is necessary, a tax on water transfers is a promising means of promoting highly efficient allocations while ensuring that third parties are fully compensated.

EXPERIMENTAL DESIGN

In this chapter, we use a controlled, laboratory setting to test three different water market institutions designed to account for third-party impacts. The first alternative facilitates direct third-party participation in the allocation mechanism. The last two institutions tested in this chapter incorporate taxes on water transfers to compensate victims. We assume that third parties derive a benefit from water consumed in their region (alternatively, an environmental benefit from instream flows at a particular location). Higher levels of water consumption imply increased regional economic activity. Similarly, exporting water out of a region generates third-party damages. We assume that third parties know with certainty the level of damages associated with a proposed set of water transfers. However, because of the need for rapid approval of transfers during droughts, government regulators do not have this information until after the transfers have been completed and the damages have been realized.

Alternative 1: Third Parties Participate in the Water Market (3PBuyer)

The first alternative, denoted 3PBuyer, tests a market structure that allows third parties to actively participate in the water allocation process. In this institution, the third parties do not have property rights to the water, but can participate in the market by subsidizing water consumption in their region. These third-party payments will increase the flow into the region, thereby reducing adverse economic impacts. This institution is consistent with the observation that some environmental groups and private parties have been active in acquiring water to provide instream flows (Anderson and Snyder, 1997; Landry, 1998). Because the nature of third-party participation in this institution is identical to one of the environmental participation treatments in Murphy et al. (2004), it serves as a link between the two studies.

Since third parties best know their own circumstances and willingness to trade, if all agents were to truthfully reveal their true willingness-to-trade, then this institution would yield the maximum possible gains-from-trade, including non-consumptive values. However, third parties receive a benefit for any water consumed in the region regardless of whether they contribute to its provision. Because of the public good nature of non-consumptive water uses, there is an incentive for third parties to under-contribute. Murphy et al. (2004) observe that some demand under-revelation by non-consumptive users exists in this institution, but not the pure free-rider outcome predicted by theory. In addition, they observe more price volatility relative to a baseline with environmental constraints but no active environmental participation.

Alternatives 2 and 3: Water Transfer Taxes and Third-Party Compensation

The California Model Water Transfer Act provides the basis for the two taxing mechanisms. Under the proposed Act, all short-term water transfers are allowed to occur, but water transfers are taxed and the revenue goes into a fund from which affected third parties can be compensated. At the end of the water year, anyone damaged by a water transfer may file a claim for compensation. An impartial arbitrator evaluates any claims and uses the tax revenue to compensate victims. Because the water transfer is decoupled from third-party compensation, these institutions have two components: (1) a taxing mechanism to generate revenue for compensating third parties, and (2) an arbitration mechanism through which victims can file claims for damages.

Taxing mechanism

In the two tax treatments, either a per-unit or a revenue tax is imposed on all transfers, and the revenue placed in a third-party compensation fund. At the end of the water year, an arbitrator evaluates any third-party claims and fully compensates them for any damages. For such a compensation mechanism to be viable, it needs to guarantee that (a) third parties are fully compensated, (b) water traders are not paying taxes in excess of damages, and (c) the fund will remain solvent over time. These three conditions yield the constraint that total (not marginal) tax revenue must exactly equal total damages in each year. The tax rate is set at the beginning of the water year by a regulator who has perfect information about all market participants. With this information, the regulator can estimate the damages that would occur in a competitive equilibrium. What he or she cannot predict, however, is how participants will actually trade. With perfect foresight, the regulator would set the tax rate such that revenues collected from water transfers exactly equalled the level of third-party damages. The fund balance at the end of each year would then be zero.[1] In reality, because estimated third-party damages and tax revenues may not exactly match actual damages and revenues, it is possible that at the end of the water year the compensation fund may run a surplus or a deficit, depending upon whether revenues or damages were greater. If there is any revenue remaining in the fund after all third parties are compensated, the residual funds are carried over to the next water year, resulting in a lower tax rate in the next year. Similarly, if there is insufficient tax revenue to fully compensate all third parties, the fund goes into a deficit and will make up for the shortfall by raising the tax rate in the subsequent year.

We consider two types of taxes: a per-unit tax (UnitTax) and a revenue or *ad valorem* tax (RevTax). Tax revenue from a per-unit tax is based on the total volume of water traded, whereas tax revenue from a revenue tax is based on the total value of the water traded. In these experiments, the water seller is responsible for collecting the tax.[2]

Arbitration mechanism

The second component is an arbitration scheme to render judgements on how the money collected from the tax is to be distributed. Those adversely affected by the transfer can file a claim for compensation to a neutral arbitrator. Clearly, in such an arbitration mechanism there are strong incentives for third parties to overestimate damages and file frivolous claims. It is incumbent upon the arbitrator to determine the true damages. In this research, we avoid this incentive problem by assuming a perfectly informed neutral arbitrator. This computerized robot arbitrator has perfect information on the value of water for all market participants, including third parties. Using this information, the arbitrator can calculate the exact level of third-party damages and fully compensate victims. Although, in reality, this is obviously not the case, this assumption allows us to take out the role of the arbitrator and award exact compensation to third parties. By taking out the vagaries of the arbitration process, we can focus solely on the ability of the tax scheme to account for actual damages.

Experimental Procedures

This research focuses on three different market institutions described in the previous section. These are: (1) third parties as Buyers in the water market (3PBuyer); (2) a per-unit tax imposed on all water trades (UnitTax); (3) a revenue tax imposed on all water trades (RevTax). Water is allocated using a computer-assisted, uniform price, sealed-bid double auction. As a price mechanism, the market's distinguishing feature is that all accepted bids to buy are filled at a price less than or equal to the lowest accepted bid price of buyers – a price that just clears the market by making the total number of units sold equal to the number purchased. Similarly, all accepted offers to sell water are filled at a price greater than or equal to the highest accepted asking price of sellers. An appealing feature of this mechanism is that there is a uniform price for the water itself; any differences in the price at a particular location represent the conveyance costs, third-party impacts and transfer taxes associated with that site.

We present the results collected from 18 computer-based experiments divided evenly across the three treatments. Participants for the experiments were recruited from the student population at the University of Massachusetts. The experiments utilized web-based water market software designed specifically for this research. Participants were required to commit to a pair of two-hour sessions. The first day was used for training. All participants read the online instructions and took part in several rounds of practice trading.[3] The parameters for the trainer were different from that used in the real data sessions, and none of the data collected on the training days was used for analysis. The second day was reserved for the experiments in which usable data were collected.

The software used for the experiments displayed the entire water network to each participant on his or her computer screen and showed information about the network. The network consisted of various buy nodes at which there was both consumptive and non-consumptive demand for water, reservoir nodes from which water was sold, and canals or rivers that connected the nodes. Water conveyance was provided by computer robot that simply revealed its supply costs.[4] Subjects were active as buyers, sellers or third parties. Each participant was randomly assigned a role that defined the location(s) at which he or she was active throughout the experiment.

All sellers received an exogenous inflow of water each period. Their induced supply schedule represented the per-unit costs of selling water. The costs were the lowest price for which the sellers could profitably sell their water. Sellers earned money by selling water at a price above these costs. Buyers submitted bids in each round based on an induced demand schedule. These values represented the benefit they received from consuming the water. Their bids represented the most they were willing to pay for a given amount of water delivered to their location, including the cost of the water, conveyance costs and transfer taxes. Buyers earned money by purchasing water at a price lower than the benefit they received from consumption. Non-consumptive users in the 3PBuyer experiments also submitted bids based on an induced demand schedule similar to that of buyers. However, the third parties did not consume the water and received a benefit from the total amount of water consumed by buyers at their location regardless of whether they contributed its the provision. The induced values for all agents are in Tables 5.1a and 5.1b.

Each experiment consisted of 16 to 20 periods in which odd numbered periods were considered 'wet' water years (higher inflows and lower buyer values) and even numbered periods were considered 'dry' water years (reduced inflows and higher buyer values). All wet years were identical, as were the dry years. Each year, trading occurred in a spot market for one-year leases. Water could not be stored for future use. During the period, participants could submit location-specific bids and asks. Subjects could divide these submitted bids and asks into as many as five separate price-quantity steps. Each period lasted about five minutes and all participants were allowed to submit bids and asks as often as they wished. Only the last submission was used by the computer. The allocation mechanism in this chapter adapts the model in Murphy et al. (2000) to include the economic benefits of non-consumptive use. When each trading period ended, the central computer took the input data from all participants and solved the following network flow problem:

$$\text{Maximize total surplus:} \quad -\sum_i c_i f_i + \sum_i b_i f_i \tag{5.1}$$

subject to:

$$\text{Balance of flow:} \quad \sum_{i \in S_k} f_k = \sum_{i \in E_j} f_j \quad (\forall \text{ nodes } j) \tag{5.2}$$

$$\text{Conveyance capacity:} \quad d_i \leq f_i \leq u_i \ (\forall \text{ arcs } i) \tag{5.3}$$

Each arc (i) in this formulation represents one bid or offer. If a buyer makes a multi-part bid, then each part is represented by separate, parallel arcs. Multi-part offers by sellers are represented similarly. Thus, each bid or offer is represented by the vector (s_i, e_i, d_i, u_i, c_i) with s_i being its starting

Table 5.1a Induced values for wet years

Role	Location		Step 1	Step 2	Step 3	Step 4	Step 5	Inflow
Buyer 1	Buy-1	Price	75	67	59	51	37	
		Quantity	8	8	6	6	16	
Buyer 2	Buy-1	Price	73	65	57	42	36	
		Quantity	8	8	6	7	16	
Buyer 3	Buy-1	Price	71	63	55	43	38	
		Quantity	8	8	6	11	14	
Buyer 4	Buy-2	Price	53	45	37	27	21	
		Quantity	8	8	7	6	16	
Buyer 5	Buy-2	Price	55	47	39	29	20	
		Quantity	8	8	6	10	16	
Buyer 6	Buy-2	Price	57	49	41	31	19	
		Quantity	8	8	6	7	16	
Buyer 7	Buy-3	Price	95	87	79	67	61	
		Quantity	4	4	4	8	6	
Buyer 8	Buy-4	Price	119	111	103	91	86	
		Quantity	4	4	4	8	6	
Seller 1	Res-1	Price	36	40	43	49	60	
		Quantity	8	8	10	10	20	56
Seller 2	Res-1	Price	36	40	47	51	58	
		Quantity	8	8	10	10	20	56
Seller 3	Res-1	Price	36	40	46	53	56	
		Quantity	8	8	10	8	20	54
Seller 4	Res-2	Price	19	23	28	33	42	
		Quantity	8	8	10	10	20	56
Seller 5	Res-2	Price	19	23	27	35	40	
		Quantity	8	8	10	8	20	54
Seller 6	Res-2	Price	19	23	31	37	38	
		Quantity	8	8	10	8	20	54
Third party 1	Buy-1	Price	24	21	16	9	5	
		Quantity	46	16	20	20	30	
Third party 2	Buy-2	Price	22	19	12	7	3	
		Quantity	46	16	20	20	30	

node, e_i its end node, d_i the least permissible flow on that arc, u_i the greatest permissible flow on that arc (determined by the bid or offer quantity entered), and c_i the bid value or offer price per-unit of flow on that arc (bid values are treated as negative costs) and b_i is the third-party bid for flow along that arc. The flow on arc i is f_i, S_j is the set of arcs which begin at node j, and E_j is the set of arcs which end at node j. Note that constraint set (5.2) maintains the balance of flow at each node j. Intuitively, equation (5.2) describes the network and equates supply and demand. Constraint

Table 5.1b Induced values for dry years

Role	Location		Step 1	Step 2	Step 3	Step 4	Step 5	Inflow
Buyer 1	Buy-1	Price	140	109	105	94	90	
		Quantity	4	4	4	8	6	
Buyer 2	Buy-1	Price	128	120	106	101	68	
		Quantity	4	4	4	4	6	
Buyer 3	Buy-1	Price	122	114	81	74	58	
		Quantity	4	4	4	8	6	
Buyer 4	Buy-2	Price	107	109	93	77	48	
		Quantity	4	4	4	8	6	
Buyer 5	Buy-2	Price	103	95	79	72	64	
		Quantity	4	4	5	8	6	
Buyer 6	Buy-2	Price	115	101	89	70	51	
		Quantity	4	4	4	8	6	
Buyer 7	Buy-3	Price	170	164	144	133	112	
		Quantity	8	8	4	8	6	
Buyer 8	Buy-4	Price	196	188	170	158	146	
		Quantity	8	8	4	8	6	
Seller 1	Res-1	Price	73	77	97	100	125	
		Quantity	6	4	4	4	20	38
Seller 2	Res-1	Price	67	79	91	98	140	
		Quantity	7	4	4	4	20	39
Seller 3	Res-1	Price	65	85	89	105	115	
		Quantity	7	4	4	6	6	27
Seller 4	Res-2	Price	48	52	64	76	97	
		Quantity	6	4	4	4	6	24
Seller 5	Res-2	Price	40	58	70	80	107	
		Quantity	7	4	4	4	20	39
Seller 6	Res-2	Price	46	60	72	87	112	
		Quantity	7	4	4	10	20	45
Third party 1	Buy-1	Price	31	29	15	10	8	
		Quantity	20	20	7	7	6	
Third party 2	Buy-2	Price	29	26	13	9	7	
		Quantity	20	20	7	7	6	

set (5.3) ensures that the flow on each conveyance arc does not exceed the stated lower or upper bounds. In the tax treatments, third parties are not active, so $b_i = 0$, and the seller's bid includes both the seller's asking price and the tax.

Solving the linear programming problem above yields not only the optimal flows (and production and consumption patterns), but also the set of location-specific shadow prices for all nodes in the network. Since the

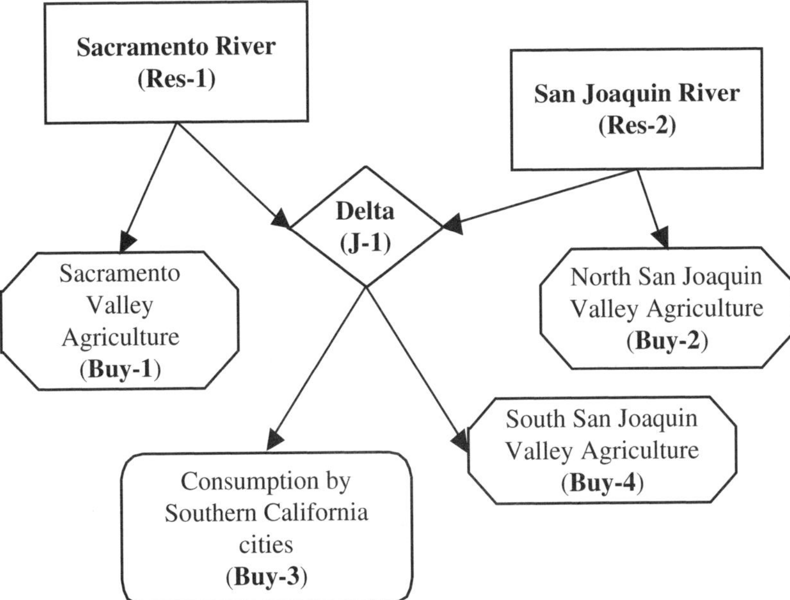

Note: The labels in parentheses correspond to the location names used in the experiment.

Figure 5.1 Diagram of water flow in the laboratory water network

shadow prices are marginal nodal values at which water is bought and sold, the difference in shadow prices at the start and end nodes of an arc yields the value of the marginal unit of flow on that arc which is the price associated with water conveyance. The software displays the results immediately following each period including profits and which bids or asks were accepted.

The laboratory water market was a simplified version of the California water network. Figure 5.1 contains an illustration of the laboratory water market. There were two main surface water sources: the Sacramento and San Joaquin rivers. These flow into the Delta from which water flows to Southern California cities through the Central Valley Project and the State Water Project. In addition to consumption by Southern California cities, there were three agricultural centres that use the water: Sacramento Valley Agriculture, North San Joaquin Valley Agriculture and South San Joaquin Valley Agriculture.

Each subject in the experiment may have played more than one role. The two upper consumption nodes, Buy-1 and Buy-2, each had three buyers active. Consumption nodes Buy-3 and Buy-4 each had a single buyer. There were three water sellers located at each of the two reservoirs. In addition to the water being traded between the buyers and sellers, third-party impacts occurred at the two regions represented by nodes Buy-1 and Buy-2.

RESULTS

In this section, we use the same criteria as Murphy et al. (2000) to evaluate market performance: efficiency, price stability, and distribution of surplus. After defining the terms, we use these criteria to evaluate the performance of the water market. Each buyer of water, b, located at node j has a resale value, or benefit, schedule B_{bj} (Q_{bj}). All buyers b at node j pay the same market price for delivered water, P_j', and each buyer b earns a profit of:

$$\Pi_{bj}' = B_{bj}(Q_{bj}') - P_j'Q_{bj}' \tag{5.4}$$

where Q_{bj}' is the equilibrium quantity of water delivered to buyer b at node j. Each seller of water, s, located at node j, has a cost schedule C_{sj} (Q_{sj}), and in equilibrium all sellers s at node j receive the same market price, P_j', and each seller s earns a profit of:

$$\Pi_{sj}' = P_j'Q_{sj}' - C_{sj}(Q_{sj}') \tag{5.5}$$

Similarly, each third party, p, located at node j, has a benefit schedule that is a function of the aggregate consumption in the region $B_{pj}(\Sigma_b Q_{bj})$. In the 3PBuyer sessions, the third party may contribute to the provision of water at his location (but will receive benefits from aggregate consumption at his node regardless of third-party contributions). Each third-party's contribution, or subsidy, to the provision of water at his location is S_j', and each third-party p at node j earns a profit of:

$$\Pi_{pj}' = B_{bj}\left(\sum_j Q_{bj}'\right) - S_j' \sum_j Q_{bj}' \tag{5.6}$$

Conveyance along each arc was provided at a constant marginal cost. The price for the water itself is uniform throughout the network, and any location-specific differences in the price for delivered water reflect conveyance costs and third-party contributions. Aggregate earnings for all buyers, Π_{Buy}', are the sum of the individual buyers' earnings: $\Pi_{Buy}' = \Sigma_b \Sigma_j \Pi_{bj}'$. Aggregate seller earnings, Π_{Sell}', and aggregate third-party earnings, Π_{3P}', are defined similarly.

Note that the computer calculates the actual market prices and allocations based on the submitted bids and asks of each agent. We can also calculate the competitive equilibrium prices, allocations, and earnings for each subject by using the induced values as shown in Tables 5.1a and 5.1b, and then applying equations (5.1)–(5.3). Because the perfectly competitive equilibrium (denoted with an asterisk *) maximizes the possible gains from trade, we use this as a baseline against which the realized market outcomes (denoted with a prime ′) can be compared. Efficiency measures the ability of the market to extract all of the potential gains from trade. It is the share of potential surplus realized by the market:

$$Efficiency = \frac{\Pi'_{Buy} + \Pi'_{Sell} + \Pi'_{3P}}{\Pi^*_{Buy} + \Pi^*_{Sell} + \Pi^*_{3P}} \in [0, 100\%] \qquad (5.7)$$

The competitive equilibrium results in an allocation that maximizes the total possible surplus for a given institution and environment, thus, a perfectly competitive market will be 100 per cent efficient.

Result 1

The revenue tax treatment produced the most efficient outcomes. The evidence is mixed about whether active third-party participation and a unit tax yield comparable levels of efficiency.

In a perfect world in which the revenue collected exactly equalled the damages compensated, the tax rate in each period would be the same. However, if a surplus or deficit in the compensation fund exists, it will be carried over into the following year. This implies that the tax rate in each period of the experiment may differ to account for this. Therefore, we define the competitive equilibrium surplus as the level of total surplus that would occur in a competitive market given the actual tax rate for that period. Table 5.2 presents the mean and median efficiency for each of the three treatments. We present the summary statistics for all periods (excluding periods 1 and 2),[5] and again after dropping periods 1 through 10 to get a sense for how these markets converge in the later rounds. By all measures, the RevTax treatment consistently yielded the highest efficiency. Mean and median efficiency in all periods (92 and 93 per cent, respectively) was greater than either of the other two treatments. Moreover, in nearly three-quarters of the RevTax periods, efficiency exceeded 90 per cent, whereas less than one-third of the periods in 3Buyer and about 40 per cent of the periods in UnitTax exceeded this benchmark. For all three treatments, performance increased in the later rounds.

The 3PBuyer treatment has the lowest median efficiency in all periods, as well as just the later rounds. 3PBuyer also has the lowest mean efficiency in the later rounds and the lowest share of periods with efficiency above 90 per

Table 5.2 Summary statistics: efficiency for each treatment

Treatment	All periods (excl. Per 1–2)				
	N	N>90%	Mean	Std dev	Median
3PBuyer	88	26 (30%)	86.0	7.8	86.4
RevTax	108	77 (71%)	92.1	6.4	93.3
UnitTax	100	39 (39%)	85.1	10.4	88.3
	Only periods ≥ 10				
3PBuyer	40	15 (38%)	87.8	5.8	87.4
RevTax	60	48 (80%)	93.6	4.9	94.3
UnitTax	52	26 (50%)	89.3	5.7	90.1

Table 5.3 Market efficiency: estimates from a random effects model

Variable	Coefficient	Standard error
Intercept	87.54***	2.25
3PBuyer	1.26	3.10
RevTax	6.87**	3.08
Dry year	−0.02	0.76
Periods 3 to 10	−5.08***	0.77

Notes:
Dependent variable: efficiency in each period (excludes periods 1–2).
Number of observations: 296.
Model significance (Pr>Chi-square): <0.0001.
*** = significant at 1%, ** = significant at 5%.

cent. We used both Wilcoxon rank sum and median two-sample tests to determine whether these differences in efficiency across treatments were statistically significant. The results of these pairwise comparisons strongly reject the null hypothesis that the efficiency in the RevTax equals that of either UnitTax or 3PBuyer ($p = 0.00$). Comparison of efficiency for UnitTax vs 3PBuyer yields a similar conclusion.

In addition to the non-parametric tests, we also used a random effects model to estimate efficiency while controlling for group effects. Table 5.3 reports the results of a random effects model in which efficiency is a function of treatment, type of water year (wet or dry), and a dummy variable that equals one for periods 3 to 10. The 18 individual sessions are the random effects. The omitted dummy variables are for UnitTax and wet years. After controlling for individual group effects, RevTax has a 6.87

Table 5.4 Efficiency comparison for dry years[a]

Treatment	Competitive equilibrium surplus	Average realized surplus	Average efficiency[b]	Avg. efficiency relative to maximum possible surplus
3PBuyer	7626	6603	87%	87%
RevTax	6872	6261	91%	82%
UnitTax	6704	5788	86%	76%

Notes:
a Excludes periods 1–2.
b Average realized surplus for each treatment divided by competitive equilibrium surplus for that treatment.
c Average realized surplus for each treatment divided by competitive equilibrium surplus for 3PBuyer treatment (7626).

percentage point higher efficiency than the UnitTax treatment. The coefficient for 3PBuyer is not statistically significant, suggesting that there is no difference in efficiency between the UnitTax and 3PBuyer treatments. The coefficient on the dummy variable for periods 3 to 10 is negative and significant, indicating that efficiency increases roughly 5 percentage points in the later rounds of an experiment.[6] There is no significant difference in efficiency between wet and dry years.

Result 2

Although 3PBuyer has lower average market efficiency than RevTax, it has the highest level of realized surplus.

The second column of Table 5.4 shows that the competitive equilibrium surplus in 3PBuyer treatment (7626) is greater than the competitive equilibrium surplus of the two tax treatments (6704 for UnitTax and 6872 for RevTax).[7, 8] The tax rates in the UnitTax and RevTax treatments are not, and cannot be, efficient because the tax rates are set to equate total (not marginal) expected damages and total expected revenue, and the tax rates are not spatially discriminative.[9] Since the 3PBuyer treatment fully accounts for the marginal costs and benefits of third-party impacts, but the tax treatments do not, the level of total surplus in the perfectly competitive equilibrium for 3PBuyer is necessarily greater than that in the tax treatments.

With our parameters, the efficiency loss in the tax treatments is around 10 per cent. This 10 per cent efficiency loss has important implications in evaluating the relative merits of each institution. Table 5.4 shows that the average level of realized surplus in the 3PBuyer treatment was greater than that of either tax treatment (6603, as compared to 6261 and 5788 for RevTax and UnitTax, respectively). Essentially, 3PBuyer offers a smaller piece of a bigger pie. What can we say about the relative merits of the different institutions if 3PBuyer has the lowest efficiency, but the highest level of available surplus? In general, we would expect that 3PBuyer will always have the highest level of potential surplus, but will be less efficient at extracting this surplus (from Result 1). However, the relationship of the levels of realized surplus from trading in the three institutions is an empirical question that will depend on the magnitude of the efficiency losses due to the tax.

Result 3

In the two tax treatments, observed prices are slightly higher than the competitive equilibrium, but prices adjust well to changes in market conditions and price volatility is low.

In addition to market efficiency, we are also interested in how the observed market price compares with the competitive equilibrium price. This evaluation has three dimensions:

1. Does the average market price equal the competitive equilibrium price?
2. Is the observed market price stable with low volatility?
3. Does the observed market price react quickly to changing circumstances?

In the two tax treatments, the observed market price performs reasonable well on all three counts.

In this analysis, we arbitrarily chose the price at node Buy-1 to serve as the 'base' price of water. In all three institutions, the price of the water itself is uniform across all locations in the network. Any differences in prices at a location are due to conveyance costs and, in the 3PBuyer sessions, to third-party contributions. Table 5.5 reports the competitive

Table 5.5 Summary statistics: price at Buy-1 for each treatment

	Wet years			Dry years		
Treatment	Comp. equil. price	Mean price	Std. dev.	Comp. equil. price	Mean price	Std. dev.
3PBuyer	54	48.1	2.4	121	99.9	7.9
RevTax	51	53.8	1.5	114	114.6	2.4
UnitTax	51	57.1	3.3	116	118.7	4.5

equilibrium and market prices of water at Buy-1 for all treatments in both wet and dry years. For the two tax treatments the mean price is slightly higher than the competitive equilibrium and, although the difference is generally small, it is statistically significant.[10] Because of this, the actual distribution of surplus tends to favour the sellers. Moreover, the market price tracks the competitive equilibrium in both wet and dry years, indicating that the market is responding well to changes in market conditions. The mean price in the RevTax treatment was the closest to the competitive equilibrium, which is consistent with the higher levels of efficiency observed in this institution.

As a measure of price volatility within an experiment, we use the mean absolute deviation (MAD) of prices, measured in percentage deviations from the mean price for each group (we use the mean for each group, rather than treatment, to control for group effects). All three treatments exhibited low volatility. RevTax had the most stable prices, with a MAD of 1.4 per cent. This indicates that, on average, the difference in prices over time for a particular group in the RevTax treatment was quite small. The MAD for UnitTax was 2.2 per cent and for 3PBuyer was 3.3 per cent.

Result 4

In the 3PBuyer treatment, third-party contributions are consistent with some demand under-revelation.

In the competitive equilibrium, third parties active at nodes Buy-1 and Buy-2 contribute money to increase water consumption in their region. However, given that these third parties receive a benefit for all water flowing into their region, regardless of their contributions, there is clearly a strong incentive to free-ride and contribute nothing. Table 5.6 provides summary statistics for the ratio of actual third-party contributions to competitive equilibrium contributions. On average, the third-party contribution at Buy-1 is 45 per cent of the competitive equilibrium price, and 69 per cent at Buy-2. These results are consistent with those reported by Murphy et al. (2004) for the same institution. With the exception of Buy-2 in wet years, contributions are clearly below the competitive equilibrium,

Table 5.6 Actual third-party contributions as a percentage of the competitive equilibrium contribution

Node	Mean	Std dev	Median
Buy-1	45.5%	33.9%	45.5%
Buy-2	68.7%	48.0%	62.5%

Table 5.7 Percentage of competitive equilibrium third-party contributions: estimates from a random effects model

Variable	Coefficient	Standard error
Intercept	78.7***	11.4
Node Buy-1	−23.7***	4.6
Dry year	−31.5***	4.6
Periods 3 to 10	12.0***	4.6

Notes:
Dependent variable: percentage of competitive equilibrium contributions by third party in each period (excludes periods 1–2).
For purposes of brevity, the group-specific random effects are not included in this table.
Number of observations: 176.
Model significance (Pr>Chi-square): <0.0001.
*** = significant at 1%.

however, there is substantial variation in the extent of the free-riding across groups. Table 5.7 presents the results of a random effects model using the percentage of the competitive equilibrium third-party contribution as the dependent variable and the group as the random effect. There is a significant difference in contributions between nodes and between water year types.[11] Consistent with results in typical public goods experiments, contributions decline by 12 percentage points in the later rounds. On average, third parties earned more than double what they would in the competitive equilibrium, but there was significant variation across individuals (mean 216 per cent, standard deviation 131 per cent, median 165 per cent). This free-riding resulted in about a 25 per cent reduction in the total quantity of water traded, and a transfer of surplus from the communities with the third parties to those without third-party impacts. Given that economic activity is dependent on the quantity of water flowing into the region, agricultural communities could face adverse long-term consequences if free-riding persists.

Result 5

The tax schemes could have equity implications if traders are not the same from year to year.

The tax rate is calculated before the market opens and assumes perfectly competitive outcomes. If the actual outcomes do not equal the competitive equilibrium, the tax rate is imperfect in the sense that total revenue collected does not equal total damages. If the tax were perfect, the tax rate would be zero in all wet years, but we consistently observed tax rates approaching $10 per-unit or 14 per cent of revenue. Although our results suggest that the mechanism is successful in its intent to compensate third parties, the results also point to important equity implications. Because no damages occur in the wet years, a non-zero tax rate in these years means that any wet-year traders are paying for damages that occurred in previous years. Essentially, part of the burden of the tax is passed on from dry-year traders to wet-year market participants. Moreover, this shift in the tax burden over time could affect the market entry decisions for some participants.

One last comment on the tax rates regards the potential bankrupting of the compensation fund. This market environment was designed so that dry years (when damages are high) alternate with wet years. We found that increasing the tax in the wet years was often sufficient to make up for any shortcomings in the dry years. However, a prolonged drought could keep the fund balance in a deficit for a number of consecutive years. Because a deficit causes the tax rate to increase in the following year, the tax rate could potentially rise to a point where it makes the water transfers prohibitively expensive. One possible means of reducing the likelihood of this occurring is to spread the surplus or deficit across multiple years.

CONCLUSION

California's drought water banks clearly demonstrated the economic benefits that voluntary short-term water transfers can provide. However, the water banks relied upon predetermined 'prices' set by the California Department of Water Resources, and these fixed 'prices' did not adjust with changes in supply or demand. The use of computer-coordinated 'smart' markets for water offer California the potential to increase the efficiency of short-term water transfers while protecting environmental, social and economic interests. This chapter extends that research by testing whether and how these computer-coordinated water markets can incorporate third-party values into the water allocation mechanism.

This research used laboratory experiments and a computer-coordinated market to analyse three alternatives designed to protect third parties. The options tested range from a free-market environment in which third parties are allowed to directly participate in the market and bid for water, to a pair of mechanisms which allow all transfers to occur but these trades are taxed to finance third-party compensation. The RevTax experiments produced the most efficient results. The UnitTax experiments exhibited some volatility in early periods but by later periods reached average efficiencies exceeding 90 per cent. The 3PBuyer experiments, on the other hand, rarely reached average efficiencies of 90 per cent in any given period. Further analysis showed that some of the losses in the 3PBuyer treatment can be attributed to partial free-riding by the third parties.

However, the lower efficiencies described here do not alone imply that any market mechanism is more or less preferred than another. As pointed out in Result 2, this is because the level of potential surplus varies across institutions. Taking this difference of available surplus into consideration, efficiency can be thought of in a second way: compare average realized surplus with competitive equilibrium surplus for the institution that yields the highest possible level of total surplus. If an institution reaches 100 per cent efficiency by this definition, then it has realized the maximum amount of total surplus for any institution. This distinction is particularly important when considering a command-and-control type mechanism to regulate water transfers. These regulated markets quickly reach high efficiencies based on the first definition and show little variation. However, because of the regulatory constraints, the amount of available surplus is lower so, although they perform well given the constraints, there may be other more flexible institutions that can increase overall welfare.

Our results show that although the 3PBuyer institution had the potential for high efficiencies by both definitions, free-riding and strategic behaviour eroded most of the potential gains. The RevTax experiments were able to realize high levels of efficiency by the first definition and still realize levels of surplus comparable to the 3PBuyer market. Although key issues such as the distribution of surplus and equity need further attention, a tax on water transfers may be appealing because it offers high levels of efficiency and market stability and is more flexible than fixed limits on water transfers. In the long-run, however, continued third-party compensation minimizes any incentives to engage in some other, more productive economic behaviour. A policy that includes third-party compensation for long-term transfers might benefit from a sunset provision that phases this compensation out over time.

NOTES

* Funding for this research was provided by the University of California Water Resources Center grant W-921, the joint NSF, EPA grant # SBR-9513406 as part of the Human Dimensions of Global Climate Change Initiative, the Center for Public Policy and Administration at the University of Massachusetts-Amherst, and the Cooperative State Research Extension, Education Service, U.S. Department of Agriculture, Massachusetts Agricultural Experiment Station, under Project No. 871. Anil Roopnarine programmed the software. We take full responsibility for any errors or omissions.

1. The tax rate is set at the start of the water year and remains fixed until the following year.
2. Although the statutory incidence of the tax falls on sellers, the economic incidence will be shared by both buyers and sellers.

3. The instructions are available at www.umass.edu/expecon/instructions/water/. The third-party buyer and tax instructions are identical, except for changes that reflect the differences that are unique to the treatments. The instructions are not neutral in the sense that subjects were aware that this was a water market experiment. Given the sensitive nature of water markets, this could introduce some biases. However, we feel it is unlikely since students at the University of Massachusetts are generally unaware of these issues.
4. Subjects were aware of this.
5. Unless otherwise noted, we drop the results from periods 1 and 2 to minimize learning and price discovery effects. This has no effect on the qualitative conclusions.
6. We also modelled learning using Period and Period^2; this yields the same conclusions.
7. The competitive equilibrium surplus of the UnitTax and RevTax treatments differs slightly due to the discrete nature of the supply and demand step functions.
8. Table 5.4 reports the efficiency comparison only for dry years. A comparison for wet years yields similar results.
9. Efficiency would require that consumption be subsidized at locations with third-party impacts. The subsidy rate would differ by location based on marginal third-party impacts. The subsidy would yield prices that are identical to the competitive equilibrium prices in the 3PBuyer treatment.
10. It is possible that these small deviations are at least partially to the discrete, step-wise nature of the supply and demand functions.
11. The reason for the difference in free-riding across nodes is unclear, however we suspect that much of it may be attributable to the individual in the role of third party. With this model, there are substantial group effects. For example, the coefficient for session 3PBuyer01 is –31.5 and is significant at the 1 per cent level. On the other hand, the coefficient for session 3PBuyer 06 is 33.4 and is also highly significant. This suggests that, although some free-riding was consistently observed, the magnitude of the free-riding depends upon the individuals. Although there is a difference in the magnitude of the effect between nodes, the qualitative conclusions about free-riding are the same. The key policy implications here are not the precise quantitative estimates, but rather the qualitative conclusions that can be drawn from the results.

REFERENCES

Anderson, T. and P. Snyder (1997), *Water Markets: Priming the Invisible Pump*, Washington, DC: Cato Institute.

California Department of Water Resources (2004), *California Water Plan – Update 2004, Advisory Committee Review Draft, Vol. 2*, Sacramento, CA: California Department of Water Resources, 7 June.

Dinar, A., R.E. Howitt, S.J. Rassenti and V.L. Smith (1998), 'Development of water markets using experimental economics', in K.W. Easter, M. Rosegrant and A. Dinar (eds), *Markets for Water Potential and Performance*, Boston, MA: Kluwer Academic.

Gray, B.E. (1996), 'The shape of transfers to come: a model water transfer act for California', *Hastings West-Northwest Journal of Environmental Law and Policy*, **4**(0), 23–61.

Griffin, R.C. and S.H. Hsu (1993), 'The potential for water market efficiency when instream flows have value', *American Journal of Agricultural Economics*, **75**(2), 292–303.

Hanak, E. (2003), *Who Should be Allowed to Sell Water in California? Third Party Issues and the Water Market*, San Francisco, CA: Public Policy Institute of California.

Huffman, J. (1983), 'Instream water use: public and private alternatives', in T. Anderson (ed.), *Water Rights: Scarce Resource Allocation, Bureaucracy, and the Environment*, San Francisco: Pacific Institute for Public Policy Research, pp. 249–82.

Landry, C. (1998), *Saving Our Streams Through Water Markets: A Practical Guide*, Bozeman, MT: Political Economy Research Center.

McCabe, K.A., S.J. Rassenti and V.L. Smith (1989), 'Designing "smart" computer-assisted markets: an experimental auction for gas networks', *European Journal of Political Economy*, **5**, 259–83.

McCabe, K.A., S.J. Rassenti and V.L. Smith (1991), 'Smart computer-assisted markets', *Science*, **254**, 534–8.

Murphy, J.J., A. Dinar, R.E. Howitt, S.J. Rassenti and V.L. Smith (2000), 'The design of "smart" water market institutions using laboratory experiments', *Environmental and Resource Economics*, **17**(4), 375–94.

Murphy, J.J., A. Dinar, R.E. Howitt, S.J. Rassenti, V.L. Smith and M. Weinberg (2004), *Incorporating Instream Flow Values into a Water Market*, University of Massachusetts-Amherst, Department of Resource Economics Working Paper 2004-08, Amherst, MA.

Vogel, N. (2002), 'Water exchanges help state through dry years', *Los Angeles Times*, 4 April, Metro, part 2, p. 1.

Water Transfer Workgroup (2002), *Water Transfer Issues in California, Final Report to the California State Water Resources Control Board*, Sacramento, CA: California State Water Resources Control Board, June.

Weber, M.L. (2001), 'Markets for water rights under environmental constraints', *Journal of Environmental Economics and Management*, **42**(1), 53–64.

6. Peer enforcement in CPR experiments: the relative effectiveness of sanctions and transfer rewards, and the role of behavioural types*

Daan van Soest and Jana Vyrastekova

6.1 INTRODUCTION

The lack of sufficiently well-defined and/or enforced property rights is at the heart of many of the major environmental problems the world is currently confronted with, including depletion of fisheries, tropical deforestation and biodiversity loss. Even if access to resources is limited to a specific group of individuals (such as a community), socially excessive resource use may occur if appropriation externalities are present, that is, if increased resource extraction by one user reduces the net yield obtained by other users either instantaneously or over time (Ostrom et al., 1994, p. 11). Without cooperation, each individual resource-user ignores the costs he/she imposes on other resource-users, and hence, from a social welfare point of view, puts too much effort into resource harvesting. As all individuals face the same situation, the resulting resource stock is smaller than the one that maximizes aggregate pay-off. The combination of appropriation externalities and lack of individualized and sufficiently well-defined property rights provides a classic case for government intervention, but socially optimal resource management may also be achieved by means of cooperation among resource-users.

A substantial amount of research has been dedicated to exploring the effectiveness of so-called 'decentralized' (or peer) regulation mechanisms where individual community members can affect the behaviour of their peers either by inflicting social or pecuniary punishment on those who over-exploit the resource, or by rewarding those who do not. Empirically analysing the effectiveness of various types of enforcement regulation is very difficult because of the many confounding factors that affect success and failure in the real world. It is seldom that one finds natural experiments with two identical resources located in identical social and geophysical environments but where two different types of regulations are in place. If such natural experiments are lacking, one may turn to analysing the effectiveness of various types of regulations in more controlled environments, such as in computer laboratories where subjects can be brought in to make decisions very similar to the ones made by resource-users in the real world. Indeed, this is the route that the bulk of the literature on regulatory design has chosen.

Most studies on peer regulation have focused on finitely repeated linear Public Goods (PG) games, and analysed the extent to which especially sanctions (monetary, but also non-monetary punishments) and rewards affect behaviour; references include Anderson and Putterman (2006), Carpenter (2006a; 2006b), Casari and Luini (2004), Cinyabuguma et al. (2005a), Fehr and Gächter (2000a; 2000b; 2002), Masclet (2003), Masclet et al. (2003), Nikiforakis (2004), Noussair and Tucker (2002), Sefton et al. (2002), Swope (2002) and Walker and Halloran (2004). In linear PG games, subjects can make contributions to a public fund, and the benefits of these contributions accrue not only to the contributor, but to all subjects in the group. This poses a social dilemma because whereas total pay-off to all members of the group is maximized if everyone contributes his/her total endowment, the benefits accruing directly to an individual contributor are smaller than the costs he/she incurs. That means that subjects who only care about their own welfare decide not to contribute. Indeed, without the possibility to reward or sanction one's peers, aggregate contributions to the public fund are observed to fall steeply over time in finitely repeated PG games.

Introducing the possibility to sanction or reward has been found to dramatically change these results. Research has focused on the consequences for aggregate contributions when transfer rewards can be given, or where punishments can be imposed in the form of financial sanctions, verbal expressions of disagreement, or ostracism (where the free-rider is excluded from the benefits of the public good). The general findings of these studies using PG games are that (1) transfer rewards are ineffective, (2) sanctions are able to increase gross efficiency (the aggregate pay-off of the public goods situation) as compared to unregulated PG games, but (3) the deadweight loss of sanctioning is such that subjects are not better off in this treatment than in the unregulated situation (Anderson and Putterman, 2006; Casari and Luini, 2004; Fehr and Gächter, 2000b; Sefton et al., 2002).

Two remarks are in place here. First, the insights from this research on PG games are obviously of direct interest to environmental economists. Indeed, in some instances investing in environmental protection is not a profitable enterprise from each individual investor's perspective, but social welfare increases if all contribute. However, the PG game focuses on positive externalities, and hence may not be a good description of many other environmental problems, especially not of those related to (renewable) natural resource use. Here, each individual's harvesting activity negatively affects the returns to activities of all other users of the resource under consideration, and in a non-linear way. A game that better captures this underlying mechanism is the Common Pool Resource (CPR) game, and the question is to what extent the results found in the literature using PG games carry over to CPR games. Note that this is not a trivial exercise, as behaviour in the CPR game is typically even more aggressive than predicted by game theory. Whereas free-riders in PG games simply fail to contribute to the welfare of others, they actually reduce their peer's welfare in CPR games. This outcome is ruled out in PG games as contributions are restricted to be non-negative.

Second, the fact that the possibility to impose sanctions improves gross efficiency is surprising, as standard economic theory predicts that neither sanctions nor rewards will be imposed in finitely repeated games. The reason for this is that whereas the costs of enforcement are incurred by the person distributing sanctions or rewards, the benefits of reduced extraction by the recipient – if enforcement is effective – accrue to all individuals having access to the resource under consideration. So why provide a public good if one can free-ride on the provision of public goods by other resource-users? If all individuals having access to a resource reason like that (as would homo economicus), the possibility of being sanctioned or rewarded does not discipline resource-users' behaviour because neither sanctions nor rewards will ever be imposed. That means that the question arises as to who these individuals are who engage in sanctioning or rewarding their peers. Whereas methods are available that can characterize subjects as being predominantly self-interested, cooperative or competitive, surprisingly few studies have yet analysed the predictive (or explanatory) power of such information with respect to subject behaviour in a social dilemma situation (such as a PG game or a CPR game).

The relevance of whether such classification has predictive power is obvious. If information on an individual's preferences obtained from a simple game is indicative of his/her behaviour in a social dilemma situation, we can also consider using this information in real-world situations. In many instances, the success of environmental projects depends crucially on the extent to which local stakeholders are willing to engage in peer monitoring and peer enforcement (cf. Baland and Platteau, 1996). If success or failure can be predicted reasonably well on the basis of a simple game, the cost-effectiveness of such projects can be increased dramatically.

This chapter takes on these two issues. In section 6.2 we briefly describe the two games that form the basis of our study; the game that aims to measure subjects' distributional preferences, and the CPR game that models the real-world environmental problems. We formulate hypotheses with respect to the social orientation of our subject pool as well as with respect to how these subjects will behave in the CPR game. In section 6.3, we (1) classify the subjects in our pool according to their distributional preferences, (2) analyse the relative effectiveness of rewards and sanctions in the CPR game, and (3) test whether indeed individual behaviour differs between subjects with different preferences. Section 6.4 concludes this chapter.

6.2 THE EXPERIMENTS

6.2.1 Measuring Preferences

In economics as well as in other social sciences, methods have been developed to collect information about the preferences humans hold with respect to the welfare of others, as compared to their own. Two approaches are most common. First, preferences can be measured on the basis of simple games, such as the Trust Game, the Ultimatum Game and also the Public Goods Game (see, for example, Fischbacher et al., 2001; Henrich et al., 2004). In these games, monetary outcomes depend not just on the decisions of the person whose preferences one wishes to measure, but also on the decisions of other participants. Second, single-person decision problems can be used where the decision-maker's choices affect his/her own pay-off, but also that of one other participant. Here, examples include the Dictator Game (Forsythe et al., 1994) and the Decomposed Game (Messick and McClintock, 1968).

The second approach has two advantages as compared to the first. In the first place, no information is needed about the decision-maker's beliefs about the behaviour of other subject(s) in order to interpret the data. Second, an individual can be asked to make several decisions in an environment where expectations about the play of others are not relevant, and hence it is possible to check the subject's consistency (as is the case in the Decomposed Game). For these reasons, we opt for the latter approach, and we use the Decomposed Game approach developed by Messick and McClintock (1968), which has been used in previous studies to classify experimental subjects according to their social orientation (see, for example, Offerman et al., 1996).

The Decomposed Game approach consists of 24 independent decision situations, which have actual financial consequences for the subject who makes the decision, as well as for one other (anonymous) participant the subject is matched with in the experimental session. Earnings are in points that represent a certain monetary value (here, one point is worth one euro cent). In each decision situation, subjects are asked to choose one of two options (Options A and B), each of which results in a number of points given to or taken from the decision-maker him/herself, and a number of points given to or taken from the other participant; see Table 6.1. These options can be plotted on a circle (not shown here), the centre of which is the origin of a system of coordinates where own pay-offs are measured along the horizontal axis (positive and negative), and the other participant's pay-offs on the vertical axis (positive and negative). By choosing between the two pay-off vectors in each decision situation, the decision-maker has to weigh his/her own pay-off gains/losses against those of the other, anonymous, participant.

Table 6.1 The 24 decision situations in the social valuation task

Situation	Order in the experiment	Option A		Option B	
		Amount self	Amount other	Amount self	Amount other
1	20	+15.0	0.0	+14.5	−3.9
2	17	+14.5	−3.9	+13.0	−7.5
3	12	+13.0	−7.5	+10.6	−10.6
4	22	+10.6	−10.6	+7.5	−13.0
5	16	+7.5	−13.0	+3.9	−14.5
6	5	+3.9	−14.5	0.0	−15.0
7	18	0.0	−15.0	−3.9	−14.5
8	23	−3.9	−14.5	−7.5	−13.0
9	19	−7.5	−13.0	−10.6	−10.6
10	4	−10.6	−10.6	−13.0	−7.5
11	21	−13.0	−7.5	−14.5	−3.9
12	2	−14.5	−3.9	−15.0	0.0
13	7	−15.0	0.0	−14.5	+3.9
14	9	−14.5	+3.9	−13.0	+7.5
15	6	−13.0	+7.5	−10.6	+10.6
16	14	−10.6	+10.6	−7.5	+13.0
17	1	−7.5	+13.0	−3.9	+14.5
18	15	−3.9	+14.5	0.0	+15.0
19	3	0.0	+15.0	+3.9	+14.5
20	13	+3.9	+14.5	+7.5	+13.0
21	11	+7.5	+13.0	+10.6	+10.6
22	8	+10.6	+10.6	+13.0	+7.5
23	10	+13.0	+7.5	+14.5	+3.9
24	24	+14.5	+3.9	+15.0	0.0

Having made all 24 choices, an individual's preferences can be determined by calculating his/her aggregate pay-off vector by adding up all chosen pay-off vectors. Subjects are labelled individualistic if they maximize their own final pay-off (resulting in approximately zero points allocated to the other participant). They are competitive if they end up with a positive number of points for themselves (but lower than the maximum) and a negative one for the other participant. And they are labelled cooperative if they end up with both a positive number of points for themselves (again lower than the maximum) as well as for the other participant. In other words, if subjects are either cooperative or competitive, they are willing to incur costs (by earning less than maximally possible) in order to either increase the pay-off to the other participant (if the decision-maker is cooperative) or to maximize the difference in points (by imposing negative points on the other participant, if the decision-maker is competitive). In the sociology literature, a subject is labelled competitive if the final (or aggregate) pay-off vector has an angle between −67.5 and −22.5 degrees, individualistic if the angle is between −22.5 and +22.5 degrees, and cooperative if the angle is between +22.5 and +67.5 degrees. Obviously, these ranges are to some extent arbitrary, and the researcher needs to be careful in checking whether there are many observations located on or close to these boundaries.

Consistency of each subject's decisions can be assessed by measuring the absolute length of his/her final pay-off vector. If a subject consistently follows the same rule (for example, own pay-off maximization if the person is individualistic), the final pay-off vector has a maximum length equal to twice the radius of the circle on which the vectors lie (in our case, this maximum length is thus 30). If the subject randomizes in every decision situation, the length of the final pay-off vector is close to zero. Thus, the length of the final vector relative to this maximum length measures each subject's consistency across the 24 decision problems.

As explained in the introduction, we will use the information on preferences thus collected to test the predictive power of the Decomposed Game approach for subjects' decisions in the CPR game. If the results of the Decomposed Game approach perform well in explaining behaviour, it may be a useful tool in the planning stage of environmental projects in the real world as it may help answer the question of which communities should be targeted.

6.2.2 The Common Pool Resource Game

The basis of the environmentally oriented part of our experiment is a finitely repeated Common Pool Resource game similar to that of Ostrom et al. (1992). There is a closed community of N resource-users (hereafter referred to as 'users'), $N > 1$, with unrestricted access to the CPR. In every period $t = 1, \ldots, T$, each user $i = 1, \ldots, N$ can allocate a fixed endowment of effort, $e > 0$, between CPR extraction and an alternative economic activity (the outside option). Extraction effort exerted by user i in period t is denoted $x_{i,t}$, and hence user i's effort devoted to the outside option equals $(e - x_{i,t})$. The outside option yields a fixed per-unit wage rate, w. When exerting extraction effort, users incur costs that are linear in extraction effort; marginal cost are constant and equal to v. The group's revenues in period t, R_t, depend on the aggregate amount of extraction effort in that period, $X_t = \Sigma_{i=1}^{N} x_{i,t}$, according to the function $R(X_t) = AX_t - BX_t^2$. User i's share in these revenues is proportional to his/her share in aggregate extraction effort $(x_{i,j} / X_t)$. Hence, user i's pay-off in period t equals:

$$\pi_{i,t}^{CPR}(x_{i,t}, X_t) = w[e - x_{i,t}] + \frac{x_{i,t}}{X_t}[AX_t - BX_t^2] - vx_{i,t}, \qquad (6.1)$$

with $A - v - w > 0$. The socially optimal extraction effort level is the one that maximizes the unweighted sum of the pay-offs of all N users in the group as defined in (6.1). Therefore, the equitable socially optimal extraction effort level is $x^* = (A - v - w) / 2NB$.

Let us use G_0 (and subscript 0 for the relevant variables) to denote the CPR game in the absence of peer regulation. Assuming that subjects are rational and aim to maximize their own pay-offs, user i's best response function to any level of aggregate extraction effort by all others $(X_{-i,t} = \Sigma_{j \neq i}^{N} x_{j,t})$ is $x_{i,t}(X_{-i,t}) = (A - v - w)/2B - x_{-i,t}/2$, and hence the unique symmetric Nash equilibrium extraction effort equals $x_0^{NE} = (A - v - w) / B(N + 1)$. Because $x_0^{NE} > x^*$ if $N > 1$, the (unregulated) CPR game poses a social dilemma.

In addition to game G_0, we analyse two other games where the basic CPR game is extended by a stage in which subjects can either give rewards to or impose sanctions on one or more of their fellow group members. In this stage, every user receives an endowment of enforcement tokens, $E > 0$, which have a unit value of one point. Let $p_{ij,t}$ denote the number of enforcement tokens individual i sends to individual j $(j \neq i)$ in period t. Given that enforcement tokens are worth one point each, the total enforcement costs in period t incurred by individual i are equal to $\Sigma_{j \neq i} p_{ij,t}$. User i may also receive enforcement points him/herself from any of the $N - 1$ other members of his/her group, and the associated benefits in each round equal $f \Sigma_{j \neq i} p_{ji,t}$, which may be positive or negative. If $f > 0$, the enforcement tokens are rewards, and the associated stage game is referred to as G_R. And if $f < 0$, the enforcement tokens are sanctions, and the stage game is referred to as G_S. Thus, user i's pay-off in period t equals $\Pi_{i,t} = \pi_{i,t}^{CPR} + E - \Sigma_{j \neq i} p_{ij,t} + f \Sigma_{j \neq i} p_{ji,t}$. In the actual experiments, a token sent to another participant in game G_S (G_R) decreases (increases) the other participant's pay-off by 3 points (1 point); $f = -3$ ($f = 1$). These two parameterizations correspond to the setup used most frequently in the literature on peer enforcement in the linear PG experiments, so that we can test whether or not the insights from these PG games carry over to the CPR game.

The order of moves and information is as follows. In each round t, each player i chooses her extraction effort $x_{i,t} \in \{0, 1, \ldots, e\}$. Then, all players are informed about the aggregate extraction effort decisions of the $N-1$ other players in the CPR game and the resulting pay-off $\pi_{i,t}^{CPR}$. In the peer regulation games G_R and G_S, all users subsequently receive the endowment of $E > 0$ enforcement tokens and decide how many of them to send to each other player $j \neq i$. Finally, they receive information on the total number of enforcement tokens received from other players, and they are also informed about the final pay-offs of all players. When the next period starts, subject identifiers are shuffled so that behaviour of individual subjects cannot be traced over time. This prevents the enforcement stage becoming a game in itself: in the sanctions (transfer rewards) treatment, subjects cannot retaliate (reciprocate) to sanctions (transfer rewards) received in previous periods, and hence the focus here is on the so-called altruistic (preference-based) sanctioning and rewarding.[1]

6.2.3 Hypotheses

As already stated in the introduction, the game-theoretic prediction with respect to the finitely repeated CPR games is that rational, own pay-off maximizing individuals would refrain from imposing sanctions or giving rewards, even if they are effective in inducing more cooperative behaviour. Imposing sanctions or rewards is costly to the individual distributing them, whereas the benefits accrue to all subjects in the group. If the subject pool consists of exclusively own pay-off maximizing individuals, the option to sanction or reward is not used, and when solving the game backwards, these subjects would choose the Nash equilibrium extraction effort x_0^{NE} in all three finitely repeated CPR games (G_0, G_S, G_R).

However, the literature on PG games shows that enforcement tokens are being used in experiments. The reason is that not all subjects are exclusively interested in their own financial gains; some take into consideration the impact of their actions on the pay-offs to their fellow group members as well. Welfare of others is a positive argument in the utility function of cooperative individuals; competitive individuals not only care about their own welfare but also about their relative position in the group (for a recent overview, see Fehr and Gächter, 2000a). Subjects of these two types are expected to allocate enforcement tokens if they play a one-shot game, and hence also in our finitely repeated game. Cooperative individuals are expected to reward cooperative behaviour of their peers. But they may or may not be willing to sanction non-cooperative behaviour: when considering to sanction, cooperative individuals have to weigh the costs of reducing another subject's pay-off against the benefits of increasing aggregate welfare. Competitive individuals are expected to be willing to incur costs to reduce other subjects' pay-offs, but not to give rewards. And they may use the sanctioning device to decrease the pay-offs of those with the highest earnings, and hence these sanctions are likely to be directed at those who overharvest the CPR most severely.

This results in the following hypotheses:

Hypothesis 1: The composition of the subject pool. The subject pool consists of individualistic individuals, but also of individuals with other-regarding preferences (competitive and cooperative individuals).

Hypothesis 2: Enforcement behaviour. Subjects use enforcement tokens as follows:

- Individualistic subjects refrain from using enforcement tokens throughout games G_R and G_S.
- Cooperative individuals use enforcement tokens in both treatments to increase (decrease) pay-offs of other subjects who put in less (more) extraction effort than the group's average.
- Competitive individuals use enforcement tokens in the sanctions treatment to decrease pay-offs of other subjects who put in more extraction effort than the group's average, but do not use enforcement tokens in the rewards treatment.

On the basis of this, we can formulate a hypothesis with respect to whether the possibility to reward or sanction is effective in increasing efficiency of resource use.

Hypothesis 3: Efficiency of CPR use. The presence of individuals with other-regarding preferences implies that enforcement will take place, but for equal group compositions, fewer enforcement tokens will be used in the transfer rewards treatment than in the sanctions treatment because competitive individuals are willing to sanction excess extraction, but not to reward low extraction effort. Hence, gross efficiency (aggregate welfare associated with CPR use) is highest in the sanctions treatment (G_S), lowest in the unregulated treatment (G_0), and intermediate in the rewards treatment (G_R).

Having argued that subjects' preferences matter for the outcome of the games, the question is whether the method we use in order to measure subjects' distributional preferences allows us to predict the behaviour described above. Actual behaviour of individuals identified as having individualistic, cooperative or competitive preferences using the Decomposed Game may differ across economic situations, especially in multi-person strategic environments. As Fehr and Schmidt (1999) pointed out, both competitive and cooperative persons may act competitively in some economic situations but cooperatively in others; emotions with regard to how play evolves can substantially affect their behaviour. Such emotions are absent in the Decomposed Game; this game only measures the unconditional, expectation-independent part of a subject's preferences. Because of the strategic character of the (unregulated) CPR game, we do not expect this measure to well explain extraction behaviour, but strategic considerations are less relevant in the enforcement stages of games G_R and G_S. The reason for this is that because we re-shuffle the subject identifiers at the beginning of every round, the use of enforcement tokens is driven purely by how each subject views his/her peers' extraction behaviour in the current period but not by their past decisions in the CPR game or in the enforcement stage. Therefore, subjects' distributional preferences measured by the Decomposed Game approach are expected to be correlated with the enforcement bahaviour, as summarized in Hypothesis 2.

6.2.4 Experimental Design

In the spring semester of 2005, we ran four experimental sessions at Tilburg University, the Netherlands. In total, 80 subjects participated, and they were students in economics, law or business. The language of the experiments was English. Upon arriving for a session, the participants were randomly assigned to a computer terminal. They were informed that the experiment consists of three tasks, and all instructions were read out aloud by the experimenter. The experiments were fully computerized; the software was programmed using z-Tree (Fischbacher, 1999).

The three tasks in the experiment were as follows. First, subjects' distributional preferences were measured using the Decomposed Game approach, then they played the unregulated repeated CPR game (G_0), and third they participated in the repeated CPR game with an enforcement stage in each round, in which subjects could either give rewards or impose sanctions (that is, they played either G_R or G_S).[2] There were two sessions of 20 subjects each for the sanctions treatment, and two sessions of 20 subjects each for the rewards treatment. So, for both treatments, we collected data on eight groups of five subjects, resulting in eight independent observations.

When measuring subjects' distributional preferences (see section 6.2.1), the 24 decision situations were offered in a random sequence which was identical for all players; see the second column in Table 6.1.[3] The subjects were informed that their decisions had real financial consequences for themselves as well as for the other participant they were matched with, but that they would not learn how much money they received as a result of the other participant's decisions until after the entire experiment was completed. Before making their actual decisions, all subjects took a small test to verify that they understood the pay-off consequences of the decisions they took in the task.

Subjects played both the unregulated and peer regulated CPR games (the second and third task) with the same group of four other subjects. The CPR game was framed neutrally as the decision how to divide an endowment of 13 hypothetical experimental units called tokens between two options, option 1 in which one's pay-off (measured in points) depends on one's own decision as well as on the decisions of the other group members (that is, extraction from the CPR), and option 2 in which one's pay-off depends purely on one's own decision (the outside option that pays a fixed wage rate; see section 6.2.2). Subjects were presented with the pay-off table of the CPR game, which summarizes the pay-off consequences of (almost all) combinations of own extraction effort and aggregate extraction effort by the other four group members. We also tested our subjects' understanding of the instructions by means of three test questions.

The enforcement stage (in the third task) was also framed neutrally. Each subject had to make a decision how many tokens from his/her endowment of 12 tokens he/she 'sends' to each other member of his/her group. Each token kept is worth 1 point to the subject. Each token sent to another subject decreases (increases) the pay-off of that subject by 3 points (1 point) in the sanctions (transfer rewards) treatment. As already stated above, we changed the 'names' of all participants at the beginning of every round, so that a subject's behaviour in one round cannot be linked to his/her decisions in previous or future rounds. The parameter values and implied values of Nash equilibrium predictions used in the experiment can be found in Tables 6.2 and 6.3.

The experiment lasted about two hours, and participants earned on average 15 euros (including 5 euros participation fee). About one-quarter of these earnings came from tasks 1 and 2, and about one-half of the earnings came from task 3 (which is, at least partly, owing to the fact that subjects received enforcement tokens which add to their earnings if not used).

Table 6.2 Experiment parameterization

Variable	Description	Value
N	Number of individuals per group	5
T	Number of rounds of the stage game	15
e	Effort endowment	13
w	Wage per unit of effort allocated to the outside option	0.5
A	Parameter of the resource revenue function	11.5
B	Parameter of the resource revenue function	0.15
v	Per unit cost of effort in resource extraction	2
E	Endowment of enforcement tokens	12
f	Impact of receiving one enforcement token in the sanctions treatment	−3
	Impact of receiving one enforcement token in the rewards treatment	1

Table 6.3 Socially optimal and Nash equilibrium levels of all variables of the stage game

Variable	Description	Value
x^*	Symmetric socially optimal individual extraction effort	6
X^*	Socially optimal group extraction effort	30
x^{NE}	Symmetric Nash equilibrium individual extraction effort	10
X^{NE}	Aggregate Nash equilibrium extraction effort	50
p_{ij}^{NE}	Nash equilibrium enforcement	0
π^*	Symmetric socially optimal pay-off to CPR use	33.5
π^{NE}	Symmetric Nash equilibrium pay-off to CPR use	21.5

6.3 DATA ANALYSIS

6.3.1 Results of the Decomposed Game Approach

The results of the Decomposed Game approach are as follows. Based on the decisions of all 80 subjects in our experiment, we classify nine subjects (11 per cent) as competitive, 57 (71 per cent) as individualistic and 14 (18 per cent) as cooperative. Distribution of types with a step of 15 degrees in the two treatments is presented in Figure 6.1. About two-thirds of population displays individualistic behaviour (that is, they aim to maximize their own pay-offs), while the remainder is symmetrically distributed on both sides of the spectrum, reflecting preferences for more competitive or more cooperative behaviour. The shares found closely resemble the results found

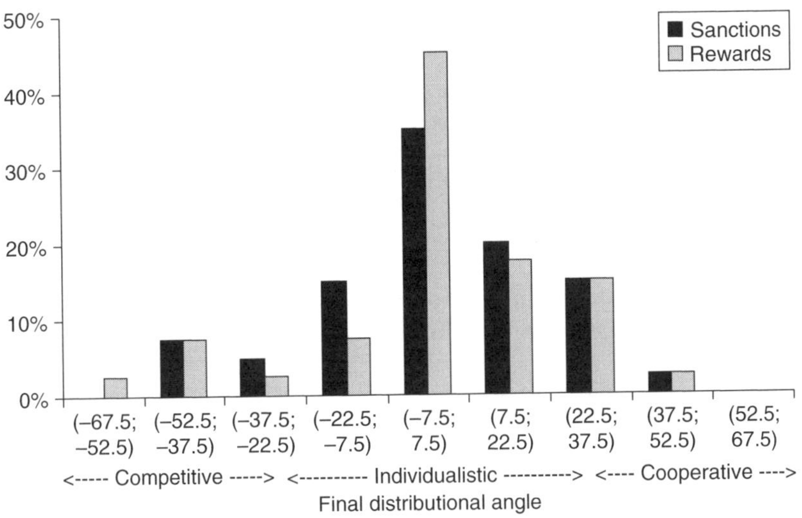

Figure 6.1 *Distribution of behavioural types in the sanctions and rewards treatments*

in earlier studies (for example, Offerman et al., 1996). Within our experiment, these shares are also not statistically different across the subpools that played either the sanctions or transfer rewards treatment (p-value of 0.959 according to the relevant Mann–Whitney U-test, 80 observations). And even at the group level (using the average distributional angle for each group), we arrive at the same conclusion ($p = 0.705$, 16 observations).

Measuring the length of the pay-off vectors, we find that subjects are quite consistent in their choices. On average, the length of our subjects' final pay-off vector is 88 per cent of the maximum length, with consistencies being 92, 81 and 76 per cent for the individualistic, cooperative and competitive subjects, respectively.

This leads us to the following observation:

> *Observation 1*: the subject pool in our experiment is heterogeneous. Preferences of about 30 per cent of the participants do not coincide with those of homo economicus.

6.3.3 The Impact of Sanctions and Rewards on the Efficiency of CPR Use

Let us now have a look at the extraction behaviour in the CPR games. Figure 6.2 presents the average group CPR extraction effort over all 30 rounds, that is those in the unregulated CPR game (rounds 1 to 15) and in the CPR games with enforcement (rounds 16 to 30), either in the form of sanctions or rewards. The development of play in the unregulated CPR game is very similar for the subjects who were subsequently exposed to either the sanctions or the transfer rewards treatment; the null hypothesis of equal aggregate extraction effort levels cannot be rejected on the basis of a Mann–Whitney U-test (eight observations in both treatments, $p = 0.878$). We also note that the average aggregate extraction effort is even above the Nash equilibrium prediction level in the second half of the 15 periods ($X^{NE} = 50$; see Table 6.3); over all 15 rounds, however, the differences between actual average group extraction effort and the Nash equilibrium level are not statistically significant for the two treatment groups.

But the performance in the peer enforcement CPR games is markedly different; see rounds 16–30. When introducing an enforcement stage in round 16, sanctions are found to be more effective in reducing aggregate extraction effort than transfer rewards (cf. Hypothesis 3 in section 6.2.3). A two-sided Wilcoxon test for paired observations allows us to reject the hypothesis of equal group extraction effort levels in the unregulated periods and in the periods of the enforcement treatment in case of sanctions ($p = 0.017$), but not so in case of transfer rewards ($p = 0.674$).

So, because of their impact on aggregate extraction effort, sanctions (rewards) result (do not result) in an increase in the direct aggregate earnings from resource extraction (that is, gross efficiency). But the real question is whether sanctions also increase total net earnings, taking into account the deadweight loss of sanctioning (that is, net efficiency). Every time an enforcement token is used in the sanctions treatment, 4 points are lost; the punisher loses 1 point, and the punished individual 3. We find that subjects are not better off in the sanctions treatment than in the unregulated CPR game; the hypothesis of equal net efficiency cannot be rejected (with a p-value of 0.327, based on a Wilcoxon matched pairs test). Obviously, because transfer rewards do not improve gross efficiency and because there is no deadweight loss associated with using enforcement tokens in this treatment, there is also no difference in net efficiency between the rewards and unregulated treatments either (p-value equals 0.674). These results are summarized in the following observation:

> *Observation 2*: Giving subjects the possibility to sanction their peers does increase the aggregate pay-offs of resource use (higher gross efficiency) over the 15 rounds the game lasts. But overall subjects are not better off in this treatment than in case of no enforcement possibilities; there is no significant difference in net efficiency. Transfer rewards also fail to increase net efficiency.

6.3.2 Analysis of the Use of Sanctions and Rewards

Having established the effectiveness (ineffectiveness) of sanctions (rewards) in improving gross efficiency of CPR use, we now turn to analysing how the two enforcement instruments are used, and whether we can explain the differences between the two treatments. Figure 6.3 shows the average number of enforcement tokens used per subject in the two regulated CPR games. In both environments, subjects use generally less than one-third of their enforcement endowment of 12 tokens. Both sanctions and transfers are used in the early periods of the treatments and both exhibit a gradual decline over time.[4]

Analysing the development of aggregate extraction effort and the use of enforcement tokens in the sanctions treatment in Figures 6.2 and 6.3, we observe that whereas the use of sanctions declines over time, there is no notable trend in aggregate CPR extraction effort in that treatment. After a few periods of severe sanctioning, subjects establish a reputation of being willing to punish, and the mere threat of sanctioning is then sufficient to deter excess extraction. Indeed, the aggregate extraction effort level in rounds 23–29 is very close to the socially optimal level $X^* = 30$ (Table 6.3); the p-values of the relevant t-tests for these rounds are all larger than 0.141. Also, when comparing net efficiency in rounds 16–22 and rounds 23–30 (on

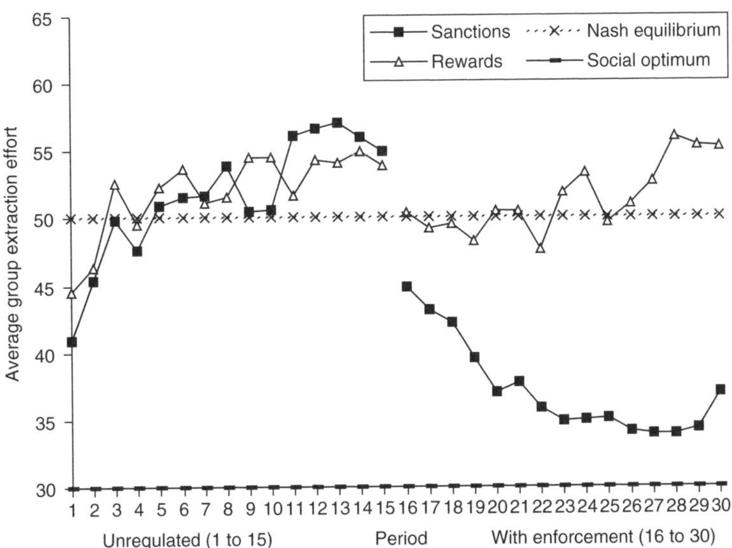

Figure 6.2 Average aggregate extraction effort in the CPR games

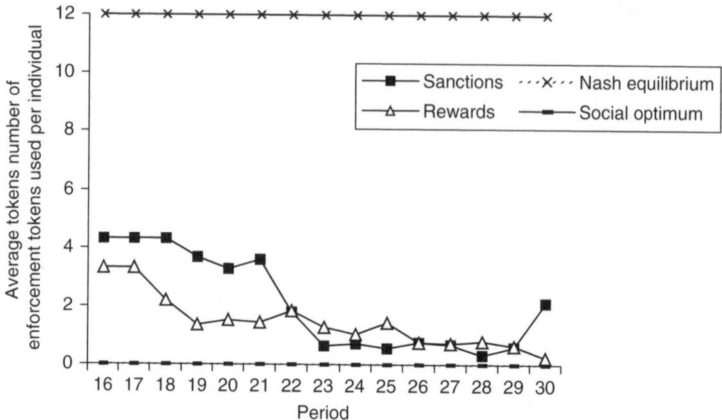

Figure 6.3 *Average number of enforcement tokens used in the sanctions and rewards treatments*

average 891.7 points and 1379.8 points, respectively), we can reject the hypothesis of equal net earnings with a p-value of 0.012 based on a Wilcoxon matched pair test. This suggests that for a number of rounds sufficiently large, net efficiency may eventually become higher than in absence of the possibility to sanction. We summarize this finding in the following observation:

> *Observation 3*: Whereas sanctions do not increase net efficiency of CPR use over all 15 rounds of the game, sanctions are imposed predominantly in the early rounds of the game; the threat of sanctioning effectively deters excess extraction effort in the later periods. Therefore, net earnings are higher in the later periods, suggesting that sanctions might be able to increase net efficiency if the experiment lasts sufficiently long.

Note that this replicates the results obtained from PG games (cf. Sefton et al., 2002), and is also consistent with findings in earlier studies of CPR games (cf. Ostrom et al., 1992).

So who is willing to use enforcement tokens in the two treatments, and who receives them? Starting with the latter question, Figure 6.4 depicts the relationship between the deviation of a subject's extraction effort from the other group members' average effort level (that is, $x_{i,t} - \frac{1}{N-1}\Sigma_{j\neq i}x_{j,t}$) on the horizontal axis, and the average number of enforcement tokens received by that subject on the vertical axis (averaged over all 15 rounds of the game). Not surprisingly, most rewards are received by subjects who put in less extraction effort than their fellow group members, while most sanctions are imposed on subjects who overextract. Indeed, there is a

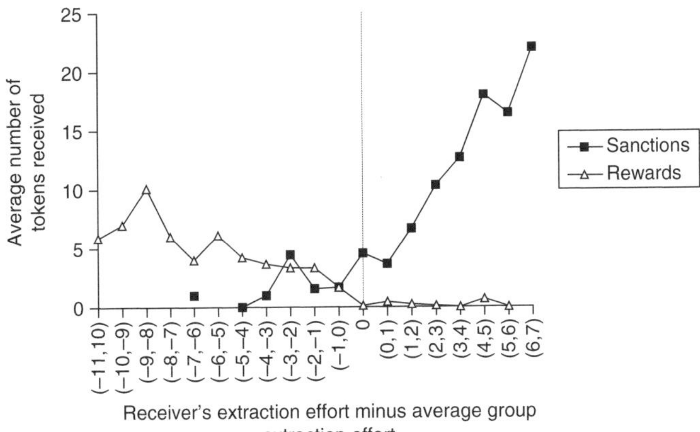

Figure 6.4 *Number of enforcement tokens received as a function of the receiver's deviation from the other group members' average extraction effort*

strong positive (negative) correlation between one's deviation from the rest of the group's average effort and the average sanction (reward) received: the Spearman rank-base correlation coefficient for the sanctions and rewards treatments equal 0.953 and –0.920, respectively, which are both significant at the 1 per cent level.

The answer to the question which subjects use the enforcement tokens can be inferred from Figure 6.5. The difference in extraction effort between enforcers and receivers is predominantly negative in case of sanctions: subjects sanction those who extract more than they do and the larger the difference, the more severe the sanction. But, surprisingly, rewards are not exchanged between individuals who act cooperatively; it is the free-riders in the CPR game who send rewards to those who extract much less than they do. So, rather than not receiving rewards being an indirect punishment on excess extraction, those who harvest relatively intensively reward those who choose extraction efforts closer to the socially optimal level, thus reducing *ex post* pay-off inequalities between the norm followers and norm violators.

To summarize,

Observation 4:

(a) The more the subject over-extracts (under-extracts) the resource relative to the group, the more sanctions (rewards) he/she receives. For comparable levels of deviation from the other participants' average extraction effort in the group, the number of enforcement tokens

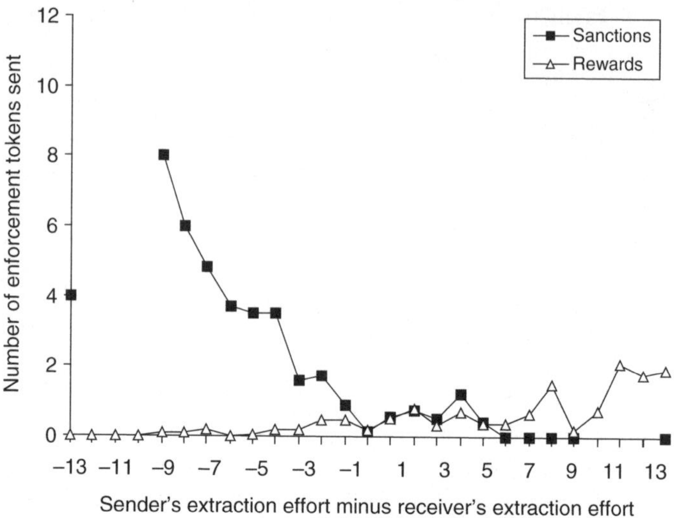

Figure 6.5 *The relationship between the difference in the sender's and receiver's extraction effort and the number of enforcement tokens sent*

exchanged is larger in the sanctions treatment than in the rewards treatment.

(b) Sanctions are imposed by those subjects who extract less than the punished subject. Transfer rewards are given to subjects who put in less extraction effort than does the sender.

So we find that rewards are used as a compensation device rather than as an indirect punishment tool. This surprising result draws attention to a very specific flaw in the experimental research on the relative effectiveness of sanctions and rewards. When using a 1:3 ratio in the sanctions treatment, the sender incurring a one-point cost results in the reduction of the recipient's revenues by 3 points. But when using the 1:1 ratio in the rewards treatment, it does not make sense for subjects who choose extraction effort levels close to the socially optimal level to reward each other. They would merely be shuffling points around between them. So, the effectiveness of rewards is likely to be highly dependent on the parameterization, as is the case with sanctions (see, for example, Egas and Riedl, 2005). This issue has not been given proper attention in the literature yet (but see Vyrastekova and van Soest, 2005). Given our 1:1 parameterization, we can only conclude that transfer rewards in the CPR game do not affect extraction behaviour as compared to the unregulated treatment, as is the case in PG games.

6.3.4 The Predictive Power of the Decomposed Game Approach

Finally, let us address the question whether the classification of individuals into three behavioural types has any explanatory power with respect to their behaviour in the extraction and enforcement stages of games G_S and G_R. This behaviour is summarized in Table 6.4, which contains information on the average number (and standard deviation) of enforcement tokens sent and received in the two treatments, either in the first round (round 16) or averaged over all 15 rounds the games last (rounds 16–30). This table is organized thus because of the following considerations.

First, with respect to presenting information about both the number of tokens sent and received, the average number of enforcement tokens each behavioural type actually sends (or uses) per period reflects their willingness to incur costs to affect earnings of their peers in connection to their behaviour in the CPR game. But analysing the average number of enforcement tokens received is also interesting, as it reflects how the extraction bahaviour of the behavioural types is perceived by their peers. This information is more useful than focusing on individual extraction effort itself. The same level of extraction can be perceived to be either excessive or moderate, depending on the average extraction effort in the subject's group. Hence a specific level of extraction effort may or may not give rise to sanctions or rewards by the other group members, depending on the relative extraction effort of other group members. Therefore, we explore the question whether subjects categorized as cooperative behave in the CPR game such that they receive more rewards and fewer sanctions than the competitive and individualistic subjects, who are predominantly interested in their private returns to CPR use.

Next, with respect to the periods analysed, including decisions over all 15 rounds is informative as these choices are determined by the subject's own distributional preferences, by his/her expectations about the behaviour of his/her fellow group members, and by the history of the game (extraction and enforcement by others). When analysing just the first round's decisions (round 16), we are able to focus on just subjects' preferences and their prior expectations.

Let us first focus on the number of sanctions and reward tokens sent. Interestingly, in the sanctions treatment, it is the individualistic subjects who impose sanctions most frequently, although the difference with respect to the other two behavioural is types is (close) to significant only when focusing on all rounds (rounds 16–30). Apparently, individualistic subjects try to increase their own long-term pay-offs by using sanctions to affect the extraction behaviour of others, even though the game is finitely repeated. In the rewards treatment, it is the competitive individuals who

Table 6.4 Average number of enforcement tokens used and received by each of the three behavioural types (with standard deviations in parentheses), and the p-values of the pairwise comparisons (as obtained by means of a two-sided Mann–Whitney U-tests)

Type	Sent (round 16)		Sent (rounds 16–30)		Received (round 16)		Received (rounds 16–30)	
	Sanctions	Rewards	Sanctions	Rewards	Sanctions	Rewards	Sanctions	Rewards
Competitive	3.4 (4.98)	6.4 (5.41)	1.8 (3.70)	1.6 (3.15)	5.4 (6.70)	2.5 (3.78)	3.6 (6.28)	1.1 (2.34)
Individual	4.7 (5.03)	3.2 (4.00)	2.4 (3.88)	1.5 (2.30)	4.9 (5.60)	3.0 (3.74)	1.9 (3.72)	1.5 (2.56)
Cooperative	3.4 (4.61)	1.4 (1.62)	1.2 (2.67)	1.4 (1.79)	1.4 (1.40)	5.0 (5.59)	1.9 (4.19)	1.5 (2.70)
p-values:								
Comp.–Indiv.	0.715	0.207	0.116	0.544	0.903	0.827	0.057	0.153
Comp.–Coop.	0.876	0.106	0.402	0.296	0.202	0.755	0.104	0.465
Indiv.–Coop.	0.406	0.454	0.002	0.500	0.079	0.454	0.855	0.521

send transfer rewards most frequently, but none of the differences with the other two types is significant at conventional levels.

When analysing how the extraction behaviour of the three types is perceived by their peers, as evidenced by the number of enforcement tokens received, we find that competitive subjects receive more sanctions and fewer rewards (in round 16, but also over the entire time period), whereas the opposite holds for cooperative subjects. Again, however, differences are small, especially in case of rewards where none are significant at conventional levels.

These results can be summarized in the following observation:

> *Observation 5:* The explanatory (or predictive) power of classifying subjects into three behavioural types is at best weak. In most instances the differences in means are as expected, but often not significant at conventional levels. Cooperative individuals are least willing to incur costs to punish others, while competitive individuals are most likely to be punished.

6.4 CONCLUSIONS

In the experimental economics literature, a substantial amount of research has been dedicated to exploring the effectiveness of so-called 'decentralized' regulation mechanisms where subjects can affect the behaviour of their peers in Public Goods Games. The peer enforcement instruments analysed most extensively are sanctions and transfer rewards, and the general finding is that the former are more effective than the latter.

This chapter takes on two issues in this literature that are relevant to environmental economics. The first is whether the conclusions on the relative effectiveness of sanctions and transfer rewards carry over to a game that has received relatively little attention, the Common Pool Resource game. This game better resembles many environmental problems the world is confronted with than the Public Goods Game because it is driven by negative rather than positive externalities. The second issue is to determine not only whether but also how the effectiveness of sanctions and transfer rewards depends on the composition of the communities' population in terms of distributional preferences.

Our results can be summarized as follows. We find that similar to the Public Goods Games' results, sanctions do increase gross efficiency of resource use, whereas transfer rewards do not. But we also find that although sanctions improve gross efficiency, the deadweight loss associated with sanctioning is such that, on aggregate, subjects in our game are equally well off in the case of the game with and without the option to sanction.

That means that neither rewards nor sanctions result in a net increase in efficiency. However, our results also suggest that in the case of sanctions this conclusion may be sensitive to the length of the experiment. The incidence of sanctions falls over time whereas aggregate extraction effort stays about constant. This suggests that at some point, the mere threat of sanctioning is sufficient to deter excess extraction and hence that for the number of rounds sufficiently large, net efficiency may eventually become higher than in absence of the possibility to sanction. This effect is absent in the rewards treatment, and this highlights an important distinction between transfer rewards and sanctions. Whereas rewards need to be given continuously in order to be effective, the presence of the possibility to punish one's peers is sufficient to affect their behaviour.

With respect to who punishes/rewards whom, we find that consistent with intuition, those who do not overexploit the resource punish those who do overexploit, but surprisingly it is the free-riders who transfer rewards to those who put in low levels of harvesting effort. That means that transfer rewards are not used by people who act cooperatively as an indirect sanctioning device (not giving rewards to those who act non-cooperatively), but by free-riders who try to encourage individuals acting cooperatively to continue doing so.

Finally, the enforcement behaviour of individuals is hypothesized to depend on their distributional preferences. We test this hypothesis having collected information on our subjects' distributional preferences using the Decomposed Game approach developed by Messick and McClintock (1968), and we find that a little more than two-thirds of our subject pool is predominantly individualistic; the remaining one-third consists of competitive and cooperative individuals in roughly equal shares. Unfortunately, the explanatory power of this classification is fairly limited at best. Results suggest that cooperative individuals are not likely to contribute much to enforcement, but are useful in sustaining cooperation as they tend to act more cooperatively than the other two types (as evidenced by the number of enforcement tokens received). Interestingly, the individualistic types are most active in sanctioning, even though imposing sanctions is costly, suggesting they are driven by strategic motivations and expectations of the impact the sanctions have on others.

NOTES

* The authors are grateful to the Netherlands Organisation for Scientific Research (NWO) for financial support as part of the research programme on Evolution and Behaviour, and Jana Vyrastekova acknowledges this organization's support in the form of a VENI grant. The authors also wish to thank an anonymous referee for excellent comments on an earlier version of this chapter. Please send all comments to Daan van Soest, Tilburg University,

Department of Economics, P.O. Box 90153, 5000 LE Tilburg, The Netherlands. Tel: +31–13–466 2072, Fax: +31–13–466 3042, E-mail: D.P.vansoest@uvt.nl.

1. Some researchers have looked at the consequences of allowing subjects to positively or negatively reciprocate to their peers' enforcement decisions; see for example Cinyabuguma et al. (2005a; 2005b), Nikiforakis (2004) and van Soest and Vyrastekova (2004). The general finding is that the possibility to reciprocate weakens the effectiveness of sanctioning but increases that of rewards.
2. In the experiment, we did not balance the order of the three tasks. The social valuation task (without feedback on the decisions of the other participant each subject was matched with) was always performed first. Thus, the obtained measure of distributional preferences is independent of (possible) emotions stirred by the interactive play of the CPR games that followed. Also, we did not change the order in which games G_0 and G_S/G_R are played. The Base treatment (game G_0) was always played first to provide subjects the opportunity to learn about the consequences of one's behaviour for the pay-offs to others, and vice versa. Any treatment effect we observe in games G_R or G_S, whether influenced by learning or not, can be attributed exclusively to the differences in the enforcement opportunities the subjects have. This is also supported by the fact that the relevant Mann–Whitney U-test does not allow us to reject the hypothesis of equal average group extraction effort in the Base treatment for all groups, independent of whether they subsequently played G_S or G_R ($p = 0.878$).
3. We are grateful to T. Offerman, J. Sonnemans and A. Schramm whose instructions we followed as closely as possible for comparability reasons when implementing this game.
4. The increase in the frequency of sanctions in the last period arises because subjects substantially increased their extraction effort in the last round of the game (see Figure 6.2), and got sanctioned.

REFERENCES

Anderson, C. and L. Putterman (2006), 'Do non-strategic sanctions obey the law of demand? The demand for punishment in the voluntary contribution mechanism', *Games and Economic Behavior*, **54**(1), 1–24.

Baland, J. and J.P. Platteau (1996), *Halting Degradation of Natural Resources: Is There a Role for Rural Communities?* Oxford: Clarendon Press.

Carpenter, J.P. (2006a), 'Punishing free-riders: how group size affects mutual monitoring and the provision of public goods', *Games and Economic Behavior*, forthcoming.

Carpenter, J.P. (2006b), 'The demand for punishment', *Journal of Economic Behavior and Organization*, forthcoming.

Casari, M. and L. Luini (2004), 'Team production with peer sanctioning', Universitat Autònoma de Barcelona, mimeo.

Cinyabuguma, M., T. Page and L. Putterman (2005a), 'On perverse and second-order punishment in public goods experiments with decentralized sanctioning', *Journal of Public Economics*, **89**(8), 1421–35.

Cinyabuguma, M., T. Page and L. Putterman (2005b), 'Cooperation under the threat of expulsion in a public goods experiment', *Journal of Public Economics*, **89**(8), 1421–35.

Egas, M. and A. Riedl (2005), 'The economics of altruistic punishment and the demise of cooperation', University of Amsterdam, mimeo.

Fehr, E. and S. Gächter (2000a), 'Fairness and retaliation: the economics of reciprocity', *Journal of Economic Perspectives*, **14**, 159–81.

Fehr, E. and S. Gächter (2000b), 'Cooperation and punishment in public goods experiments', *American Economic Review*, **90**, 980–94.

Fehr, E. and S. Gächter (2002), 'Altruistic punishment in humans', *Nature*, **415**, 137–40.

Fehr, E. and K. Schmidt (1999), 'A theory of fairness, competition, and cooperation', *Quarterly Journal of Economics*, **114**(3), 817–68.

Fischbacher, U. (1999), 'z–Tree: toolbox for readymade economic experiments', IEW working paper 21, University of Zurich.

Fischbacher, U., S. Gächter and E. Fehr (2001), 'Are people conditionally cooperative? Evidence from a public goods experiment', *Economics Letters*, **71**(3), 397–404.

Forsythe, R., J. Horowitz, N.E. Savin and M. Sefton (1994), 'Fairness in simple bargaining experiments', *Games and Economic Behavior*, **6**, 347–69.

Henrich, J., R. Boyd, S. Bowles, C. Camerer, E. Fehr and H. Gintis (eds) (2004), *Foundations of Human Sociality: Economic Experiments and Ethnographic Evidence from Fifteen Small-Scale Societies*, New York: Oxford University Press.

Masclet, D. (2003), 'Ostracism in work teams: a public good experiment', *International Journal of Manpower*, **24**(7), 867–87.

Masclet, D., C. Noussair, S. Tucker and M.C. Villeval (2003), 'Monetary and non-monetary punishment in the voluntary contributions mechanism', *American Economic Review*, **93**(1), 366–80.

Messick, D.M. and C.G. McClintock (1968), 'Motivational bases of choice in experimental games', *Journal of Experimental Social Psychology*, **4**, 1–25.

Nikiforakis, N.S. (2004), 'Punishment and counter-punishment in public goods games: can we still govern ourselves?', Royal Holloway University of London, discussion paper 2004–5, London.

Noussair, C. and S. Tucker (2002), 'Combining monetary and social sanctions to promote cooperation', Emory University, Department of Economics, mimeo.

Offerman, T., J. Sonnemans and A. Schram (1996), 'Value orientations, expectations and voluntary contributions in public goods', *Economic Journal*, **106**, 817–45.

Ostrom, E., R. Gardner and J. Walker (1992), 'Covenants with and without sword: self-governance is possible', *American Political Science Review*, **86**, 404–17.

Ostrom, E., R. Gardner and J. Walker (1994), *Rules, Games and Common Pool Resources*, Ann Arbor, MI: The University of Michigan Press.

Sefton, M., R. Shupp and J. Walker (2002), 'The effect of rewards and sanctions in provision of public goods', CEDEX working paper 2002–2, University of Nottingham.

Swope, K.J. (2002), 'An experimental investigation of excludable public goods', *Experimental Economics*, **5**, 209–22.

Van Soest, D.P. and J. Vyrastekova (2004), 'Economic ties and social dilemmas: an economic experiment', CentER Discussion Paper 2004–55, Tilburg: Tilburg University.

Vyrastekova, J. and D.P. van Soest (2005), 'Demand for rewards', Tilburg University, Department of Economics, mimeo.

Walker, J.M. and W.A. Halloran (2004), 'Rewards and sanctions and the provision of public goods in one-shot settings', *Experimental Economics*, **7**, 235–47.

7. Experimental approaches to understanding inter-cultural conflict over resources

Paul J. Ferraro and Ronald G. Cummings

INTRODUCTION

Throughout the world, ethnic, racial and religious conflicts over limited resources persist in the face of potential settlements that plainly serve the interests of all sides. Environmental economists have generally left the study of such conflicts to sociologists, political scientists and anthropologists. Research in these other disciplines has highlighted the role that cultural differences among competing groups can have in determining environmental outcomes. In summarizing the main thrust of this area of research, Adams et al. (2003, p. 1915) argue that

> [a]lthough conflict is a feature of many resource management regimes, it is often assumed to reflect differences in material interests between stakeholders . . . Conflicts over the management of common pool resources are not simply material . . . and the origins of conflict go beyond material incompatibilities. They arise at a deeper cognitive level . . . One cannot, therefore, simply analyze the economic interests of different claimants to rights over a defined resource. Different people will see different resources in a landscape.

Kim (2003), a political scientist analysing a conservation and development project in Korea, argues that conflicts can be 'culturally constructed' and difficult to resolve because of the way in which interacting cultures frame the resource dilemmas in which they are playing. In a recent edited volume on local-level environmental outcomes, Agrawal and Gibson (2001: 15) emphasize that explicitly considering the heterogeneity of communities along gender and ethnic lines ('differentiated relations of community actors') is one 'of the most important issues confronting the research and practice of local-level conservation efforts'. Of the 11 authors in the edited volume, none are economists.

The absence of economists in this area of research is unfortunate. By building on advances in behavioural economics and experimental methods, economists can make important contributions to our understanding of the ways in which 'culture' affects economic decision-making. Through a combination of simple economic theory and experimental methods, we offer a demonstration of how economists can contribute to knowledge about the role of cultural diversity and conflict in competition and cooperation over environmental resources.

We are not the first economists to explore the role of culture in economic decision-making. In an experimental application of the Ultimatum Game, Roth et al. (1991) found cross-cultural behavioural differences across four countries.[1] More recent inquiries have also found behavioural differences across countries (for example, Brandts et al., 2004; Burlando and Hey, 1997; Croson and Buchan, 1999; Henrich, 2000; Oosterbeek et al., 2004) and across ethnicities in a country (for example, the 'Hispanic effect' in Holt and Laury, 2002). In particular, a recent initiative to explore the effect of culture in 15 small-scale societies across the globe has found striking variability in the outcomes of Ultimatum Game experiments (Henrich et al., 2001).

Considering these cross-cultural studies, we were led to a closely related issue that takes the 'cultural effects' inquiry in a different direction of direct relevance to environmental economics: if cultural differences affect economic behaviour (or indeed even if they do not), do *inter*-cultural *relationships* affect such behaviour? Thus, as opposed to the question addressed in previous cross-culture studies – 'Do individuals in one culture behave differently from individuals in another culture?' – we pose the question, 'Do individuals interacting with others sharing the same culture behave differently than when interacting with others from a *different* culture?' If the answer is 'Yes', then important issues arise concerning economic behaviour and outcomes in societies of mixed ethnicity, race and religion.

To answer our question, we organized experimental sessions of a simple bargaining game with members of two ethnic groups from New Mexico: Navajo Indians and Hispanic Americans. We varied the ethnic mix of our experimental sessions in order to infer the effect of inter-cultural interactions on economic behaviour. In the next section, we describe the way in which our study builds on previous research. In 'Experiment design', we describe the design of our experiments. We report results in two 'Results' sections, and a simulation based on these results in 'Simulated societies'. Concluding remarks are offered in the final section.

CULTURE, ETHNICITY AND RACE

Our experiments were conducted in Albuquerque, New Mexico, during July 2002. New Mexico is arguably the most unique state in the USA in terms of ethnic diversity, with three major ethnic groups each accounting for a sizeable proportion of the population. In 2001, New Mexico's population was 42.1 per cent Hispanic, 45 per cent Anglo and 10 per cent Native American, with Blacks and Asians accounting for the remaining 2.9 per cent.[2] New Mexico has a higher Hispanic population, in terms of percentage of total population, than any other state in the USA. Other states have a higher proportion of Native Americans, but no other state has a mix of Anglos, Hispanics and Native Americans comparable to New Mexico. Native American and Hispanic cultures are distinct and dominant in the state, and in the city of Albuquerque.

Economists who work with concepts like culture, ethnicity and race rarely attempt to define such words. Their definitions, however, are subject to much debate in other disciplines (McElreath et al., 2003).[3] We use the word 'culture' to refer to the statistical distribution of beliefs, values and modes of thinking that shape behaviour among a group of people (for example, notions of fairness). 'Ethnicity' is related to symbolically marked groups (for example, marked by language, dialect or clothing). Cultural differences may be present in a population when ethnicity is not marked (for example, southern-born and northern-born whites in the USA; Nisbett and Cohen, 1996). Similarly, ethnic differences may exist when no cultural differences exist (except for the ethnic marking). 'Race' is like ethnicity, except the 'markers' are genetically transmitted (Gil-White, 2001).

We assume that self-reported Navajo and Hispanic individuals in our experiments are distinct culturally, ethnically and racially. We are testing whether such distinctions make any difference in the bargaining behaviour of our subjects. In our experiment, we cannot differentiate the separate effects of culture, ethnicity and race; empirically, they are identical for our purposes. Thus we will use the term 'cultural differences' to describe any differences that result from differences in culture, ethnicity or race. As in previous papers that find relationships between an individual's culture, ethnicity or race and his or her behaviour or economic status, we can never be certain that what we describe as cultural determinants are not actually non-cultural determinants, for which we have no data, that are correlated with our cultural categories. In this sense, what we call 'culture' in our analysis is best viewed as a residual category. By controlling for differences in behaviour that stem from variability in the socio-economic attributes of our subjects, we attribute to 'cultural differences' any remaining variability in behaviour across ethnic groups.

As mentioned above, experimental economists have generally ignored the question, 'Do individuals interacting with others sharing the same culture behave differently than when interacting with others from a *different* culture?' We find only two published studies that address the inter-cultural question: Fershtman and Gneezy (2001; hereafter FG) and List (2004).[4]

In a series of experiments with two major Israeli ethnic groups, the Ashkenazic Jews (European and American immigrants and their Israeli-born offspring) and the Eastern Jews (Asian and African immigrants and their Israeli-born offspring), FG addressed the effects of ethnic stereotyping on trust and the ability of two players to cooperate. In their application of the Ultimatum Game, FG found significantly larger offers were proposed to Eastern players.[5] However, they found no significant difference between the percentage of Eastern and Ashkenazic players that rejected a proposed split of 25 per cent of the pie.

Fershtman and Gneezy write (2001: 370) that the observed discrimination 'is probably an outcome of a common ethnic stereotype in Israeli society, according to which men of Eastern origin are believed to react more harshly if treated unfairly'. Although FG do not explicitly refer to their Dictator Game experimental results to interpret their Ultimatum Game results, one could interpret the absence of any discrimination in the Dictator Game as indirect evidence that behaviour in the Ultimatum Game results from erroneous statistical discrimination. However, absent information about players' expectations of partner responses, one has only indirect evidence for this conclusion.

List (2004) examined the bargaining behaviours of participants in a real sportscard market. He observed starting and final offers for a specific card and collected information on basic attributes of the bargainers (age, experience, gender, education, income, height and weight) and the length of the bargaining session. He had subjects from four categories: white males aged 20–30, white females aged 20–30, white males aged 60+, and 'non-white' males aged 20–30. Given that race was not asked on the questionnaire, it is unclear as to how the author determined race and what race, or races, the term 'non-white' includes for his sample.

List found that average initial and final offers from dealers to 'minority' buyers (females, older males and non-white males) were higher than those received by young white males. After controlling for experience, the differences among final offers were small for experienced buyers (but minority buyers did have to spend more time to obtain their final offers) and were only significantly different among inexperienced older male and young female buyers.[6] Like FG, List used complementary 'laboratory' experiments (Dictator Game, Decentralized Chamberlain Market, and a Vickery second-price auction for a real card) to elucidate the underlying reasons for the observed discrimination in the real sportscard market. The data in the complementary experiments suggest that the observations in the real sportscard market were a result of statistical discrimination by dealers rather than preference-based discrimination.

Two interrelated issues motivate our analysis below. First, we wish to ensure that we do not attribute to 'culture' any differences in behaviour that stem from variability in the socio-economic attributes of our subjects. For example, FG analysed only the behaviour of the male Proposers in their Ultimatum Game and did not analyse rejections controlling for the gender (or ethnicity) of the subject making the offer. Other studies, however, have found significant gender effects in the Ultimatum Game (Botelho et al., 2002; Eckel and Grossman, 2001; Solnick, 2001). Fershtman and Gneezy (2001) also did not control for socio-economic differences across subjects (for example, Ashkenazic Jews tend to be wealthier). List, in contrast, controls for gender, length of bargaining session, average frequency of buyer transactions per month, years of market experience, income and education.

Our second motivation relates to common practices used by economists to control for subject characteristics, particularly ethnicity, and is relevant whether or not subjects from the two cultures behave differently in the Ultimatum Game when each player's partner is from the same culture. We wish to determine if the *ethnic mix* of the experimental session affects how subjects make decisions. Fershtman and Gneezy's inquiry into the existence of inter-cultural discrimination is based on a design wherein players attempt to infer the ethnicity of their partners, who are in a different location, from the partners' surnames – subjects assume they are either playing with a partner of the same or a different ethnic group. In List, subjects can either observe the race, gender or approximate age of their partner or are told these attributes by the experimenter.

While these may be important contexts, we wish to explore behavioural variability in response to changes in the *proportional representation* of the two ethnic groups in an experimental session. In other words, we wish to determine if subjects behave differently in the following three contexts: (1) all players share the subject's ethnicity, (2) the player's ethnic group makes up a large majority of the players, and (3) the player's ethnic group is a small minority of the players. If subject behaviour is affected by the ethnic mix of a session, several considerations arise that are relevant for public policy and for the manner in which economists control for ethnicity in empirical analyses. Public administration often takes place in societies characterized by mixed ethnicities, in which one or two ethnicities dominate. In empirical economic analyses, economists commonly use simple dummy (zero-one) variables to control for ethnicity, race and religion. If, however, subject behaviour is affected by the cultural mix rather than (or in addition to) the subject's own culture, economists may need to reconsider the way in which they control for cultural differences in empirical analyses.

EXPERIMENT DESIGN

We analyse our problem in the simplest of bargaining environments: the Ultimatum bargaining game. Two players, a Proposer and a Responder, bargain over \$10. The Proposer offers \$$x$ to the Responder, leaving himself \$$10 - x$. The Responder can either take the offer, in which case each obtains the proposed split of the \$10 pie, or reject it and both get nothing. As noted by Camerer (2003: 8), the Ultimatum Game is too simple to be a good model of the complicated processes of most real-world bargaining. Yet because it is simple, it offers a useful environment for testing hypotheses about the factors that influence how people feel about the allocations of money between themselves and others. It is thus unsurprising that previous cross-cultural studies and the Fershtman–Gneezy inter-cultural study have used the Ultimatum Game as a vehicle for understanding the way in which culture affects economic behaviour.

The experimental sessions were held in a large room rented at the Menaul School, centrally located in Albuquerque. A portable experimental laboratory was used that consists of 32 networked notebook computers with wireless connection to a laptop computer that acts as a server. The subjects' computers are situated in folding partitions to ensure private decisions. The instructions for the experiments were conveyed orally and in writing. A portable projector demonstrated the subject interface (see appendix for instructions). Prior to each session, subjects were placed in a room in which some food and refreshments were offered. We grouped subjects prior to entering the experimental room for two reasons: (1) such grouping allowed subjects to observe the ethnic make-up of their session (Navajo and Hispanic subjects are visually very different) and (2) it allowed us to conduct back-to-back sessions without risking cross-session observation or communication. This simple and efficient approach allows one to highlight the cultural composition of the session without emphasizing it in a way that allows subjects to infer the purpose of the experiment.

Sixty Hispanic subjects were recruited by distributing flyers in Hispanic neighbourhoods. All Hispanic subjects were raised in the USA. Sixty Navajo subjects were recruited primarily by distributing flyers at three Navajo organizations: the Southwest Indian Polytechnic Institute (SIPI), the PHS Indian Hospital, and the Albuquerque Indian Center. 'Navajo neighbourhoods' do not exist and these organizations serve as the closest equivalent. Overall, 45 per cent of the subject pool was male, 59 per cent reported an annual income of less than $15 000, 47 per cent of the sample was full- or part-time students, 15 per cent was married and the mean age was 29 years.

In order to explore cross-cultural and inter-cultural effects on behaviour, we scheduled four experimental sessions. The ethnic composition of each session was as follows:[7]

Session 1 (All-Hispanic)	30 Hispanic subjects
Session 2 (Majority-Hispanic)	21 Hispanic and 6 Navajo subjects
Session 3 (All-Navajo)	29 Navajo and 1 Hispanic subject[8]
Session 4 (Majority-Navajo)	23 Navajo and 7 Hispanic subjects.

Session 1 followed immediately by Session 2 took place on one night, and Session 3 followed immediately by Session 4 took place the next night.

The standard rules of the Ultimatum Game were explained to subjects and subjects were required to complete a practice question to ensure they understood how their earnings would be calculated (see Davis and Holt, 1993, or Roth, 1995, for more information on Ultimatum Games). Subjects played the role of *both* Responder and Proposer (as was done in the original application of the Ultimatum Game by Güth et al. (1982) and in more recent studies like Andreoni et al. (2003), Carter and Irons (1991) and Kahneman et al. (1986)). Subjects were told that they would make decisions as a Responder and as a Proposer. At the end of the experiment, the computer randomly assigned each subject to the role of Responder or Proposer, and randomly paired the subject with another subject in the room (not known to him or her) who played the opposite role. Subjects were cautioned to take each role seriously given the equal chance that each person had of being assigned the role of Responder or Proposer. With the exception of the All-Navajo and All-Hispanic sessions, the ethnicity of a subject's partner was uncertain but the ethnic composition of the session was obvious: the subject's ethnic group constituted either a large majority or a small minority of the subjects.

As an aside, we note that our design differs from FG's in that subjects from one culture interact *directly* with subjects from the other culture. The only contact that an Ashkenazic subject in FG's experiment had with an Eastern subject was a visual inspection of the Eastern subject's name on a form.[9]

The amount of money given to the Proposer, known by all subjects, was $10.00. Subjects first saw a screen (Figure 7.1) that asked them to make the decisions of a Responder. They were asked to indicate, for each dollar amount between $0 and $10, *if* they were assigned the role of Responder and *if* that dollar amount were sent to them, whether they would accept it

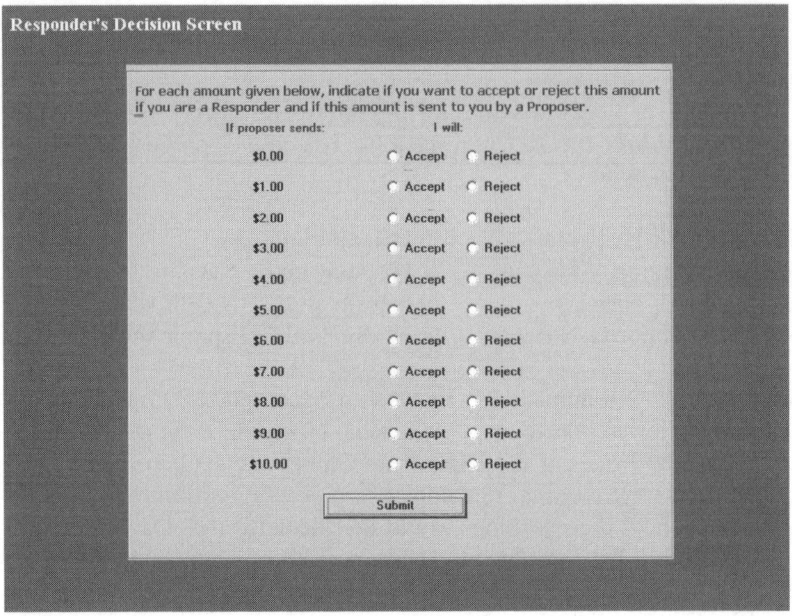

Responder's Decision Screen

For each amount given below, indicate if you want to accept or reject this amount if you are a Responder and if this amount is sent to you by a Proposer.

If proposer sends:	I will:	
$0.00	Accept	Reject
$1.00	Accept	Reject
$2.00	Accept	Reject
$3.00	Accept	Reject
$4.00	Accept	Reject
$5.00	Accept	Reject
$6.00	Accept	Reject
$7.00	Accept	Reject
$8.00	Accept	Reject
$9.00	Accept	Reject
$10.00	Accept	Reject

Submit

Figure 7.1 Responder screen

or reject it; that is, we used the strategy method. Eliciting the behaviour of Responders through the strategy method allowed us to collect data on all information sets of the game, not just those that were actually reached in the course of the game. Subjects were cautioned that, if assigned the role of Responder, they would be bound by the decisions that they recorded on this screen.

Subjects were then asked to play the role of a Proposer. To allow us to make inferences about discriminatory behaviour that may be observed in the laboratory, subjects were first asked *to predict* how they believed Responders would respond to each possible amount that they might send to a Responder, from $0 to $10 (Figure 7.2). Subjects predicted the *percentage* of Responders in the session that would accept each amount. To create incentives for subjects to think about their estimates, subjects were informed that the individual whose estimates were the closest to the actual per cent of Responders accepting each amount would win $10.00.[10]

Subjects were then asked to decide how much they would send to a Responder *if* they were assigned the role of a Proposer (Figure 7.3). Subjects were advised that if assigned the role of Proposer, the amount they chose on this screen would be sent to the Responder.

Proposer's Estimation Screen

For each amount given below that you might send to a Responder, indicate what you think the chance is that a Responder in this room will accept the amount. (For example, 10% chance, 47% chance, 99% chance, etc.)

If you send	Chance that it would be accepted		
$0.00	0%	0	100%
$1.00	0%	0	100%
$2.00	0%	0	100%
$3.00	0%	0	100%
$4.00	0%	0	100%
$5.00	0%	0	100%
$6.00	0%	0	100%
$7.00	0%	0	100%
$8.00	0%	0	100%
$9.00	0%	0	100%
$10.00	0%	0	100%

Submit

Figure 7.2 Proposer's expectations of the likelihood of offer rejection

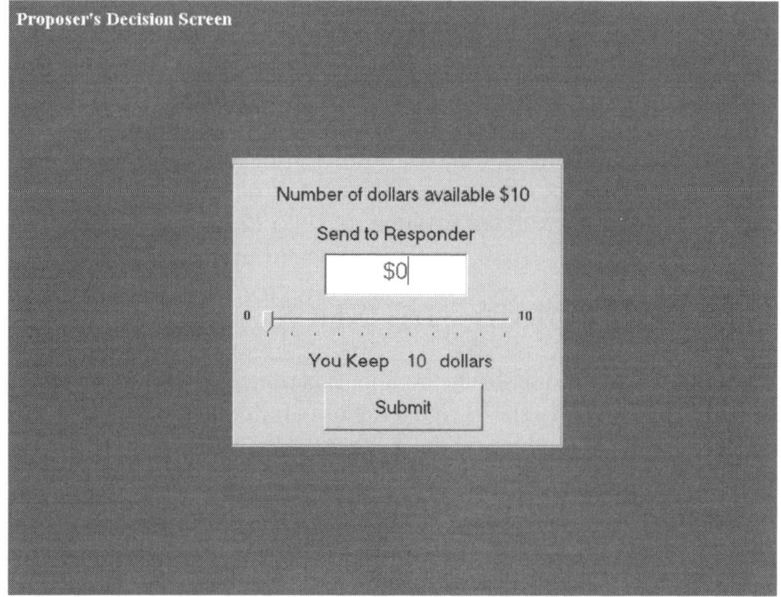

Figure 7.3 Proposer's screen

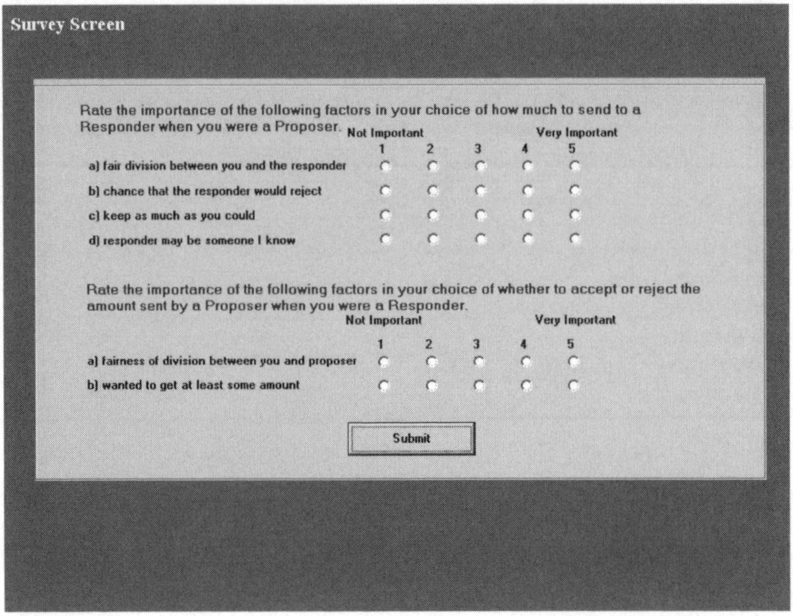

Survey Screen

Rate the importance of the following factors in your choice of how much to send to a Responder when you were a Proposer.

	Not Important 1	2	3	4	Very Important 5
a) fair division between you and the responder					
b) chance that the responder would reject					
c) keep as much as you could					
d) responder may be someone I know					

Rate the importance of the following factors in your choice of whether to accept or reject the amount sent by a Proposer when you were a Responder.

	Not Important 1	2	3	4	Very Important 5
a) fairness of division between you and proposer					
b) wanted to get at least some amount					

Submit

Figure 7.4 Post-experiment questionnaire and subject motivations

Finally, subjects responded to a questionnaire (Figure 7.4) that inquired about the motivations for the decisions made by the subject as a Responder (Figure 7.1) and as a Proposer (Figure 7.3). At the end of the session, the computer randomly assigned each subject to the role of Responder or Proposer and randomly paired the subject with another subject in the room. Demographic information was then obtained from each subject. The same person conducted all the sessions.

RESULTS: SUMMARY STATISTICS

A summary of the results from the four experimental sessions is given in Table 7.1. This summary shows rough trends in the data. In the next section, we control for demographic and other subject characteristics in the analysis.

Responders

We begin by examining the behaviour of Responders (that is, compare Hispanic Responders in All-Hispanic session to Navajo Responders in the All-Navajo session, and so on). Hispanic Responders have higher minimum

Table 7.1 General summary of experiment results

	Responder				Proposer	
	Average reservation price		% responders accepting $1.00 offer		Average	
Session	Navajo	Hispanic	Navajo	Hispanic	Navajo	Hispanic
All subjects same ethnicity	$1.31	$1.83	62	60	$3.83	$4.90
Subject's ethnicity is a majority	$1.78	$2.73	61	33	$5.13	$4.77
Subject's ethnicity is a minority	$2.00	$3.38	50	13	$4.17[12]	$4.50

acceptable offers, on average, than Navajo Responders in all sessions (significant at 2 per cent to 11 per cent level, depending on the comparison and whether one uses a Mann–Whitney or t-test). In the All-Navajo and All-Hispanic sessions, 60 per cent of both ethnicities were willing to accept an offer of 10 per cent of the pie ($1). These acceptance rates are substantially higher than those observed in previous Ultimatum Game experiments in industrialized nations. Güth et al. (2003) report that anything over 33 per cent is much higher than the rates typically observed in Ultimatum Game experiments that use the strategy method (including experiments in which subjects played both roles).[11]

Furthermore, both Hispanics and Navajos appear to discriminate against the other ethnic group – there is an increase in the minimum offer that they would accept as the relative proportion of their ethnic group in the session decreases. This increase is particularly notable for the Hispanics.[13] The same pattern appears in the percentage of subjects willing to accept an offer of one dollar. Both Hispanics and Navajo become more willing to accept the 1-dollar offer as the proportion of their ethnic group in the session increases. Again, the behaviour on the part of Hispanics is more striking. Thus Navajo are willing to accept low offers at much higher rates than most other subjects in previous Ultimatum Game experiments, whereas Hispanic acceptance rates are only unusually high when playing in an All-Hispanic group.

Proposers

Offers by both Hispanic and Navajo Proposers are in the range observed in earlier studies regardless of their proportion of the session: between

38 per cent and about 50 per cent of the $10.00 to be divided. When playing with members of one's own ethnic group, however, Navajos make significantly lower offers than Hispanics (significant at 1 per cent level under both a Mann-Whitney and t-test). In addition, Hispanics appear to persistently discriminate against the Navajo–Hispanic offers appear to decline as their majority status diminishes – while Navajos appear to make higher offers when Hispanics are in the session.[14]

RESULTS: REGRESSION ANALYSES

The summary statistics in the previous section do not, of course, control for demographic variability among subjects or the differences in ethnic proportions across sessions. There was a high degree of variability in our subject pool with, for example, ages ranging from 16 to 50 years old and annual incomes ranging from less than $5000 to more than $50 000. Such variability affected the demographic composition across sessions. For example, among Hispanic subjects in the All-Hispanic session, the mean age was 32.3 years and 40 per cent reported incomes less than $5000 per year. For Hispanic subjects in the Majority-Navajo session, the mean age was 22.1 years and 12.5 per cent reported incomes less than $5000 per year. Similar variability existed among Navajos across sessions. As we wrote in the second section, some studies have found that demographic attributes are important determinants of behaviour in the Ultimatum Game (Botelho et al., 2002; Carter and Irons, 1991; Eckel and Grossman, 2001; Harbaugh et al., 2000; Kahneman et al., 1986; Solnick, 2001; Stanley and Tran, 1998).[15] To control for their effects, and to allow us to focus on our two major questions, we conduct regression analyses of Proposers' offers and Responders' minimum acceptable offers (reservation prices) against the variables listed in Table 7.2.

Hispanic ethnicity is the omitted ethnicity variable in the models. Inter-ethnic effects are measured by the variables (2), (3), and (3.a) (3.a is used only in Offer regression). The squared interaction term (3.a) between Navajo and per cent of subjects in a session from a different ethnic group is included as a result of our finding a non-linear relationship between Navajo Proposer behaviour and the ethnic composition of the session.[16] As we will note, however, this non-linearity is largely a result of the behaviour of two subjects. Such non-linearity was not observed among Hispanics.

We also estimated a model in which behavioural variables (that is, responses from questions in Figures 7.2 and 7.4) and expectations were included, but these regressions do not change the qualitative results of our analysis of cross-cultural and inter-cultural effects on decision-making (see Ferraro and Cummings, 2003, for other regressions). Given evidence of

Table 7.2 Variables used in regression analyses

Variable	Description
Dependent variables:	
RESERV	Responder's reservation price
OFFER	Proposer's offer
Independent variables:	
1. Navajo	Dummy variable = 1 if subject is Navajo
2. PercentOther	Percentage of subjects in session from an ethnic group *different* from that of the subject's [0%, 96.9%]
3. NavPercentOther	Interaction between (1) and (2)
3.a $(\text{NavPercentOther})^2$	(3) squared, used only in Offer equation
4. Age	Subject's age
5. Male	Dummy variable = 1 if subject is male
6. Econ	Number of economics courses taken by subject
7. Less$15 000	Dummy variable = 1 if subject's income is less than $15 000
8. $15–$45 000	Dummy variable = 1 if subject's income is between $15 000 and $45 000
9. NavLess$15 000	Interaction term between (1) and (7)
10. Nav$15–$45 000	Interaction term between (1) and (8)
11. Married	Dummy variable = 1 if subject is married

heteroskedasticity, we use the Huber/White/sandwich estimator of variance (White, 1980), which produces robust estimates of the standard errors.[17]

Results from the regressions of Responder behaviour (RESERV) and Proposer behaviour (OFFER) are presented in Tables 7.3 and 7.4. These results will serve as a basis for responses to the two questions raised in the second section: (1) Do we observed cross-cultural differences in Ultimatum Game behaviour of subjects from these two cultures that share the same geographic area? (2) Do changes in the proportional representation of an ethnic group substantially affect behaviour in the Ultimatum Game? We answer these questions by first examining the behaviour of Responders, and then the behaviour of Proposers.

Responders

With respect to *cross*-cultural effects, Navajos have significantly lower reservation prices, on average, than Hispanics (Table 7.3). For example, the ethnicity coefficients suggest that, depending on income, a Navajo subject will accept, on average, between $0.35 and $2.80 *less* than a Hispanic subject.

Table 7.3 Responder's reservation price as dependent variable

Independent variable	Coefficient (Standard error)	t-statistic (p-value)
Constant	4.165 (0.801)	5.20 (0.000)
Navajo	−2.793 (0.642)	−4.35 (0.000)
PercentOther	0.019 (0.007)	2.88 (0.005)
NavPercentOther	−0.010 (0.013)	−0.77 (0.443)
Age	0.011 (0.017)	0.64 (0.527)
Male	−0.446 (0.292)	−1.53 (0.130)
Econ	−0.079 (0.032)	−2.31 (0.023)
Married	−0.969 (0.385)	−2.52 (0.013)
Less$15 000	−2.355 (0.509)	−4.63 (0.000)
$15–$45 000	−1.793 (0.456)	−3.94 (0.000)
NavLess$15 000	2.445 (1.027)	3.20 (0.002)
Nav$15–$45 000	1.970 (0.838)	2.35 (0.021)

Note: Model 1: F(11,105) = 10.27 (Prob>F = 0.000);[18] R-squared = 0.24; Root MSE = 1.50.

With respect to our second question concerning *inter*-cultural effects, the behaviours of both Hispanic and Navajo Proposers are significantly affected by the ethnic composition of the session in both models. Both Hispanics and Navajo discriminate against the other ethnic group in the sense that their mean reservation prices increase with an increase in the proportion of subjects from the other ethnic group; this effect is most pronounced with Hispanic subjects. If, for example, the subject pool were 25 per cent Hispanic and 75 per cent Navajo, the model predicts that the average minimum acceptable offer of Hispanics would be about $1.44 more than if the pool were 100 per cent Hispanic.

With regard to the demographic variables, we observe that Hispanic reservation prices are significantly and positively related to income, whereas such

Table 7.4 Proposer's offer as dependent variable

Independent variable	Coefficient (Standard error)	t-statistic (p-value)
Constant	6.642	7.27
	(0.914)	(0.000)
Navajo	−2.502	−2.17
	(1.151)	(0.032)
PercentOther	−0.013	−1.98
	(0.007)	(0.050)
NavPercentOther	0.107	3.18
	(0.034)	(0.002)
NavPercentOther^2	−0.001	−2.75
	(0.000)	(0.007)
Age	−0.029	−1.54
	(0.019)	(0.126)
Male	0.092	0.29
	(0.314)	(0.771)
Econ	0.052	1.62
	(0.032)	(0.109)
Married	−0.245	−0.55
	(0.442)	(0.580)
Less$15 000	−1.060	−2.26
	(0.470)	(0.026)
$15-$45 000	−0.689	−1.46
	(0.472)	(0.147)
NavLess$15 000	1.232	1.20
	(1.027)	(0.233)
Nav$15-$45 000	1.050	0.90
	(1.170)	(0.372)

Note: Model 1: $F(12,104) = 1.97$ (Prob>F = 0.034); R-squared = 0.15; Root MSE = 1.56.

a relationship was not observed for the Navajo (if anything, poorer Navajos demand a little more of the pie). Married subjects, both Hispanic and Navajo, have significantly lower reservation prices than single subjects by almost $1 on average. Evidence of gender effects on a Responder's reservation price is weak, at best, with males requiring about $0.45 less than females on average. A negative effect also derives from exposure to economics courses.[19]

Proposers

In terms of *cross*-cultural effects among Proposers, we find a significant difference in the behaviour of our two cultural groups in both specifications

(Table 7.4). On average, Navajos offer less than Hispanics. For example, the ethnicity coefficients suggest that, depending on income levels, a Navajo subject offers, on average, between \$1.27 and \$2.50 *less* than a Hispanic subject.

In terms of our *inter*-cultural question – Does the ethnic mix of the session 'matter'? – we find the ethnic composition of the session has significant effects on offers. Hispanics make the highest offers to a Responder *when all subjects are Hispanic*, and persistently lower offers as the percentage of Hispanics in the group decreases. For example, a Hispanic subject offers, on average, \$1 less if Hispanics make up only 25 per cent of the session rather than 100 per cent.

Turning to Navajo Proposers, the non-linear response to ethnic composition that was evident in Table 7.1 is also reflected in our regression results: mean Navajo offers rise and then fall as their proportional representation of the session decreases (reflected in the significantly positive sum of 'PercentOther' and 'NavPercentOther' and the significantly negative sign on 'NavPercentOther^2'). However, much of this non-linearity is driven by two influential observations. Using Cook's (1997) distance to identify influential observations, we identified two Navajo subjects who offered \$0 as the two most influential observations (number 29 in the All-Navajo session; number 33 in the Majority-Hispanic session). Removing these observations from the data-set removes the observed non-linearity in the data: the coefficient on NavPercentOther^2 is statistically no different from zero. Removing the two influential observations and the squared variable from the regression yields the following coefficients: PercentOther = −0.015 ($p = 0.013$) and NavPercentOther = 0.033 ($p = 0.006$). This result implies that Hispanic offers decrease linearly in the proportion of Navajo subjects in the session (almost 2 cents for every 1 per cent increase in the proportion of Navajos), while Navajo offers *increase* linearly in the proportion of Hispanic subjects in the session (almost 2 cents for every 1 per cent increase in the proportion of Hispanics).

Predicted Proposer and Responder Behaviour

In an effort to make clear the nature of these cross-cultural and inter-cultural effects, an example is given in Table 7.5 where we consider two hypothetical subjects: a Navajo and a Hispanic subject, both 25-year-old single females with incomes in the \$15 000–\$45 000 range. For various ethnic mixes, Table 7.5 gives the Responder reservation prices and Proposer offers that are predicted by the regressions reported in Tables 7.3 and 7.4. Because the non-linearity observed for Proposer Offers was driven by two influential observations, we drop these two observations and use a re-

Table 7.5 Comparison of hypothetical Navajo and Hispanic subjects with identical attributes

Percentage of 'other' ethnic group in session	Navajo		Hispanic	
	Minimum acceptable offer	Offer	Minimum acceptable offer	Offer
0	\$1.19	\$3.13	\$2.14	\$4.33
20	\$1.37	\$3.46	\$2.50	\$3.95
50	\$1.63	\$3.96	\$3.03	\$3.38
80	\$1.89	\$4.45	\$3.57	\$2.81

estimated Offer model without the squared term 'NavPercentOther^2' (from Ferraro and Cummings, 2003).

In the ethnically homogeneous sessions, reservation prices *and* offers are substantially different between the Navajo and Hispanic 'subjects'. Most importantly for our purpose, as the percentage of Navajo subjects in a session increases, reservation prices increase and offers decrease for the Hispanic subject. For the Navajo subject, increases in the percentage of Hispanics in the session also results in increasing reservation prices; his/her offer, however, also increases as the percentage of Hispanic subjects in a session increases.

Statistical versus Preference-based Discrimination

In another paper (Ferraro and Cummings, 2003), we analyse the reasons for the observed discrimination across sessions. If rational agents have no information about the behaviour of the partner with whom they are bargaining, but have information about the *average* behaviour of the group to which the partner belongs (for example, an ethnic group), they may condition their decision on the average behaviour of the group to which the partner belongs. Such behaviour is called 'statistical discrimination' (or 'rational stereotyping'). If, in contrast, a rational agent simply prefers to behave differently when paired with a bargaining partner of particular characteristics, such behaviour is called 'preference-based discrimination' (or 'a taste for discrimination'). The extent to which these two types of discrimination are empirically relevant in real-world societies is controversial (Ladd, 1998).

Explaining the behaviour of Responders as stemming from anything other than preference-based discrimination is difficult (how would the average *behaviour* of the Proposers affect what a Responder would be willing to accept?), but the behaviour of Hispanic and Navajo Proposers could be explained as statistical discrimination because Navajos are generally more likely to accept low offers in mixed sessions. Incorporating our data on subject expectations, however, led us to conclude that although expectations do play a role, they cannot completely explain the behaviour we observe. A taste for discrimination against Navajo Responders by Navajo and Hispanic Proposers represents the strongest explanation for the observed Proposer behaviour.

A reader may find strange the conclusion drawn from the regression analyses that Navajos discriminate against Hispanics when they are Responders but against Navajos when they are Proposers. Previous Ultimatum Game analyses, however, suggest that the framing of the Responder's decision is different from the framing of the Proposer's decision, and thus the operative decision variables are different. In the former decision, issues associated with justice, fairness and equity are operative, but in the latter decision, strategic concerns and other-regarding preferences are operative. We do not pretend to understand *why* these observed patterns of preference-based discrimination take place, but we note that the results are consistent across alternative model specifications.

SIMULATED SOCIETIES

Subjects in the experiment described above were only matched once at random. What if these subjects in each session were matched repeatedly, as they would be in a larger society? How would members of the Navajo and Hispanic cultures fare in such simulated societies? To explore this question, we take the subjects in each session and create 10 000 random matches (thus we are implicitly assuming no learning or updating of prior beliefs among our subjects). We are able to randomly re-match subjects because we have each Responder's decision for every dollar offer a Proposer can make in this game.

We present the results from this simulation in Table 7.6. For each simulated society, we present the average pay-off to Proposers and Responders broken down by culture. We also present the 'agreement rate' for the society, which is the percentage of interactions that resulted in positive pay-offs for the bargainers. For example, the average pay-off to Navajo Proposers in the All-Navajo simulated society was $4.15, while the average pay-off to Navajo Responders was $3.41. These pay-offs are substantially lower than the pay-offs to Hispanic Proposers ($4.95) and Responders (4.84) in the All-Hispanic society.

Thus the Hispanic bargainers in a culturally homogenous society were better able to extract the available surplus than the Navajo bargainers in a culturally homogenous society. The differences stem from the larger

Table 7.6 Summary of simulation results

Society	Average proposer pay-off		Agreement rate	Average responder pay-off	
	Navajo	Hispanic		Navajo	Hispanic
All-Navajo	$4.15	—	75.59%	$3.41	—
All-Hispanic	—	$4.95	97.91%	—	$4.84
Majority-Navajo	$4.60	$4.79	93.53%	$4.64	$4.82
Majority-Hispanic	$4.08	$4.37	85.50%	$4.01	$4.31

agreement rate among Hispanic bargainers – Hispanic Proposers in the All-Hispanic society tend to make higher offers and Responders are willing to accept low offers (recall mean values in Table 7.1).[20] As indicated in the last two rows of Table 7.6, Navajo bargainers would do better in a mixed society with Hispanic members, but Hispanic members do best in a culturally homogenous society.

Do such simulations offer insights into current day behaviours and outcomes? Without further experimentation, we cannot say. We do, however, note intriguing anecdotes from the real world that are consistent with the data in Table 7.6 and imply further study might be warranted. For example, the well-known trend of Hispanic self-segregation is generally thought of as largely an issue of language preferences. Our results suggest that Hispanics may also prefer self-segregation because it yields greater surplus gains in everyday negotiations. Indeed, among Hispanic communities in Chicago, Aaronson (2004) found that Hispanic-owned firms had access to more trade credit when working with Hispanic suppliers.

On the Navajo side, we note two observations from the field. First, the Navajo reservations continue to lose members to off-reservation towns and cities in which Navajos find themselves in the minority. The incomes of these off-reservation Navajos is higher, on average, than the incomes of on-reservation Navajos. Second, establishing businesses on Navajo reservations is notoriously difficult because of intense negotiations that often fail to achieve a mutually agreeable outcome. A Navajo businessman who opened the first national brand restaurant and hotel near a Navajo reservation chose to build them just over the reservation's borders. He is quoted as saying, 'The number of businesses that are formed on Navajo lands is very small compared to other areas. The same project that would take three to four months to complete in Show Low, Ariz., for instance, could take three to four years on Navajo land'.[21] The President of the Navajo nation acknowledged such difficulties in a recent interview and stated that the nation was 'working on making it a little bit easier for businesses to get established'.[22]

CONCLUDING REMARKS

Our results clearly demonstrate that culture does matter, and in more ways than previous research had suggested. Hispanic and Navajo subjects not only behave differently in the Ultimatum Game, but they also respond differently to the ethnic composition of the session.

As noted in the 'Introduction', these results have implications of general interest to economists. Throughout the world, policies are formulated in societies characterized by mixed ethnicity, race and religion, in which there are clear majority and minority groups. Allocating the costs and benefits of public decisions across citizens (for example, setting tax policy, providing public goods) is a crucial policy issue. The way in which citizens value the potential policy outcomes, however, may not only be affected by the cultural group to which they belong, but also by the group's relative size in the society. The experimental approach we advocate can also shed light on current research programmes analysing endogenous preferences across different socio cultural structures (Palacios-Huerta and Santos, 2004), and the role of cultural diversity in economic growth (Alesina, 2003; Fearon, 2003) and social policies towards the poor (Alesina and Glaeser, 2004).

Furthermore, the results suggest that economists may need to reconsider the way in which they control for ethnicity in empirical analyses. Economists traditionally use simple dummy (zero-one) variables for each ethnic group. Twenty-five years ago, Thomas Schelling (1978: 108) observed that 'undoubtedly for some behaviors . . . it is proportions that influence people, not absolute numbers'. Our results provide empirical support for Professor Schelling's observation.

The increased global relevance of diverse institutional arrangements for mediating the bargaining over natural resources (for example, participatory resource management, community-based natural resource management, and so on) ensures that inter-cultural relationships will continue to have an impact on economic outcomes related to environmental resource for the foreseeable future. Economists cannot continue to sit on the sidelines. We hope that our analysis has shed light on an initial path for economists to begin participating in this growing area of research.

NOTES

1. In the Ultimatum Game, one player (the Proposer) makes an offer to another player (the Responder) to divide a fixed amount of money. The Responder can accept or reject the Proposer's offer. If the offer is accepted, the money is divided as proposed; if the offer is rejected, both players earn zero.

2. Tables 23 and 24, from US Department of Commerce (2002), *Statistical Abstracts of the United States, 2001*, Washington, DC: Bureau of the Census, Department of Commerce.
3. The authors thank anthropologist Joseph Henrich (Emory University) for helping us to come to grips with these terms and directing us to the relevant literature.
4. We note, however, the interesting unpublished study of the ultimatum game with ethnicity manipulation (between two Mongolian tribes) by Gil-White (no date).
5. FG do not make clear whether this discrimination was observed only with Ashkenazic Proposers or both Eastern (n = 33) and Ashkenazic (n = 24) Proposers.
6. Similar results are presented for the offers made by dealers to minority sellers, but the differences are not statistically as meaningful.
7. Only 117 of 120 observations were usable. Given our concern with offending subjects or the organizations providing subjects, we chose to allow subjects to complete the experiment even if they were unable to successfully complete practice questions or were demonstrably unable to comprehend questions. As a result, we exclude data from three subjects: one Navajo subject from the All-Navajo session who could not respond to the practice question (even after repeated explanations by the experimenter), could not understand how to use the mouse, and rejected every possible offer; and one Navajo subject from the All-Navajo session and one Hispanic subject from the Majority-Hispanic session, both of whom had obvious difficulty completing the practice question and who then clicked reject and accept in alternating fashion for every potential offer that could be sent to them. For these three subjects, the idea of a minimum acceptable offer makes no sense and it is unlikely that these subjects understood the main components of the experiment. We note, however, that including these subjects in the analysis by treating their first accepted offers as their Responder reservation prices does not affect our results. When estimating the percentage of Navajo and Hispanic in a session, we include these subjects because they were observable to every subject in the room (removing them from the percentage calculation does not affect our results).
8. Native American ethnicity is a requirement for entry into these organizations. Thus, presumably all subjects in the All-Navajo session were Navajo. However, one subject selected 'Hispanic' on the post-experiment questionnaire. We are unsure if the subject was indeed Hispanic, was of mixed heritage and did not see the option for mixed ethnicity, or made a mistake filling out the questionnaire, which was completed on a computer. We treat the subject as Hispanic, but note that deleting this subject or re-coding her as 'Navajo' does not affect our results.
9. In Gil-White's (no date) experiment, subjects' viewed photographs of the 20 potential partners. We note, however, that our methodology has the same drawback as most laboratory experiments in which subjects can see members of their session: we cannot definitively rule out subject familiarity with other subjects prior to the experiment as a cause of behavioural variability. However, we include a post-experiment question (Figure 7.4) that inquires if the belief that the Responder may be someone they know influenced Proposer behaviour. Few subjects said this factor was important (less than 10 per cent and no difference by cultural group). Adding this variable to the regressions yields a coefficient insignificantly different from zero.
10. More specifically, they were told that the absolute values of the differences between their predicted percentages and the actual percentages for each potential offer would be summed. The subject with the *lowest sum* wins the $10.00. We do not claim that this method is incentive-compatible (we gratefully acknowledge related comments offered by Uri Gneezy). However, our payment rule is highly transparent and can include truth-telling as one best response, while a best response that deviates from true beliefs under this rule requires sophisticated strategizing about the beliefs of others in the session and mathematical acumen to solve for a best-response conditional on those beliefs. Moreover, a recent study by two economists who have published numerous experiments using incentive-compatible quadratic scoring rules (Sonnemans and Offerman, 2001) found no significant difference between the beliefs elicited from a sophisticated quadratic scoring rule that corrects for undesired effects of risk attitudes and probability weighting and beliefs elicited from a method that simply pays subjects a fixed (unconditional)

payment: the offer of some compensation for effort was enough to induce subjects to think carefully about their beliefs.

11. Our anomalous results are not likely to be a result of having players play both roles. Conducting the same experiment at Georgia State University, we find only one-third willing to accept $1 *or* $2 (mean reservation price was $2.77). The mean offer in this session was $4.17. This session of 30 subjects had no culture in a majority or substantial minority: 16 males, 14 foreign subjects from 10 different nations, 5 Hispanic, 3 African-American and 8 White.
12. The mean offer increases from $4.17 to $5 if one influential subject is removed. We will discuss this influential observation (subject number 33) in the next section.
13. Results from a Jonckheere-Terpstra test (with exact p-values) indicate a significant difference in Hispanic Responder behaviour across the independent sessions ($p = 0.0015$). No such significant difference is found among Navajo Responders ($p = 0.2837$). The J-T test is a non-parametric test for ordered differences (trend) among classes and is preferable in this context to tests of more general class differences (for example, Kruskal-Wallis H test; Hollander and Wolfe, 1999). In our experiment, it tests the hypothesis that as one decreases the proportional representation of the cultural group, the within-sample magnitude of the reservation price increases for members of that cultural group.
14. Results from a Jonckheere-Terpstra test indicate significant differences in Proposer behaviour across sessions for both the Navajos ($p = 0.0237$) and Hispanics ($p = 0.0590$).
15. Although previous Ultimatum Game studies have not included marital status (probably because most of the subjects were young college students), 15 per cent of our subject pool was married and we hypothesized that married subjects may behave differently in a bargaining situation.
16. We detected this non-linearity using Mallows (1986) augmented component-plus-residuals plot, a sensitive test of non-linearity.
17. We also used Davidson and MacKinnon's (1993) more conservative HC3 estimator without a substantial change in the standard errors. All regressions were run in Stata v.7.
18. Values of '0.000' imply a value less than 0.001.
19. Removing one subject who reported taking 26 economics courses makes the coefficient smaller (−0.04) and insignificantly different from zero ($p = 0.65$).
20. In the All-Navajo session, there are also a few Responders who reject both low amounts and high amounts (called 'non-monotonic' preferences and examined in Ferraro and Cummings, 2003).
21. www.hirediversity.com/news/newsbyid.asp?id=11971.
22. www.indiancountry.com/?1061221789.

REFERENCES

Aaronson, D. (2004), 'Supplier relationships and small business use of trade Credit', *Journal of Urban Economics*, **55**(1), 46–67.

Adams, W.M., D. Brockington, J. Dyson and V. Bhaskar (2003), 'Managing tragedies: understanding conflict over common pool resources', *Science*, **302**(5652), 1915–16.

Agrawal, A. and C.C. Gibson (eds) (2001), *Communities and the Environment: Ethnicity, Gender and the State in Community-based Conservation*', New Brunswick, NJ: Rutgers University Press.

Alesina, A. (2003), 'Fractionalization', '*Journal of Economic Growth*', **8**(2), 155–94.

Alesina, A. and E. Glaeser (2004), *Fighting Poverty in the US and Europe: A World of Difference*, Oxford: Oxford University Press.

Andreoni, J., M. Castillo and R. Petrie (2003), 'What do bargainers' preferences look like? Exploring a convex Ultimatum Game', *American Economic Review*, **93**(3), 672–85.

Botelho, A., G.W. Harrison, M.A. Hirsch and E.E. Rutström (2002), 'Bargaining Behavior, Demographics and Nationality: what can the experimental evidence show?', working paper. October.

Brandts, J., T. Saijo and A. Schram (2004), 'How universal is behavior? A four country comparison of spite, cooperation and errors in voluntary contribution mechanisms', *Public Choice*, **119**: 381–424.

Burlando, R. and J.D. Hey (1997), 'Do Anglo-Saxons free-ride more?', *Journal of Public Economics*, **64**(1), 41–60.

Camerer, C.F. (2003), *Behavioural Game Theory: Experiments in Strategic Interaction*, Princeton, NJ: Princeton University Press.

Carpenter, J., S. Burks and E. Verhoogen (2002), 'Comparing students to workers: the effects of stakes, social framing and demographics on bargaining outcomes', working paper, June.

Carter, J.R. and M.D. Irons (1991), 'Are economists different, and if so, why?', *Journal of Economic Perspectives*, **5**(2), 171–7.

Cook, R.D. (1997), 'Detection of influential observations in linear regression', *Technometrics*, **19**, 15–18.

Croson, R.T.A. and N.R. Buchan (1999), 'Gender and culture: international experimental evidence from Trust Games', *American Economic Review*, **2**(2), 386–91.

Davidson, R. and J.D. MacKinnon (1993), *Estimation and Inference in Econometrics*, New York, Oxford University Press.

Davis, D.D. and C.A. Holt (1993), *Experimental Economics*, Princeton, NJ: Princeton University Press.

Eckel, C.C. and P.J. Grossman (2001), 'Chivalry and solidarity in ultimatum games', *Economic Inquiry*, **39**(2), 171–88.

Fearon, J. (2003), 'Ethnic and cultural diversity by country', *Journal of Economic Growth*, **8**(2), pp. 195–222.

Ferraro, P.J. and R.G. Cummings (2003), 'Inter-cultural discrimination in the ultimatum game: ethnic bias and statistical discrimination', *Environmental Policy & Experimental Laboratory Working Paper Series #2003-002*, Department of Economics, Andrew Young School of Policy Studies, Atlanta, GA.

Fershtman, C. and U. Gneezy (2001), 'Discrimination in a segmented society: an experimental approach', *Quarterly Journal of Economics*, **116**(1), 351–7.

Gil-White, F.J. (no date), '*Ultimatum game with an ethnicity manipulation: results from Bulgan Sum, Mongolia*', Solomon Asch Center for the Study of Ethnopolitical Conflict, University of Pennsylvania, Philadelphia, PA.

Gil-White, F.J. (2001), 'Are ethnic groups biological "species" to the human brain?', *Current Anthropology*, **42**(4), 515–54.

Güth, W., R. Schmittberger and B. Schwarz (1982), 'An experimental analysis of ultimatum bargaining', *Journal of Economic Behavior and Organization*, **3**(4), 367–88.

Güth, W., C. Schmidt and M. Sutter (2003), 'Fairness in the mail and opportunism in the Internet: a newspaper experiment on ultimatum bargaining', *German Economic Review*, **4**(2), 243–65.

Harbaugh, W.T., K. Krause and S. Liday (2000), 'Children's Bargaining Behavior: differences by age, gender and height', working paper, October.

Henrich, J. (2000), 'Does culture matter in economic behavior? Ultimatum game bargaining among the Machiguenga of the Peruvian Amazon', *American Economic Review*, **90**(4), 973–9.

Henrich, J., R. Boyd, S. Bowles, C. Camerer, E. Fehr, H. Gintis and R. McElreath (2001), 'In search of homo economicus: behavioural experiments in 15 small-scale societies', *American Economic Review*, **91**(2), 73–8.

Hollander, M. and D.A. Wolfe (1999), *Nonparametric Statistical Methods*, 2nd edition, Etobicoke, Ontario: John Wiley and Sons.

Holt, C.A. and S.K. Laury (2002), 'Risk aversion and incentive effects', *American Economic Review*, **92**(5), 1644–55.

Kahneman, D., J.L. Knetsch and R.H. Thaler (1988), 'Fairness and assumptions of economics', *Journal of Business*, **59**(4, Part 2), pp. 285–300.

Kim, S. (2003), 'Irresolvable cultural conflicts and conservation/development arguments: analysis of Korea's Saemangeum Project', *Policy Sciences*, **36**(2), 125–49.

Ladd, H.F. (1998), 'Evidence of discrimination in mortgage lending', *Journal of Economic Perspectives*, **12**(2), 41–62.

List, J.A. (2004), 'The nature and extent of discrimination in the marketplace: evidence from the field', *Quarterly Journal of Economics*, **119**(1), 49–89.

Mallows, C.L. (1986), 'Augmented partial residuals', *Technometrics*, **28**, 313–19.

McElreath, R., R. Boyd and P.J. Richerson (2003), 'Shared norms can lead to the evolution of ethnic markers', *Current Anthropology*, **44**(1), 122–9.

Nisbett, Richard E. and D. Cohen (1996), *Culture of Honor*, Boulder, CO: Westview Press.

Oosterbeek, H., R. Sloof and G. van de Kuilen (2004), 'Cultural differences in ultimatum game experiments: evidence from a meta-analysis', *Experimental Economics*, **7**(2), 171–88.

Palacios-Huerta, I. and T.J. Santos (2004), 'A theory of markets, institutions, and endogenous preferences', *Journal of Public Economics*, **88**, 601–27.

Roth, A.E. (1995), 'Bargaining experiments', in J.H. Kagel and A.E. Roth (eds), *The Handbook of Experimental Economics*, Princeton, NJ: Princeton University Press, pp. 253–348.

Roth, A.E., V. Prasnikar, M. Okuno-Fujiwara and S. Zamir (1991), 'Bargaining and market behavior in Jerusalem, Ljubljana, Pittsburgh, and Tokyo: an experimental study', *American Economic Review*, **81**(5),1068–95.

Schelling, T.C. (1978), *Micromotives and Macrobehavior*, New York: Norton.

Solnick, S.J. (2001), 'Gender differences in the ultimatum game', *Economic Inquiry*, **39**(2), 189–200.

Sonnemans, J. and T. Offerman (2001), 'Is the quadratic scoring rule really incentive compatible?', working paper, December.

Stanley, T.D. and U. Tran (1998), 'Economics students need not be greedy: fairness and the ultimatum game', *Journal of Socio-Economics*, **27**(6), 657–64.

White, H. (1980), 'A heteroskedasticity-consistent covariance matrix estimator and a direct test for heteroskedasticity', *Econometrica*, **48**(4), 817–38.

8. Behavioural economics and the valuation of non-marketed goods and services: the lab, the behavioural anomalies and the policy-maker

Wiktor Adamowicz, Jonathan E. Alevy and John A. List

8.1 INTRODUCTION

Economists and public policy-makers have only begun to contemplate the value of psychology and its close cousin, behavioural economics, when making normative and positive prescriptions. The study of preference reversals over *evaluation scales*, such as choices or prices, is one example of a research programme at the intersection of economics and psychology that has yielded fruitful advances (Grether and Plott, 1979; Kagel and Roth, 1995; Slovic and Lichtenstein, 1968). More recently another type of preference reversal has been explored, this one resulting from choices over different *evaluation modes*. Evaluation mode reversals arise when relative values or rankings of goods depend on whether their evaluation is made jointly or in isolation. As with the earlier literature on evaluation scales, the bulk of the initial research on the effects of evaluation modes has been conducted by psychologists. In this chapter we summarize this initial research and discuss additional recent results that should be of interest to economists. Both theoretical and practical issues, particularly those associated with non-market valuation for environmental policy, are associated with the issues raised by the evaluation mode studies.[1]

At the theoretical level, interest in preference reversals arises because a fundamental tenet of neoclassical theory is called into question when reversals are shown to persist in economically relevant settings. While the economic theory pioneered by Jeremy Bentham and James Mill characterizes utility maximization as a process in which decision-makers' preferences are consistent and stable, a large body of research in psychology and behavioural economics suggests that contextual cues can have a strong influence on choice (Gilovich et al., 2002; Kahneman and Tversky, 2000). Evaluation modes are one avenue through which contextual cues for goods can be altered.

The distinction between joint and separate evaluation modes is simple and also ubiquitous – in every choice we are in one or the other mode. In the separate evaluation mode a single alternative is evaluated on its own; in the joint evaluation mode two or more alternatives are evaluated simultaneously. Several examples are discussed by Shafir (2002) who observes that, in test design, true/false and multiple choice questions are examples, respectively, of the isolated and joint evaluation modes. The distinction in experimental science of within- and between-subject designs is another example that we return to in more detail below. More fundamentally, it has been argued that the distinction between reflective and active aspects of life can be understood as differences across evaluation modes. Ethical principles are derived from a comparative reflection on alternatives, in order to guide a life that is experienced sequentially as 'one thing after another'.

The significance of evaluation mode for the formulation of environmental policy is straightforward. Since environmental goods and services are often unobtainable in markets, stated preference techniques have been devised to elicit their economic value. Two of these methodologies, contingent valuation (CV), and conjoint or attribute-based methods (CJ) differ, in many applications, precisely across the joint and separate evaluation modes. CV methods elicit willingness-to-pay (WTP) or willingness-to-accept (WTA) in the isolated evaluation mode, most typically by asking one or more closed-ended dichotomous choice questions.[2] The attribute-based, or CJ, methods elicit preferences through joint evaluations of related goods that are created by varying specific attributes of interest to researchers and policy-makers (Adamowicz, 2000; Louviere et al., 2000).

A common use of the stated preference methods is the valuation, at trial, of environmental damages in order to estimate the amount required to compensate the public for oil spills and other such damages. Perhaps more importantly, environmental values are used in benefit–cost analysis to inform policy decisions regarding regulatory standards (ever since President Reagan's 1981 Executive Order 12291, federal agencies are required to consider both the benefits and costs of regulations prior to their implementation). Indeed, in the most recent revision of the benefit–cost guidelines that federal agencies must comply with, the role of stated preference techniques is highlighted as an effective methodology in those cases where non-use values are important (OMB, 2003). However, the possibility of large differences between the methods, including preference reversals, makes the use of such values in policy analysis potentially troublesome.[3]

This chapter makes a contribution to what has been termed the 'second wave' of behavioural economics research, which attempts to consolidate a number of behavioural findings and explore their policy implications (Camerer et al., 2003). This literature has begun to examine time-inconsistent and reference-dependent preferences, probability distortions, as well as the role of affect, availability, and overconfidence, in areas as disparate as addictive behaviours, retirement planning and environmental policy (Camerer et al., 2003; Knetsch, 2002; Patt and Zeckhauser, 2002; Shafir, 2002). While our contribution is narrowly focused with respect to its substantive content, we believe that we also make a methodological contribution through the use of field experiments that can be more broadly applied to work of interest to policy-makers.

In a recent study, List (2003) surveyed policy-makers in the federal government to gauge their familiarity with the results of behavioural economics research and to determine whether their knowledge affected policy implementation. List concluded that, while many decision-makers are aware of the results, they are not convinced of their relevance and are not incorporating the findings in their decision-making. A frequent criticism from the sampled population is that experimental studies, often run with student subjects and without salient incentives, do not provide sufficiently weighty evidence to alter policy practice.

In the study of preference reversals across evaluation modes, laboratory experiments have begun to be complemented by experiments in the field. This approach has yielded results of scientific interest, and the broad confirmation of laboratory studies with field experimental data supports the notion that evaluation mode alters choice in a way that is important for policy-makers to consider. More generally, we believe that testing the validity of laboratory findings in the field can have an important effect on how experimental results are received by the policy-making community.

The balance of our chapter proceeds as follows. In section 8.2 we review the literature that has demonstrated the importance of evaluation mode, particularly with regard to the possibility of preference reversals across both laboratory and field environments. Section 8.3 discusses results that investigate the importance of evaluation modes for environmental policy, including our own recent work that emphasizes the possibility of preference reversals. Section 8.4 examines relevant theoretical contributions from the literature on behavioural decision theory that explain underlying processes from which differences across modes arise. Section 8.5 raises several open research questions and section 8.6 concludes.

8.2 EVALUATION MODE STUDIES

Bazerman et al. (1992) were the first to demonstrate the existence of preference reversals over joint and separate evaluation modes. They presented subjects with a hypothetical dispute between neighbours and asked subjects to evaluate alternative resolutions. In the separate evaluation modes, equitable settlements, in terms of monetary pay-offs were preferred. When settlements were evaluated together, the preference for equity was overturned in favour of settlements that maximized own pay-offs. A number of studies have followed and preference reversals have been elicited in a variety of contexts, including ice-cream consumption, hiring practices, public versus private good provision, and so on (see, for example, Hsee, 1996; 1998; Irwin et al., 1993). We present two examples from this literature in some detail so that the character of the reversal is made clear.

Hsee (1996) presented participants with the following problem: consider hiring a computer programmer to program in the KY programming language. Two individuals with the following qualifications are under consideration.

Candidate J: GPA 3.0 Has written 70 KY programs in last 2 years.
Candidate S: GPA 4.9 Has written 10 KY programs in last 2 years.

The evaluation scale, held constant across evaluation modes, is salary; hence the subject's willingness-to-pay for each of the job candidates was elicited. In the joint evaluation mode, candidate J, the experienced jobseeker, received higher offers. In the isolated mode candidate S was preferred.

A second example, also due to Hsee (1998), considered a problem in which one of the goods, here called Set I (where I represents 'Inferior'), is a proper subset of the other good, Set S (Superior). Hsee compares choices over two sets of dinnerware with the following characteristics:

Set S: 40 pieces 31 in good condition, 9 are broken.
Set I: 24 pieces all in good condition.

The two sets share the same 24 pieces (eight dinner plates, eight salad plates, eight dessert plates) in good condition. In addition, set S contains cups and saucers of which seven are intact and nine are broken. The evaluation scale, as in the example above, was the subject's willingness-to-pay, and the preference reversal occurred since the Inferior set was preferred in the isolated evaluation mode and the Superior set was preferred when the two were evaluated jointly. This reversal has been characterized as a 'more is less' result since the dominated good is preferred in isolated evaluation (Hsee, 1998).

In the economics literature, List (2002) presents subjects with a problem that is similar in character to Hsee's dinnerware example in that an inferior and superior good are used. The 'inferior good' is 10 1982 Topps baseball cards and the 'superior good' is the same 10 sportscards *and* three other 1982 Topps baseball cards. The 10 baseball cards shared across the two baskets are graded 'mint/near mint condition' by a professional grading company and are clearly labelled as such. The three additional cards are graded 'poor' and also clearly labelled. An important difference between List's study and those discussed above is that List's is carried out in a naturally occurring marketplace, where subjects endogenously select into the market (and select their roles in the market). Subjects in the experiment voluntarily use their own funds to bid on the goods in an incentive-compatible elicitation mechanism.[4] Winners of the goods receive the cards in exchange for money. List's study is therefore the first to investigate the effect of markets and monetary incentives on the existence and persistence of the evaluation mode preference reversals. List finds that the 'more is less' reversal is alive and well in the market setting, although attenuated among a group of super-experienced subjects, those who deal professionally in the sportscard market.

Alevy et al. (2003; hereafter ALA) conduct a follow-up study to examine the impact of information about quality on the potential for reversals across evaluation modes. This study alters List's original field study in a simple way, by removing the cards from their sealed cardholders effectively taking away the quality signal provided by the professional grading company. The informational treatment provides a bridge to the investigation of environmental public goods since the quality of the public goods may be more difficult to discern than that of the graded sportscards.

With the ungraded cards ALA find that the evidence for the more is less preference reversal is even more pronounced, with bidding behaviour affected by the apparent 'contamination' of the 10-card bundle by the additional low-quality cards, particularly in the non-expert subject pool.[5] In the isolated evaluation modes, on average, non-dealers bid \$4.05 in for the inferior 10-card bundle, and only \$1.82 for the superior 13-card bundle, a difference of approximately 121 per cent. This compares with prices of \$4.86 and \$3.06 for the inferior and superior goods in the original study with graded cards. Moving to the joint evaluation mode the preference reversal is evidenced by non-dealer bids of \$2.89 and \$3.32 for the inferior and superior goods in the ungraded treatment, and \$3.72 and \$4.52 in the graded treatment.[6] Table 8.1 provides details on the bidding behaviour for both treatments and Figures 8.1 and 8.2 summarize these findings. These results lead ALA to conclude that

Table 8.1 Experimental results

Treatment	Bundle		
	10 cards		13 cards
Non-dealers		Bidding data	
IS (n=35)	*$4.86 (0.65)*		—
IS (n=33)	**4.05 (0.45)**		—
SS (n=37)	—		*$3.06 (0.60)*
SS(n=30)	—		**1.82 (0.26)**
J (n=33)	*$3.72 (0.53)*		*$4.52 (0.69)*
J (n=31)	**2.89 (0.51)**		**3.32 (0.55)**
		Choices	
C (n=25)	*2/25 (8%)*		*23/25 (92%)*
C (n=20)	**1/20 (5%)**		**19/20 (95%)**
Dealers		Bidding data	
IS (n=35)	*$3.20 (0.44)*		—
IS (n=30)	**$3.52 (0.33)**		—
SS (n=35)	—		*$2.70 (0.41)*
SS (n=30)	—		**$3.36 (0.65)**
J (n=28)	*$3.09 (0.47)*		*$3.45 (0.50)*
J (n=30)	**$3.21 (0.53)**		**$3.48 (0.53)**
		Choices	
C (n=13)	*0/13 (0%)*		*13/13 (100%)*
C (n=15)	**0/15 (0%)**		**15/15 (100%)**

Notes:
Mean bids are reported.
Numbers adjacent to bids in parentheses are standard errors (percentages for choice treatments).

Sources: Results from List (2002) in italics and Alevy et al. (2003) in bold.

when uncertainty about the goods' values increases, the evidence in favour of a more is less preference reversal is even more pronounced. We believe this result is fundamental to valuation of non-market goods and services, where survey responders may be uncertain about the good's quality.

8.3 ENVIRONMENTAL PUBLIC GOODS

A small number of studies have investigated the evaluation of environmental or other public goods across joint and separate evaluation modes and most have suggested substantial differences in results across methods

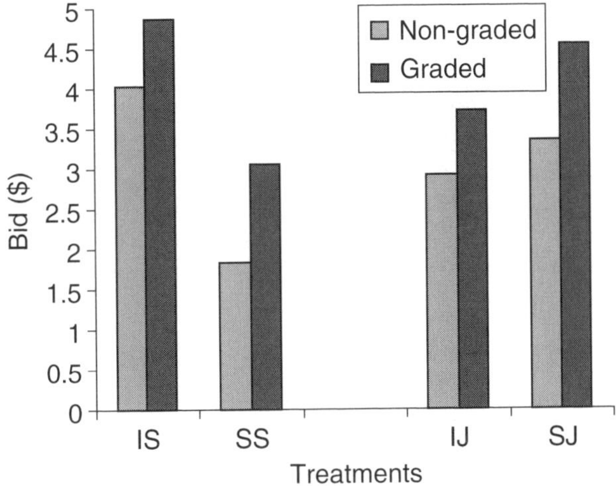

Note: Data on graded cards is from List (2002), and the non graded from Alevy et al. (2003). The first letter of the treatment codes indicates the good type with I = Inferior, S = Superior. The second letter of the treatment code indicates the evaluation mode with S = Separate and J = Joint.

Figure 8.1 Market data (non-dealers)

(Boxall et al., 1996; Irwin et al., 1993; Magat et al., 1988; Takatsuka et al., 2002). Interestingly, the direction of differences is not uniform across studies. Boxall et al., studying environmental quality related to moose habitat, find higher WTP in the contingent valuation setting, with CV estimates roughly 20 times those in the joint evaluation mode, CJ study. Magat et al. find the reverse in a study related to risk reduction in the purchase of private goods with CV WTP 58 per cent below the CJ results. Takatsuka et al. also found WTP to be much lower in the CV setting, approximately 13 per cent of their CJ estimates in a study of ecosystem attributes in Tennessee's Clinch River Valley. These studies generate welfare measures for changes in quality but, by design, do not investigate the possibility of preference reversals across evaluation modes since they limit the CV investigation to a single choice and compare this finding to the results of the CJ study for that particular public good. The magnitude of the differences they report however is a matter of concern.

Boxall et al. (1996) demonstrate that the limited substitution possibilities in the CV questions may be an important factor that gives rise to the different results. They analyse the attribute based method as if the substitution possibilities were limited to those available in the CV study and show that this eliminates a large share of the difference between the CV and CJ results.

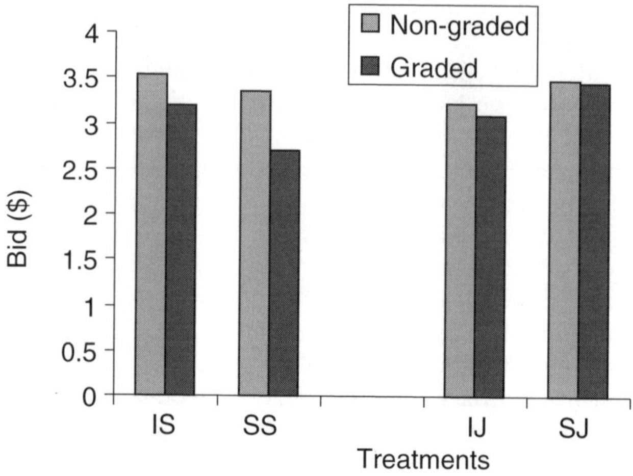

Note: Data on graded cards is from List (2002), and the non-graded from Alevy et al. (2003). The first letter of the treatment codes indicates the good type with I = Inferior, S = Superior. The second letter of the treatment code indicates the evaluation mode with S = Separate and J = Joint.

Figure 8.2 Market data (dealers)

Irwin et al. (1993) were the first to investigate the possibility of preference reversals with environmental public goods by comparing the valuation of private and public goods across the evaluation modes. They find that preferences for public goods are accentuated in the joint evaluation mode. While not directly comparable, these results are consistent with those of ALA which are discussed in more detail below.

The ALA study of sportscard quality also included surveys to study the impact of evaluation mode on the valuation of environmental public goods. The basic structure of the survey methodology follows that used in both Hsee's chipped-plate study and the sportscard-market studies, by using superior and inferior goods with quality variation. The superior good provides an additional quantity of the public good, although the extra amount of the good is provided with lower quality. Both farmland preservation and watershed restoration were studied with the basic good, a unit preserved or restored, augmented by temporary preservation or partial restoration.

In the farmland preservation treatments the inferior good is the permanent preservation of 500 acres of farmland. The superior good augments the inferior good with an additional 50 acres preserved for five years. The watershed restoration offers a full clean-up of 500 acres, for the inferior good, augmented with 50 acres of partial clean-up for the superior good.

Alevy et al. (2003) elicited willingness to contribute to the public goods from people visiting a University of Maryland 'open-house'. Each treatment followed the within- and between-subject protocol that had previously been applied by Bazerman, Hsee, List and their colleagues. Thus each individual answered one of three questions, two of which were associated with the isolated evaluation mode and one with the joint evaluation mode. The isolated evaluation mode questions were dichotomous choice CV questions and the joint evaluation mode question included a 'no-contribution' or status quo option in addition to the inferior and superior options.

Both open-ended and closed-ended questions were implemented in distinct treatments. For the wetlands study, two closed-ended treatments were implemented by varying the required contribution amount for the public good from $50 to $100. These treatments are denoted as W50 and W100 in Table 8.2. Pooled data from these treatments is denoted WP. The two farmland preservation treatments, included a $50 closed-ended treatment, F50, as well as an open-ended question (FO). The open-ended treatment provides a link between this study and the psychology literature, which typically uses an open-ended elicitation mechanism.

The results from the public goods treatments show differences across evaluation modes that are consistent with the 'more is less' preference reversal. In all treatments the data are consistent in direction with the more is less result, although the magnitude and statistical significance of the results varies considerably across treatments. Alevy et al. (2003) report another significant finding across evaluation modes: aggregate willingness to contribute to the public good is significantly *greater* in the joint evaluation mode than in the separate evaluation mode.[7]

Results of the public good treatments are summarized in Table 8.2 and Figure 8.3 for the closed-ended treatments, and Table 8.3 for the open-ended treatment. Table 8.4 contains results regarding overall contribution rates across treatments and is supplemented by Figure 8.4. Valuations in the separate and joint modes as well as differences across modes are discussed below.

Valuation of Public Goods in the Separate Evaluation Mode

Proportions of subjects willing to contribute to the public good for each question are presented in columns IS and SS of Table 8.2; where IS and SS denote inferior and superior goods in the separate evaluation mode. While there are small proportions in the direction of favouring the inferior good in each of the isolated valuation tasks, in all cases the null hypothesis of homogeneity across evaluation modes was not rejected. This result provides

Table 8.2 Proportion contributing to public good

Treatment	IS	SS	J	ISNJ χ^2_2	ISJ χ^2_1
W50	0.67 n = 30	0.63 n = 30	I = 0.30, S = 0.50, N = 0.20 n = 29	4.20	1.50
W100	0.62 n = 29	0.61 n = 31	I = 0.31, S = 0.45, N = 0.21 n = 30	1.93	0.73
WP	0.64 n = 59	0.62 n = 61	I = 0.30, S = 0.48, N = 0.22 n = 59	5.93**	2.17
F50	0.58 n = 36	0.51 n = 39	I = 0.17, S = 0.53, N = 0.30 n = 30	6.20**	5.76**
FO	1.00 n = 23	0.97 n = 29	I = 0.32, S = 0.68, N = 0.00 n = 25	17.36***	3.24*

Notes:
IS and SS columns present the portion contributing to the public good in the separate evaluation modes. Although contributions to the inferior good are uniformly higher, these differences are not significant in any treatment.
Column J: Joint evaluation mode, with I, S, N representing proportions contributing to inferior (I), superior (S) public goods or not contributing (N).
Columns ISNJ and ISJ report on the significance of one-sample tests of proportions for the joint evaluation mode.
The level at which the null hypothesis is rejected is indicated by * (10 per cent), ** (5 per cent) and *** (1 per cent).

Source: From Alevy et al. (2003).

weak support for the 'more is less' hypothesis since we find no support for the alternative that 'more is more.'

Data from the open-ended question, summarized in Table 8.4, suggest that the elicited willingness-to-pay across the isolated judgements is not significantly different across the inferior and superior questions. The large variance in responses to both questions is responsible for this result. In Table 8.4 the results are reported with one outlying observation removed. This observation was for an individual who expressed a willingness-to-pay of $100000 to preserve 1/10 of an acre. With this result omitted ALA find that the mean WTP for the inferior good is greater than for the superior good, although, again, the difference is not statistically significant at conventional levels.

Valuation of Public Goods in the Joint Evaluation Mode

Column J in Table 8.2 contains the proportions choosing Inferior (I) and Superior (S) public goods as well as those declining to contribute (N) in the

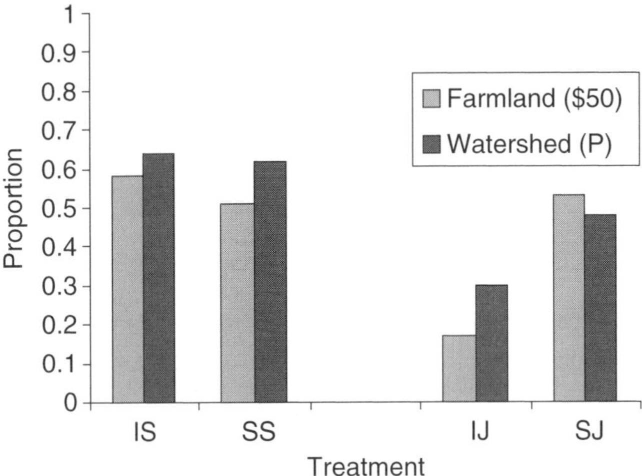

Note: The first letter of the treatment codes indicates the good type with I = Inferior, S = Superior. The second letter of the treatment code indicates the evaluation mode with S = Separate and J = Joint.

Figure 8.3 Proportions contributing to closed-ended Public good treatments

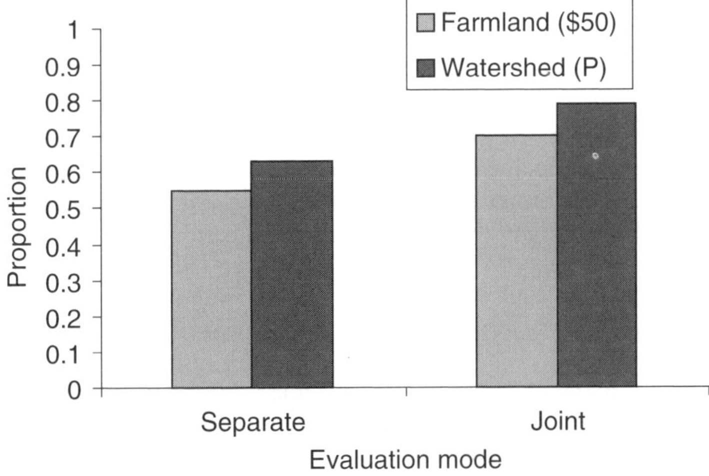

Note: The first letter of the treatment codes indicates the good type with I = Inferior, S = Superior. The second letter of the treatment code indicates the evaluation mode with S = Separate and J = Joint.

Figure 8.4 Proportions contributing to public goods by evaluation mode

Table 8.3 Mean and standard deviation of the contribution for FO treatment

	S	I	S vs. I t
FO	4923.37 (20763.6) n = 23	871.3793 (2557.061) n = 29	−0.9303
FO*	601.7045 (1278.80) n = 22	871.3793 (2557.06) n = 29	0.4925

Note: FO* displays the results when a single outlying observation, representing a stated willingness-to-pay of $100 000 is deleted from the sample. In this case the mean price for the inferior public good is greater than that for the superior good.

Table 8.4 Contribution rates across isolated and juxtaposed evaluation modes

Treatments	Isolated (pooled SS & IS)	Juxtaposed	I vs. J χ^2
WP	0.63 n = 120	0.79 n = 59	3.90**
F50	0.55 n = 75	0.70 n = 30	2.08
WFP	0.60 n = 195	0.75 n = 89	6.26**

Note: Entries provide insights into the probability of contributing to the public good. For example, 0.63 in row 1, column 1 suggests that 63 per cent of respondents chose to contribute in the isolated treatments.
The level at which the null hypothesis is rejected is indicated by * (10 per cent), ** (5 per cent) and *** (1 per cent).

joint evaluation mode. An initial test of differences in proportions between the W50 and W100 treatments reveals that the responses across treatments are statistically indistinguishable, and the two treatments are therefore pooled (WP). Two measures of treatment effects in the joint evaluation mode are reported. Column ISNJ reports on treatment effects that, in addition to accounting for responses to the inferior and superior goods include the status quo, no contribution response, N. The column ISJ reports on tests of proportions between inferior and superior goods only. In the ISNJ data, both with the pooled watershed data (WP) and the farmland preservation treatments F50 and F0 the null hypothesis that the Inferior and Superior goods are indistinguishable in the joint evaluation mode is rejected. In the ISJ comparison, the farmland preservation treatments also show significant differences.

Contributions across Evaluation Modes

Table 8.4 summarizes the data in order to compare contribution rates in the joint and separate evaluation modes, where a contribution represents a willingness to contribute to either the inferior or superior public good. Unexpectedly, the contribution rates are uniformly higher in the joint evaluation mode. Significant differences in contribution rates occur in the pooled watershed data and in the pooled data over both the watershed and farmland closed-ended treatments (treatment WFP).

The difference in contribution rates across evaluation modes raises important policy issues unrelated to the preference reversal phenomenon which motivated the ALA study. The difference in contribution rates is consistent with the valuation work of Irwin et al. and Takatsuka et al. that finds higher WTP for environmental quality in the CJ than in the CV mode. As with the preference reversals the different results across techniques can affect decisions about whether or to what extent a particular policy should be pursued.

8.4 THEORETICAL EXPLANATIONS

Psychologists who took the lead in investigating the preference reversals have also taken steps to explain the evaluation mode preference reversal phenomenon. Recent reviews of the literature have put forward theoretical explanations for the observed reversals. Of particular interest for the public good results are the 'evaluability hypothesis' and the 'want/should' dichotomy that arises from an application of the theory of multiple selves (Bazerman et al., 1998; 1999; Hsee, 1996; Hsee et al., 1999). The evaluability hypothesis proposes that each decision-maker has some 'evaluability information' about the attributes of an option that serves to inform them about how important different attribute levels are for choice. Preference reversals may arise because access to evaluability information can differ across evaluation modes. Thus, in Hsee's hiring example discussed earlier, it is known that GPAs in universities in the midwestern USA can range from zero to five. This evaluability information is equally available in either the joint or separate evaluation mode. By contrast, the experience factor in the hiring decision has less evaluability information associated with it in the separate evaluation mode since there is no objective scale through which to evaluate experience in isolation. As a result, the GPA information has additional weight when the judgement process occurs in isolation. The value of the GPA data is reduced when the comparison of job candidates enables the decision-maker to better utilize the experience data in the joint evaluation mode. In the cases presented above, the strength of the shift in evaluability information was sufficient to cause a reversal of preferences (Hsee et al., 1999).

We believe that further insights into how information is evaluated across joint and separate evaluation modes can be gained from dual-process models of cognition. These theories posit two systems: (1) 'System 1' is quick, associative, and intuitive; and (2) 'System 2' is slower, based on rules and reasoning (Chaikin and Trope, 1999; Kahneman and Frederick, 2002). The use of heuristics, such as representativeness or affect in judgment and valuation, by System 1, has been shown to produce biases that may be mitigated by System 2's supervision of intuitive judgments.

In examining valuations and judgements across evaluation modes, it is clear that the conditions required for System 2 to carry out its role may be compromised in isolated evaluation. Consider the examples above which resulted in the 'more is less' phenomenon. Both in the case of the cracked dinnerware and with the sportscards, it seems plausible that an affective response to the poor-quality items substituted for the target characteristic, that of an overall evaluation of the bundle. In the joint evaluation mode, the information was available to promote System 2 responses and ameliorate the effects of the affective response, in the separate evaluation mode it was not. The different behaviour across experience levels that List (2002) reported, with professional dealers much less affected by the different evaluation modes, can also be understood in the context of the dual-process theory, which suggests that complex cognitive operations can migrate from System 2 to System 1 with repeated exposure to similar tasks (Kahneman and Frederick, 2002).

Another line of research, which in some applications bears a strong resemblance to the dual-process theories, suggests that behaviour can be understood as if multiple internal selves are agents in the decision process (Schelling, 1984). Recently, Bazerman et al. (1998) have applied the multiple-selves theory to studies of decision-making over joint and separate evaluation modes. These authors posit a *want* self and a *should* self, with the *want* self invoking primarily, affective, impulsive processes associated with System 1, and the *should* self more rational and 'cool headed' primarily accessing System 2. The authors argue that the resolution of conflicts between the two selves is highly sensitive to the evaluation mode, arguing that the *want* self may dominate in isolated evaluation modes and the *should* self under joint evaluation. Alevy et al.'s (2003) finding that there are more contributions to the public goods in the joint evaluation mode is consistent with this understanding and with interpretations of previous findings of preference reversals over evaluation modes (Bazerman et al., 1998; Irwin et al., 1993).

8.5 OPEN RESEARCH QUESTIONS

Initial research on valuations made across joint and separate evaluation modes suggests that significant issues remain in order to determine how best to utilize CV and CJ techniques. Both the preference reversals and the differing contribution rates across modes imply that policy decisions regarding environmental improvements can differ simply as a result of the methodology chosen. We suggest two primary areas of research in order to clarify the importance of these issues. The first is suggested by the preference reversals arising from the differences in information evaluability across modes, as evidenced most clearly in the sportscard market results. The second, and more broadly based area of research, is motivated by the dual-process theories and requires an engagement with issues regarding which 'self' is the relevant one for the elicitation of environmental values.

With regard to issues raised by information evaluability the results from the sportscard market suggest that the manner in which quality differences are perceived varies significantly across evaluation modes. Extending the understanding of how characteristics of environmental quality are perceived across modes is one area where additional research would be useful. This research could provide a helpful taxonomy for researchers who must choose between the CJ and CV methods and should address the argument that environmental concerns are permeated with the qualities that make rational choice difficult (Patt and Zeckhauser, 2002). Both the timescale of effects and the complexity of interactions lead to large uncertainties about outcomes and their likelihood. The interaction of evaluation modes with these specific characteristics is an area that is largely unexplored.

Theories of multiple selves provide another avenue to tee-up how to choose between non-market valuation methods, explicitly raising the question of what kind of context is appropriate for cost–benefit analysis. Thus the joint mode, which elicits the 'should self', and is associated with methods of ethical decision-making may seem superior, particularly when it is clear that informational problems may be ameliorated by joint comparisons. Alternatively, since valuation exercises usually result in the implementation of a single policy from an array of possibilities, the isolated mode may have more external validity in the sense that it is tied more closely to the experienced utility of individuals living under a given policy regime.

8.6 CONCLUSION

This chapter discusses and summarizes recent findings from behavioural economics that potentially have sharp implications for environmental policy-makers. Given that past attention has primarily been paid to the WTA/WTP disparity, we purposely shift the attention to a new set of results that should also be of importance to policy-makers and scholars alike. This is not an attempt to suggest the value disparity results are not important or interesting, as we believe implications of this fundamental result are substantial in both a positive and normative sense. From a positive perspective, the disparity between WTA and WTP essentially renders the invariance result of Coase invalid. In a normative sense, reference-dependent preferences call into question commonly held interpretations of indifference curves, make cost–benefit analysis illegitimate and change the procedure necessary to resolve damage disputes.

Rather, our shift in focus is to highlight what we believe to be a new result that should be more thoroughly explored and documented. In addition, this chapter highlights that field experiments can play an important complementary role to laboratory findings in that the natural next step in generalizing laboratory results is to explore their robustness in naturally occurring markets where market participants are engaging in activities that are ordinary to them. Without this next step, behaviouralists are in danger of taking a back seat in the policy community. This would be unfortunate, as this line of research has much to offer both today and in expected value terms.

NOTES

1. The terminology of evaluation scales and evaluation modes has not been used uniformly in the literature and is adopted from Bazerman et al. (1999).
2. Some of this dichotomy depends on presentation. A discrete choice CV, for example, can be considered a choice between a current situation and an improved situation. In this format the context is more like a joint evaluation mode. In the more traditional format of 'would you pay $X' for this good, the evaluation mode appears to be separate. The assessment of joint versus separate evaluation mode may thus depend on the individual's perception of the choice problem/context.
3. Note that the issue we raise relates to the evaluation mode differences and not to the issue that the techniques elicit stated preferences. As we will see below, similar concerns over evaluation modes also arise in market environments.

4. A random nth-price auction was used to elicit values. List (2002) discusses the characteristics of this mechanism.
5. As with the graded cards, professional dealers' behaviour is not significantly different across the evaluation modes, at conventional levels, although the actual bid prices are consistent with the 'more is less' preference reversal.
6. Subjects in the isolated evaluation modes bid on only one good and those in the joint evaluation mode bid on two. In order to keep budget sets comparable across treatments, those in the joint evaluation mode were told that, if they won both goods at auction, they would only purchase one of them, with the choice of good determined by the toss of a coin.
7. Stevens et al. (2000) report a related result – more contribute when given a polychotomous choice question, intended to elicit intensity of preference, than to dichotomous choice CV.

REFERENCES

Adamowicz, W.L. (2000), 'Environmental valuation case studies', J. Louviere, D. Hensher and J. Swait (eds), *Stated Choice Methods: Analysis and Application*, Cambridge: Cambridge University Press, pp. 329–53.

Adamowicz, W.L., P. Boxall, M. Williams and J. Louviere (1998), 'Stated preference approaches for measuring passive use values: choice experiments and contingent valuation', *American Journal of Agricultural Economics*, **80**(1), 64–75.

Alevy, J.E., J.A. List and W. Adamowicz (2003), 'More is less preference reversals and nonmarket valuation', University of Maryland College Park working paper.

Bazerman, M.H., G.F. Loewenstein and S.B. White (1992), 'Reversals of preference in allocation decisions: judging an alternative versus choosing among alternatives', *Administrative Science Quarterly*, **37**(2), pp. 220–40.

Bazerman, M.H., D.A. Moore, A.E. Tenbrunsel, K.A. Wade-Benzoni and S. Blount (1999), 'Explaining how preferences change across joint versus separate evaluation', *Journal of Economic Behavior and Organization*, **39**, 41–58.

Bazerman, M.H., A.E. Tenbrunsel and K. Wade-Benzoni (1998), 'Negotiating with yourself and losing: making decisions with competing internal preferences', *Acadamy of Management Review*, **23**(2), 225–41.

Boxall, P.C., W.L. Adamowicz, J. Swait, M. Williams and J. Louviere (1996), 'A comparison of stated preference methods for environmental valuation', *Ecological Economics*, **18**(3), 243–53.

Camerer, C., S. Issacharoff, G. Loewenstein, T. O'Donoghue and M. Rabin (2003), 'Regulation for conservatives: behavioral economics and the case for "asymmetric paternalism"', *Penn Law Review*, **151**, 1211–54.

Chaikin, S. and Y. Trope (1999), *Dual-Process Theories in Social Psychology*, New York: Guilford Press.

Gilovich, T., D. Griffin and D. Kahneman (2002), *Heuristics and Biases: The Psychology of Intuitive Judgment*, Cambridge: Cambridge University Press.

Grether, D. and C. Plott (1979), 'Economic theory of choice and the preference reversal phenomenon', *American Economic Review*, **69**, 623–38.

Hsee, C.K. (1996), 'The evaluability hypothesis: an explanation of preference reversals between joint and separate evaluations of alternatives', *Organizational Behavior and Human Decision Processes*, **46**, 247–57.

Hsee, C.K. (1998), 'Less is better: when low-value options are valued more highly than high-value options', *Journal of Economic Behavior and Decision-Making*, **11**, 107–21.

Hsee, C.K., G.F. Loewenstein, S. Blount and M.A. Bazerman (1999), 'Preference reversals between joint and separate evaluations of options: a review and theoretical analysis', *Psychological Bulletin*, **125**(5), 576–90.

Irwin, J.R., P. Slovic, S. Lichtenstein and G.H. McClelland (1993), 'Preference reversals and the measurement of environmental values', *Journal of Risk and Uncertainty*, **6**, 5–18.

Kagel, J.H. and A.E. Roth (1995), *The Handbook of Experimental Economics*, Princeton, NJ: Princeton University Press.

Kahneman, D. and S. Frederick (2002), 'Representativeness revisited: attribute substitution in intuitive judgment', in T. Gilovich, D. Griffin and D. Kahneman (eds), *Heuristics and Biases: The Psychology of Intuitive Thought*, New York: Cambridge University Press, pp. 49–81.

Kahneman, D. and A. Tversky (2000), *Choices, Value and Frames*, Cambridge: Cambridge University Press.

Knetsch, J.L. (2002), 'Policy analysis and design with losses valued more than gains and varying rates of time preference', in R. Gowda and J.C. Fox (eds), *Judgments, Decisions, and Public Policy*, Cambridge: Cambridge University Press, pp. 91–115.

List, J.A. (2002), 'Preference reversals of a different kind: the "more is less" phenomenon', *American Economic Review*, **92**(5), 1636–43.

List, J.A. (2003), 'Scientific numerology, preference anomalies, and environmental policymaking', *Environmental and Resource Economics*.

Louviere, J.J., D.A. Hensher and J.D. Swait (2000), *Stated Choice Models: Analysis and Application*, Cambridge: Cambridge University Press.

Magat, W.A., W.K. Viscusi and J. Huber (1988), 'Paired comparison and contingent valuation approaches to morbidity risk valuation', *Journal of Environmental Economics and Management*, **15**(4), 395–411.

OMB (2003), 'Draft 2003 report to Congress on the costs and benefits of federal regulations', at www.whitehouse.gov/omb/fedreg/2003draft_cost-benefit_rpt.pdf.

Patt, A. and R.J. Zeckhauser (2002), 'Behavioral perceptions and policies toward the environment', R. Gowda and J.C. Fox (eds), *Judgments, Decisions, and Public Policy*, Cambridge: Cambridge University Press, pp. 265–302.

Schelling, T.C. (1984), *Choice and Consequence: Perspectives of an Errant Economist*, Cambridge, MA: Harvard University Press.

Shafir, E. (2002), 'Cognition, intuition, and policy guidelines', in R. Gowda and J.C. Fox (eds), *Judgments, Decisions, and Public Policy*, Cambridge: Cambridge University Press, pp. 71–88.

Slovic, P. and S. Lichtenstein (1968), 'Relative importance of probabilities and payoffs in risk taking', *Journal of Experimental Psychology*, **78**, 1–18.

Stevens, T.H., R. Belkner, D. Dennis, D. Kittredge and C. Willis (2000), 'Comparison of contingent valuation and conjoint analysis in ecosystem management', *Ecological Economics*, **32**(1), 63–74.

Takatsuka, Y., J. Kahn and S. Stewart (2002), 'Choice model and contingent valuation estimates of the value of ecosystem attributes', working paper, University of Tennessee.

Index